SQUEEZE THIS!

FOLKLORE STUDIES
IN A MULTICULTURAL
WORLD

FOLKLORE STUDIES IN A MULTICULTURAL WORLD

The Folklore Studies in a Multicultural World
series is a collaborative venture of the University of
Illinois Press, the University Press of Mississippi, the
University of Wisconsin Press, and the American
Folklore Society, made possible by a generous grant
from the Andrew W. Mellon Foundation. The series
emphasizes the interdisciplinary and international
nature of current folklore scholarship, documenting
connections between communities and their cultural
production. Series volumes highlight aspects of
folklore studies such as world folk cultures, folk art and
music, foodways, dance, African American and ethnic
studies, gender and queer studies, and popular culture.

SQUEEZE THIS!

A Cultural History
of the Accordion
in America

MARION JACOBSON

UNIVERSITY OF ILLINOIS PRESS

Urbana, Chicago, and Springfield

Publication of this book is supported by a grant
from the Andrew W. Mellon Foundation.

Library of Congress Cataloging-in-Publication Data
Jacobson, Marion S.
Squeeze this! : a cultural history of the accordion
in America / Marion Jacobson.
p. cm. — (Folklore studies in a multicultural world)
Includes bibliographical references and index.
ISBN 978-0-252-03675-0 (hardcover : alk. paper) —
ISBN 978-0-252-09385-2 (e-book)
1. Accordion—United States—History.
2. Accordionists—United States.
I. Title.
ML1083.J33   2012
788.8'650973—dc23   2011034681

A fearful instrument that looks like a cash register, and sounds worse, produces gasps of pleasure at the Orpheum this week. It is called a piano accordion and its behavior is shameless.

    —*Minneapolis Journal,* December 16, 1912

Welcome to Hell. Here's your accordion.

    —Gary Larson, *The Complete Far Side, 1980–1994*

I still have to overcome skeptics. But after hearing me play, they say, "I've never heard anything like this."

    —Eddie Monteiro, noted jazz and classical accordion artist

CONTENTS

Color illustrations appear after page 90

ACKNOWLEDGMENTS

I AM LUCKY TO BE ABLE TO THANK a long roll call of people who helped make this book both doable and fun to write. If it weren't for my accordion teachers, Walter Kuehr and Charlie Giordano in New York City and Peggy Minore Hart in Albany, New York, my involvement with the accordion would not have built up enough momentum for a book. The commitment, knowledge, and generosity of all the accordion people I have interviewed over the years inspires sincere gratitude. I am also grateful to the American Accordionists Association, the Accordion Teachers Guild, and all the "accordion people" who have made this topic so rich.

I am so grateful to my advisors at New York University, Gage Averill and Michael Beckerman, for encouraging me to go forward with this project, which was full of challenges and uncertainty from the outset. My colleagues at the Albany College of Pharmacy, especially Erika Muse, Kevin Hickey, and Kenneth Blume, gave me intellectual support and the will to continue with the project while negotiating the challenges of my early academic career. The American Philosophical Society granted me research and travel funds without which my "accordion festival tour" would have been impossible. It was a great honor, as well, to receive the Parsons Fund Award for Ethnography from the Library of Congress in 2009. As a researcher, I received red carpet treatment from the World of Accordions Museum in Superior, Wisconsin, the Library of Congress, the New York Public Library's Research Division, and the Center for the Study of Free Reed Instruments at the CUNY Graduate Center in Manhattan. There Allan Atlas spent hours helping me sift thorough hundreds of photos and documents from the Pietro Deiro Archives, stashed in every nook and cranny of his office.

The list of people who lifted my spirits with advice, music, photos, kind words, and free CDs would fill an entire chapter. I cannot express enough gratitude to Helmi Harrington, curator of the World of Accordions Museum, a wellspring of accordion knowledge and a supporter of this project. For making available photographs and rare materials from the Museum's personal collections, I am also indebted to Alex Carozza of Alex & Bell Accordions, Guido Deiro, Jr., Tom Torriglia, Joan Grauman, Faithe Deffner, Robert Young McMahan, William Schimmel, Henry Doktorski, and Jacob C. Neupauer. Each of them also contributed valuable insights and comments on the project.

Without images, this would have been an uninviting book. I am deeply thankful to all the talented photographers and artists who answered my desperate call at the eleventh hour, when I realized that only a handful of the hundreds of photos I had taken at museums and field trips would meet UIP's publication standards. There is a place in accordion heaven for each of the amazing photographers who donated their work to this project: Jane Finch, Jayme Thornton, Bengt Alm, Danny Clinch, John Clayton, Martin Cooper, Brian McLernon, Jim Merithew, Hai Zhang, Sean Vallely (with a little graphic wizardry from Renee de la Prade, Tim Gennert, Rosie Steffy), Larry Utley, Frank Lima, Maria Sonevytski, Shannon Conyers, Michael Macioce, and Patti Davi. I especially benefited from Patti's outstanding visual documentation of the Cotati Accordion Festival.

I am especially thankful to the editors of *World of Music* for allowing me to guest edit their "Accordion issue." Each author contributed an original perspective on the topic that helped inspire me and get out of my little piano-accordion box: Maria Sonevytski, Graeme Smith, Sydney Hutchinson, and Yin-Yee Kwan. Other incredibly supportive and helpful researchers of accordion-related topics who were often in my thoughts as I was writing this book were ethnomusicologist Helene Simonett and folklorist James Leary, who helped me track down information on Finnish-American music and culture. Without James Leary's guidance—and his encyclopedic knowledge of Upper Midwest accordion traditions—there would be no chapter 4.

Many thanks to my razor-sharp editor, Laurie Matheson, and the UIP copy editing team for shaping the book from the table of contents to the conclusion, and to the Mellon Foundation for funding this book series. I was lucky enough to participate in a round table for first-time authors at the American Folklore Society meeting in Boise in 2009, where I benefited from the insights of distinguished mentors and expert editors from the University Press of Mississippi, the University of Wisconsin Press, and the University of Illinois Press. I would especially like to thank Judith McCullough, Sheila Leary, and Simon Bronner for their input. Above all, this book would truly not be possible without the love, support, and inspiration provided by my family. Sabina and Bob Jacobson kept beaming it from Bethesda, Maryland. Their enthusiasm and pride in my work will stay with me forever. My itinerant in-laws Tom and Carolyn Hilliard were always there for our family, wherever they were, in Nashville, Dallas, or on the road. Thanks to my sister Alice Jacobson for proofreading the first three chapters. Thanks to Simone and Jasper, who fill each day with love, excitement, and joy. Thanks to my kids for reminding me what really matters in life. The tender love and steadfast support of my husband, Tom Hilliard, have enriched my life and work in too many ways to describe. He is always the first to comment and critique my work, and he helped with editing. What a pleasure it is to be able to share ideas with and be inspired by one's life companion.

SQUEEZE THIS!

INTRODUCTION

LIKE MANY WHO STARTED PLAYING the accordion in the late twentieth century, my introduction to the instrument happened quite unexpectedly, resulting from a series of chance encounters. While strolling down Essex Street in Manhattan's Lower East Side on a brilliant fall day in 2002, I impulsively ducked into Main Squeeze Accordions. I do not recall what drove me into the store to examine the used and new squeezeboxes, browse through sheet music, and talk at length with owner Walter Kuehr. Perhaps I was curious as to what an accordion store was doing in this neighborhood, at the crossroads of Orthodox Jewish and hipster cultures. I was vaguely aware that accordion shops had once populated Mulberry Street, but that neighborhood was further west and significantly more Italian. I do recall my feeling of awe when Kuehr strapped on one of his wood-framed accordions, made to his specifications in a factory in the Czech Republic, and a velvety carpet of free-reed sound washed over me. "Here's a little Cajun tune," he said, launching into "Jambalaya." He then gave his interpretations of klezmer, French musette, and an Italian song, each time flipping another switch to alternate from the dark, low reeds of the Cajun and klezmer tunes (the bandoneon switch) to the lighter, sweeter textures of French and Italian music (the musette switch, with two reeds tuned slightly apart, creating a reedy vibrato). *With only one instrument, you can travel the world*. I was also fascinated by the physical dynamics of the instrument, the way Walter and the accordion seemed to breathe together, and how this awkward-looking box could be transformed into something that looked like an extension of the player's body. "You hold it close, you practically embrace it, and it breathes. And you can get every effect you want out of it," said Kuehr. "You can sound sad or silly, and you can make someone laugh or cry. That's harder to do on a piano."

Funny that Walter should have mentioned the piano. I had taken lessons and played piano for most of my life but had been thinking of getting rid of mine, to make room for a second child in our cramped Brooklyn house. But I still wanted to make music, so I decided to get an accordion—as the right-hand keyboard, at least, would no doubt be easy to learn. The idea of owning an accordion seemed completely irrelevant to the musical tastes and habits of my generation. Those of us who grew up in the 1970s were more likely to base their instrument choices on seeing Paul McCartney or Pete Townshend playing keyboards or electric guitar than Myron Floren or Lawrence Welk playing an accordion. Like many who began playing accordion in the twentieth century, I acquired my instrument from someone who didn't want it any more. I have observed thousands of orphaned accordions sitting in museums and hundreds for sale on Ebay. This wave of neglect came for various reasons discussed in this book: the Lawrence Welk stigma; the emerging appeal of electronic instruments in the 1960s; and, simply, these instruments' need for expensive repairs or attainment of the ends of their fifty-year life spans. But an accordion fell into my hands under different circumstances, ones that proved to be highly significant for this book. Alyssa Lamb, a singer and musician who lived near me in Brooklyn, played accordion with a local band called Las Rubias del Norte. After many nights standing up and playing the thirty-five-pound instrument for two or three hours, Lamb's back had given out. Her boyfriend, Olivier Conan, was the owner of Barbès, a popular bar and music venue in Park Slope. Conan needed a piano for visiting musicians. Within a matter of days, we arranged a trade: Barbès got my Baldwin Acrosonic spinet, and I got Lamb's ruby-red Delecia Carmen accordion.

I made frequent visits to Barbès to hear local accordionists like Ben Ickies and Rachelle Garniez (accordion and vocals) and bands that made use of the accordion and free-reed instruments: Slavic Soul Party (Peter Stan, accordion), Matt Munisteri & Brockmumford (Will Holshouser, accordion), and One Ring Zero (Joshua Camp, accordion). So my interest in the accordion was a product of an entirely new phenomenon, apparently unrelated to the wave of popularity the accordion experienced during the Lawrence Welk era. But what was this phenomenon, exactly? Who were all these people who played accordion? Why did they choose their instrument, and what kinds of sounds and styles did they relate it to? Under what circumstances did the accordion make a reappearance in the late twentieth century, and how did these new uses of the accordion relate to the its history? And why, when I began to learn and play the accordion in public, did people seem so amazed to see and hear the accordion? ("I haven't seen one of those in awhile" was a frequent comment I heard.) Judging from the lineup at Barbès, accordionists and bands with accordions symbolized an appealing and popular manifestation of alternative musical cultures in the postpunk area. Had we returned to some version of the era when accordion bands, accordion orchestras, and accordion-playing virtuosi on television had symbolized an appealing and popular manifestation of American mainstream musical cultures, pre-Elvis and pre-Beatles? Were we returning to the past, and under what conditions?

Attempting to answer some of these questions, I attended my first Accordion Seminars, an annual ritual sponsored by the American Accordionists Association (AAA) in New York City. I was not prepared for what I was witnessing—northern Italian accordion music, Mozart opera overtures transcribed for the accordion, and atonal improvisations for digitally enhanced accordions, interspersed with maniacally satirical and dark commentary by curatormusician William Schimmel. I was amazed to visit Joan Grauman's house in Potomac, Maryland, in which every room was filled with accordions, accordion memorabilia, accordion-playing troll figurines, and drawings and paintings of accordionists. This was a world in itself, different from anything I had seen as a pianist or even as a player of klezmer and other ethnic styles of music. I became intrigued by the stories older people told about their experiences with the accordion—which seemed to consist of episodes like being enticed into lessons by a door-to-door salesmen, followed by intensive study at a studio, followed by neglect, and later, rediscovery. But how did that relate to what I was observing in New York City? And what of the accordion's history—right here in New York, a manufacturing center? At that point, I had no inkling of the century's worth of historical research that lay ahead of me, detailed in chapters 2, 3, and 4 of this book.

I learned that there were accordion festivals and conventions in most major cities and many small towns across the country; that there were workshops on specific ethnic styles featuring the accordion; that one could travel to an accordion festival somewhere in the world every month. I learned of the many people who played and composed for the accordion as a "classical" instrument, as well as those who played accordion in the context of ethnic and traditional folk music. In this way I discovered the conventionally ethnographic material in this book. All of these phenomena were vaguely familiar to me as an ethnomusicologist, but it was hard to determine—once I decided to turn my accordion investigations into a book—where to locate my "field" of study. The community with which I became involved was bound by no single repertoire, ethnic background, or specific location. This "world" owed its existence almost entirely to a shared interest in a particular instrument. In this sense, it differed markedly from the traditional fieldwork situations in which the location of the field is obvious. One of my first discoveries was that these "accordion people," as they called themselves, were extremely mobile, traveling to conventions and conferences and competitions all over the globe.

Since the origins of ethnomusicology as a discipline, scholars have been concerned with the collection and documentation of musical instruments from around the world. The discipline's major thrust has been the investigation of their sound quality and the materials and techniques of their construction. The centuries of work in this area has privileged scientific modes of inquiry such as classification and acoustic analysis.[1] This book addresses the ongoing reexamination of organology, the science of musical instruments. Like some other contemporary scholars of ethnomusicology, I conceive the study of musical instruments not as the study of objects but as the study of tools for making culture. Two scholars in this endeavor, Alan Merriam and Paul Berliner, have made significant, early progress toward enhancing our knowledge of the meaning of musical instruments. Merriam's magisterial account of drum-making among the Bala Basongye introduced a comprehensively ethnographic approach to the study of musical instruments, revealing important findings about how they operate at the intersection of material, social, spiritual, and cultural worlds, and how their meanings are constructed on multiple symbolic levels.[2] Paul Berliner's unique contribution was to fuse the study of a musical instrument (the Shona mbira) with all aspects of music making in people's lives.[3] Recent books have deepened our understanding of the cultural work musical instruments perform: how they visually and publicly display a culture's mores and values, retain cultural memory, delineate gender roles, construct ethnic identity, embody meaning, and act as indicators of place, self, and community. In these studies, particularly Kevin Dawe's study of the Cretan lyre, the themes and ideas come from observations in situ of the instruments' and performers' relationships with their geographic, economic, and cultural contexts. Studies such Richard Leppert's analysis of the role of seventeenth- and eighteenth-century keyboard instruments in European domestic culture offer a valuable contribution toward the understanding of iconographic representations of musical instruments.[4]

In all of these studies, musical instruments are viewed not just as soundmaking objects but as part of an active web of meaning, whether they are rooted in a single tradition or community or circulate transnationally, acquiring a different range of meanings for which they were not originally intended, as Karen

Linn certainly demonstrates in her study of the banjo, tracing its circulation from Africa to American minstrel shows to middle-class American parlors.[5] Clearly, instruments can be problematic; their meanings are never neutral. But few instruments—perhaps only the banjo—have had as wide a range of meanings as the accordion, whose role, from the rock band to the Dutchman band to the symphony orchestra, has been hotly contested.

Scholars exploring new symbolic and sonic dimensions of musical instruments in human experience find themselves increasingly drawn into conversations about transnational networks and industries that circulate and transmit musical instruments, along with other ethnic commodities. These conversations often reference James Clifford's "traveling cultures" and his analysis of issues surrounding the display and performance of objects in postmodern contexts.[6] For example, Karl Neuenfeldt's (1997) work views the didjeridu as a symbol both of aboriginality and resistance, in Australia, and of essentialized primitivism, where it is played on the streets of large cosmopolitan cities from Berlin and Boston.[7] Likewise, Kevin Dawe and Andrew Bennett reveal strikingly different dimensions of the guitar's ubiquity in world cultures, where it "circulates in cultural spaces created at the convergence of local and global forces."[8] Like the mass-produced guitars of Gibson and Fender, the piano accordions of Excelsior and Titano offer a uniform and consistent prototype with which to contend as a hegemonic force. These types of accordion have followed a consistent pattern—replacing local indigenous instruments and sounds—yet people subvert that hegemony by appropriating the instrument in local ways, as in the customized models used in conjunto music and Dominican *merengue típico*.[9] Less prone today to frame their analyses of instruments in closed or static cultural systems, scholars are increasingly attracted to postmodern formations such as the "global cultural flows" described by Arjun Appadurai and Igor Kopytoff.[10] The "cultural biographical" approach prescribed by Kopytoff can be productive and helpful in transforming the classic "organology orthodoxy"[11] that has held on for too long in the field of ethnomusicology.

Accordingly, in writing this biography of the accordion, I move away from traditional organological concerns (the collection of data on materials, construction, and design of musical instruments) and focus on the accordion as a thing with a complex "social life," career, and networks of exchange. I pose questions similar to those Kopytoff asks about material objects in general: Where do accordions come from and who made them? For what purpose? What are the major markers and periods in the thing's life, and what are the possibilities inherent in its status? How does it function as an object of exchange? When the accordion moved from local artisan production in small shops to the global market, it did so with a force Kopytoff might recognize as a "drive toward commoditization."[12] In a general sense, the mass-produced, factory-made piano accordion emerged as a "colonizing" force in the modern European and American world, reshaping tastes and musical practices as it replaced the traditional diatonic button accordions that had long been popular with European national and ethnic groups. But people also appropriate and "recolonize" musical instruments, subverting the meanings and uses for which they were invented.[13] My cultural biography of the accordion offers a compelling model for scholars concerned with how instruments become situated in wider networks of social and symbolic exchange across a broad spectrum of time and space in the twentieth century.

A second conversation with which this book will engage scholars of music is the idea of the accordion as a cultural technology, which I define (after Jon Frederickson) as a network of circulating objects and relationships involving musical skills and a means of organizing cultural work.[14] Like scholars such as Paul Théberge and Timothy Taylor, who have been concerned with musical instruments as consumer technologies, I view the accordion and its manufacture as rooted in an American midcentury cultural sphere in which issues of authenticity and power come into play.[15] Throughout the book, relating debates about the free-bass accordion and whether or not and how people should play Bach and rock on piano accordions, I explore the routes by which accordionists became "consumers of technology" in a way that represented a break from earlier practices.[16] Paralleling Théberge's study of music technologies in North America, this book will address accordion manufacture, design, and marketing. The reader will see that some of the same processes that produced the American accordion phenomenon also produced the Hammond organ and the Moog synthesizer, enhancing the presence of technology in the musical lives of Americans. I will also show how the accordion contributed to a backlash against technology and the desire for the more "embodied" experience of music making that the accordion offers.

Another of my early observations was how marginal the accordion was to a topic that would appear to fit the aims of my academic discipline. As studies of American vernacular music have proliferated in ethnomusicology and folklore studies lately, various American popular instruments such as the reed organ, the steel-pedal guitar, and the banjo have received long overdue attention from scholars, including folklorists, historians, and anthropologists, as well as authors without scholarly credentials.[17] Meanwhile, the accordion has fallen through the disciplinary cracks. Although it is a Western instrument, invented in nineteenth-century Vienna and used to play classical repertoire, it is seen as too "folk" for musicologists to study, and therefore, few scholarly studies of the accordion exist apart from encyclopedia articles. Yet it is not "other" enough to attract ethnomusicologists, who have traditionally avoided Western musical practices and instruments. A number of fine books written about accordion luminaries and about ethnic American traditions such as Cajun/zydeco and Tejano/conjunto have helped to shed light on accordion icons like Dick Contino, Peewee King, and Frankie Yankovic, as well as the role of the accordion as a frontline or solo instrument in oldtime ethnic musical styles and western swing, in Nashville and beyond.[18] However, these studies have contributed little to an understanding of the accordion's cultural evolution and its wider cultural relevance. As studies of individual genres or regional styles, these books cannot help us in interpreting the instrument's unique crosscultural appeal. This relative neglect of the instrument has its roots in the trivialization of the accordion, which began during the peak of its commercial appeal in the early twentieth century and accelerated as early virtuosi incorporated it into their vaudeville routines. To many scholars and composers, the accordion represents a novelty, shtick, corniness, sentimentality. To ethnomusicologists, the accordionist suggests polka, a faux pas of ethnic revivalism, or both.

Nevertheless, the themes sounded by accordion advocates recur in the major American cultural movements of the twentieth century, and the accordion was at the center of developments in American vernacular music before it was displaced by the guitar. Even the most banal evocations of the accordion at the hands of Lawrence Welk and Dick Contino have significant importance, having exercised an alluring hold over images of the American past and collective identity. These evocations have been recycled and parodied in pop cultural representations in radio, television, film, and advertising and have played a vital role in consumer culture. Accordion advocates fought to establish the accordion in playing a significant role in what Americans recognize as "serious" musical culture, and it still does, although in a limited way. This book examines the accordion as cultural icon, identifying its role in American musical life and explicating its appeal to a large segment of the American public.

The instrument discussed in this book is the piano accordion, which evolved from different types of free-reed instruments invented and popularized in Europe and the British Isles. A definition of this modern instrument that would be acceptable to its contemporary scholars and performers would run as follows: it is a chromatic, bellows-driven, free-reed instrument that produces multiple chord tones with buttons on the left side manual and a piano keyboard on the right. Accordion reeds, like their counterparts in harmonicas, are "free" because of the way air passes over them inside reed blocks. As opposed to diatonic free-reeds, which necessitate bellows changes in order to play different pitches, the chromatic accordions can produce multiple tones, and entire phrases, on a single draw or press of the bellows. All accordions feature at least two or three switches that can vary the number and combinations of reeds, producing a variety of tone colors and a dense "symphonic" texture, and many accordions are equipped with five or seven switches, making possible dozens of reed combinations. All accordions, diatonic and chromatic, are equipped with straps that hold them on the body.[19]

Piano accordions differ from diatonic button boxes mainly in their function. In most folk musical traditions making use of the button box, the accordion is paired with a second instrument; for example, accordion and rubboard in zydeco, the accordion and *bajo sexto* in conjunto music. Such pairings provide the rhythmic armature that is characteristic of these dynamic dance music traditions. Unlike the button box, which is seen as a band instrument, the piano accordion came into its own as a solo instrument.

The typical midcentury piano accordionist student repertoire reflects a fondness for earlier (dated) styles of ethnic and popular styles of music, along with an intense commitment to Western classical repertoire that is often overlooked by today's accordionists, who admire the instrument for its folksy qualities. What are the origins of this particular instrument and the styles of playing associated with it? What does the instrument signify for its users and audiences in North America, and how has it evolved? What are the reasons for its dramatic rise to popularity and sudden fall? These are some of the basic questions that inspired this book.

Beginning with the first accordion craze in the 1900s, this book chronicles the accordion's rise to popularity in vaudeville, recreational groups and clubs, radio, recordings, television, and film, and the present "accordion revival" that took root with the help of Those Darn Accordions and many other groups based in San Francisco and New York in the 1990s. I argue that the accordion has played a significant and overlooked role in the American musical landscape and that it has reflected and shaped an eclectic mix of mainstream, folk, and classical cultural forms. It has served as a lightning rod for debate about high versus low culture and amateur and professional performance, as framed by American accordion advocates in the 1940s and 1950s who demanded equal opportunities for their instrument in America's elite cultural institutions. Polemical discussions taking shape in accordion magazines, as well as in mainstream music periodicals, shaped an idealized vision of the accordion as a classical musician worthy of a chair in the symphony orchestra, while discounting the role of the accordion in folk and popular musical genres. More significantly, the piano accordion was one of America's most popular instruments between 1938 and 1963, and in the peak year of 1953, its sales rivaled those of all the band instruments combined.

Like other grassroots American musical movements, such as barbershopping and banjo playing, the accordion movement revolved around themes of self-improvement, wholesomeness, and elevation. These notions, galvanized by visions of the piano accordion as one accordion for all Americans, paralleled the development of industrialization and suburbanization in America after World War II. Accordions produced in midwestern factories reached a peak of innovation (and pricing) in the 1940s and 1950s, contributing to pride in American ingenuity.

Accordion playing, motivated by a commitment to core community values as well as a fascination with technology, helped to support dominant modes of production, creating national and local communities of accordion players. At the same time, the piano accordion displaced the variety of diatonic button accordions (and their associated repertoires) played by immigrant Americans into a homogenized mainstream culture for a large proportion of white middle-class Americans.

Chapter 1 begins to answer some of the questions that sparked my curiosity after leaving Main Squeeze Accordions that brilliant fall day in Manhattan. I introduce the piano accordion and explain its modern evolution from earlier free-reed instruments. My exploration begins with mid-nineteenth-century Europe and moves on to the accordion's emerging audience in American cities at the turn of the century, this book's point of entry into the accordion world. I explain how the piano accordion became the most ubiquitous and popular free-reed instrument in the United States and many other parts of the world. I explore the development of the modern piano accordion through a look at its European roots, followed by a discussion of its evolution as a uniquely American instrument. Some of the early designs helped to create fascination with the instrument on the vaudeville stage and beyond. Some of these new accordions—and some of the debates surrounding their design and construction—demonstrate the unique visual and material culture surrounding the accordion. This chapter sets the stage for discussions of the accordion's emerging social capital—its capacity to express social status and power, and what accounted for its increasingly visible role in popular culture.

Next comes the story of the career of vaudeville star Guido Deiro (1886–1951), whose triumph as a vaudeville showman lay chiefly in his ability to use the accordion to bridge the gulf between notions of "high" and "low" entertainments and "classical" and "folk" that were widening in American culture. Laying the groundwork for later accordion artists, Deiro's presentations shaped the accordion's image as "an instrument for all." In contrast to earlier perspectives on the piano accordion that have overemphasized the contributions of Guido's brother Pietro, this chapter sheds light on Guido's pioneering role as a popular culture figure and his significant role in cementing a place for the accordion in American musical culture.

Continuing to look at the early roots of accordion culture in the United States, chapter 2 tells of a moment when the artistic value of the accordion came into greater focus. From conservatories to concert halls to competition stages, the absence of the accordion was touted as evidence of injustice. What's more, the improvement of the accordion's repertoire, pedagogy, and physical construction were prescribed as an urgent undertaking—and as vital contributions to the elevation of American cultural sensibilities. Although accordion personalities are not the primary focus of this book, I discuss the work of some of the accordion's most outstanding midcentury practitioners and promoters and the importance of innovations such as the free-bass converter system—the accordion's bid to be recognized not only as a legitimate instrument but an artist's instrument, worthy of the concert hall. Here we encounter some of the most significant classical repertoire for the accordion, still widely circulated today in accordion concerts and competitions.

This chapter concludes with a profile of Guido Deiro's younger brother Pietro Deiro (1888–1954), the self-described "Daddy of the Accordion." While his brother was capturing the admiration of vaudeville and theater audiences, Pietro was busy laying the groundwork for a popular accordion movement that would sustain itself in the American heartland. Unlike his dissolute brother Guido, Pietro was a calculating businessman who established and profited from accordion studios, schools, and his own publications. Beginning in the 1930s, Pietro organized a "rear guard" of professional accordionists to wage war against the "wrong" music for accordion and made it their mission to elevate the instrument. They continued in this mission until the rock 'n' roll revolution changed the American musical landscape forever.

Having described the workings of highbrow accordion culture in chapter 2, I pay tribute to the instrument's ethnic American roots in chapter 3. I discuss its ongoing importance in particular regions of the country—particularly the Upper Midwest—and in several ethnic styles of music: Slovenian and "Dutchman" style polka in the Midwest and Upper Peninsula and Valtaro musette in Manhattan's Italian neighborhoods. These communities generated many accomplished accordionists, a few of whom became popular "crossover" entertainers with international careers. These worlds predated and coexisted alongside the "accordion industrial complex", described in chapter 2, but few eminent accordion teachers valued or drew on any of these folk traditions. A discussion of conflict and continuity between the accordion's role in "folk communities" and the accordion industrial complex sets the stage for my examination of the later revival of the accordion (chapters 5 and 6).

Chapter 4 resumes the story around 1963, after the accordion had reached the height of its popularity and America's youth were beginning to embrace new music and new instruments. Looking at the accordion in the context of the rock 'n' roll invasion and the rise of youth culture, this chapter examines the accordion industrial complex's efforts to extend its popularity—focusing on a trickle of new models equipped with features for rock accordionists. Yet this new sense of excitement about the future of the accordion subsided. What's more, playing the accordion became, for all intents and purposes, geeky and uncool.

The accordion and its music come into focus in different sectors of the mainstream music world of the 1980s and 1990s (chapter 5). The accordion was presented as a counterbalance to the ubiquitous electronic soundscape of techno and punk. In world music, pop, and country, in the music of Bruce Springsteen, Peter Gabriel, Los Lobos, Paul Simon, and John Mellencamp, the accordion was presented in a folksy vein and as a counterpart to the artist's working-class and/or ethnic identity. Zydeco accordionist Clifton Chenier and Tex-Mex conjunto players Flaco Jimenez and Esteban Jordan (for whom Hohner designed its special Rockordeon model) were among those who helped to bring the instrument to wider attention in the 1980s. Although many of the newly "revived" folk styles (especially Irish traditional music) featured the button diatonic accordion or melodeon, I argue that these instruments gave piano accordionists a new impetus to explore what they perceived as a more "folk" or "authentic" style of playing. In the academic music world, the accordion fueled an ongoing hunger for new sounds and new cultural experiences. There were attempts to bridge the traditional divide between the highbrow and lowbrow aspects of the accordion. This chapter also profiles Carl Finch and accordionist-composer Guy Klucevsek. Their experimental uses of the accordion have opened up new possibilities for the potential of the accordion and the polka, now signifying the "cutting edge" and the avant-garde.

At the end of the twentieth century and the beginning of the twenty-first, Americans renewed their fascination with the accordion, as well as with a variety of world-music instruments. Attempting to go beyond conventional and obvious explanations that focus on nostalgia and the heightened ethnic self-awareness of Americans in the post-*Roots* era, in chapter 6 I trace some diverse aspects of the accordion's current popularity that have yet to come to light: the San Francisco neo-vaudeville scene; the accordion festival phenomenon with its emphasis on the ludic, participatory aspects of accordion playing; and Internet-based accordion communities. Newly created festivals and organizations, often in conjunction with local tourism boards and business councils, became focal points for diversity and provided the accordion scene with a core identity. I explore the rise of festivals such as the International Accordion Festival in San Antonio and the Cotati Accordion Festival in Sonoma County, California. Their performer lineups and audiences reflect a wide range of age groups, ethnicities, and musical interests. Another notable, undocumented development is a renewed interest in learning to play folk and traditional music. Today's accordion enthusiasts are more likely to play Tejano, klezmer, Cajun, and zydeco than transcriptions of the classics. Festival attendees are as eager to participate in workshops as they are to sit through concerts. Accordion collecting and the material culture of the accordion are again on the rise. Accordion conventions and festivals are bustling with sales of accordion-related merchandise, ephemera, and tokens of self-identification with the global "accordion community." I conclude the chapter with reflections on the cultural work the accordion has been doing in the late twentieth and early twenty-first centuries—embracing the idea of "difference" and recapturing genres, cultures, and repertoires that were previously marginalized in the accordion world.

In the conclusion, I chart the relationships between all the different communities, regions, and phases of the accordion's life I have discussed, exploring common threads and disjunctions throughout this book's historical period. While attempting to adhere to a chronological narrative, I emphasize that this "biography" of the accordion does not follow a smooth arc of rise, fall, and revival; nor is it the province of one social group or place or of a fixed body of repertoire. Although I trace the evolution of one single free-reed prototype, the piano accordion, I also reference other instruments, such as the diatonic button accordion and the chromatic accordion, which helped to shape the piano accordion's development and influence the tastes and playing style of its practitioners. In many phenomena that can be described as postmodern, global, transnational, virtual, and commercial, boundaries are often blurry and difficult to define. How can the ethnographer approach musical instruments? Are they fixed objects of study, or moving targets? My intention is to move the study of the accordion away from the traditional subdiscipline of organology and to say something about the processes through which instruments evolve. Musical instruments entail a great deal of disjunctions between the makers, individuals, institutions, and ideas that shape them at different phases in their history. The large number of variables involved in all the repertoires, practices, and ideas of accordionists have frequently led me to question the wisdom of attempting a single book on this topic. Yet it is this very breadth that allows me to define my object of study, as if it were expanding in bellows-like fashion. Such a perspective enables us to see, among all the variables, continuity and harmony among different sectors of the accordion world.

Remarkably cohesive ideas of authenticity, technological progress, elevation of taste, and—ultimately—self-improvement surface over the course of the accordion's hundred-year history in the United States. Some of the ideologies and institutions that promoted these ideas deserve close scrutiny. Hence this work can be seen, in part, as a missing piece of this nation's social history and a collection of ideas—their emergence and transformation within different American communities. To return to the metaphor of the accordion bellows: both push and pull factors, observable over long periods of time, shape the accordion's life span. The reasons for the accordion's ebb and flow, and what it reveals about the American cultural experience, should become clear by the end of the book.

$\mathcal{A}$DVENT OF THE $\mathcal{P}$IANO $\mathcal{A}$CCORDION

THE LUSHLY SYMPHONIC SOUNDS of the accordion filled the parlors, salons, and concert halls of nineteenth-century Europe. Accordion scholars generally trace the beginnings of their instrument's history to the "Demian," a new free-reed instrument patented by Austrian organ builder and inventor Cyril Demian in 1828.[1] These diatonic button accordions were equipped with two, three, or four rows for a variety of harmonies, and could create multivoiced textures and simple rhythms suitable for folk and traditional dance music. Demian brought about the first significant transformations with an instrument he called the *akkordeon*, from the Italian word *accordare* ("sound together"), a name he chose shrewdly. "Sounding together" implied that it could play chords—glorious harmony. The button system with its preset chords enabled the player to produce multiple harmonies without the need for a band. The patent stated that it could play rhythm (waltzes, marches, and polkas)—a small orchestra substitute. The neologism *akkordeon* highlights the instrument's novelty appeal. The wording of Demian's patent implies that it was conceived as a convenience for travelers and a portable substitute for other instruments.[2] The Demian was the instrument that would ultimately evolve into the modern piano accordion and serve a broader range of constituencies than its inventor had imagined. But at the time of its invention, other inventors were hoping to profit from the new free-reed instruments. Only a month after the Demian was patented in May 1829, Charles Wheatstone followed with his concertina, which drew an enthusiastic following in the United Kingdom and beyond.[3] There were German, French, Russian, Swedish, and American versions of Demian's accordion as well, varying in size and numbers of keys.

After 1914, the accordion underwent another dramatic transformation: global sales and marketing. That would not have happened were it not for the plastics industry, advances in manufacturing, and the development of many features of the accordion—new arrangements of keyboards and buttons that made an expanded range of notes accessible to the fingers and ultimately more suited to the needs of solo virtuoso artists. Changing tastes and the rise of radio and sound recording played a significant role in bringing the accordion to wider attention. Nevertheless, the familiar piano accordion design that became standard by the mid-1930s—as well as its playing conventions and repertoire—is a direct descendant of what Paolo Soprani and the Italian accordion industry developed. The Italians were significant in the popularization of the accordion, with their vision not only of how to design and perform the accordion artistically but also of how to get large numbers of them into the hands of Americans. The story of the accordion after 1908 is about people who at critical moments redefined the technology of the instrument as well as the culture surrounding the instrument. In so doing, they opened for it new markets, new repertoires, and a new place in the social order.

The early Italian firms were the first of many who would effect such transformations. They took an expensive, fragile, and exotic instrument and with the cooperation of manufacturers turned it into a product that could be mass-produced and sold, if only in limited quantities at first. Italians made the first mass-produced accordions, and American firms followed with scores of others that came to surpass the Italian ones in ingenuity and sophistication. The Americans' timing was excellent. Turn-of-the century vaudeville, the subsequent jazz craze of the 1920s, and the emerging role of the accordion in dance bands all helped to pave the way for the accordion's wider popularity. The era witnessed the first (and only) accordion-playing vaudeville celebrity, Guido Deiro, whose career is discussed in this chapter. With remarkable self-confidence and musical acumen, Deiro transformed the accordion into a tool with which to enrich one's musical tastes and sensibilities and set the stage for the accordion's "golden age." This golden age was not just invented by a single artist; it was willed into existence by a broad constituency of people. This process of reinvention and redefinition is still going on. To account for the incredible success of a single free-reed instrument—the piano accordion—one must also understand how the descendants of the Demian, the diatonic button accordions, were used and how their limitations were understood. It was these limitations that made room for the piano accordion, which broke with past practices in many ways.

Throughout the nineteenth century, the age of Romanticism in Europe, the most popular type of free-reed instrument in circulation—and the one pioneered by Demian—was the diatonic accordion, which produces two notes on a single button upon the opening and closing of the bellows. These were manufactured throughout Europe and circulated to the United States; by 1902, Sears Roebuck was featuring European accordions in its retail catalogs.[4]

Italian makers developed the Demian prototype—flat and no larger than a harmonica—into its iconic shape and gave it protection from dust and moisture, extending its life span.[5] Italian makers offered many choices of models with highly ornamented, elegant, and allegorical case designs. On one of Dallapé's earliest models, neoclassical muse-like figures float in midair, holding lyres. Skilled craftsmen carved shimmering mother-of-pearl (abalone) embellishments for the grilles, working through the standard visual vocabulary of neoclassicism and Art Deco: grapevines, flowers, naked cherubs, and scantily clad Greco-Roman Muses. These alluring (and sometimes erotic) images not only provided eye candy but also served a practical function: covering the screws and joints and concealing the instrument's otherwise boxy shape. Such iconography, rendered in expensive materials, suggests that the some of the accordion's early makers wished to present it as a "classical" or "high-class" instrument, worthy of the salons of Europe in which it was circulated.[6] Such designs would later leave their iconographic traces on the much fancier accordions developed by Italian immigrants for the American vaudeville scene.

The names of manufacturers always appear on the grilles, helping to identify their dates and places of origin. The fronts of the grilles feature ornate hand-cut covers. The buttons on the right-hand keyboard are arranged in rows of ten, containing a major scale. The push of the bellows produces a major triad, and the pull produces the other tones of the scale (the left-hand buttons sound the bass notes). The number of rows and the tuning system used often reflect the unique characteristics of the musical genre deployed.[7] Although popular in many ethnic and traditional musical styles, diatonic button accordions could only produce a limited number of bass tones, and hence they were not seen as complete instruments in their own right.[8]

In 1850, the Viennese musician Franz Walther built an instrument with forty-six buttons arranged in three rows of minor thirds, each row a half step apart. (The bass section was a diatonic row, divided between single bass notes and two-note chords). In this three-row chromatic pattern, the two additional rows duplicated the first two rows to provide alternative fingering (only one finger pattern was necessary to play all the keys). To change to another key, the player shifted the finger pattern across the keyboard and began another note, as one might do on a guitar fingerboard. On a chromatic keyboard, the hand can span two and a half octaves, as compared to a single octave on a piano keyboard prior to the introduction of treble shifts. Another feature that distinguished this accordion from the earlier diatonic button box was its ability to produce the same note upon different directions of the bellows. These instruments came to be called chromatic accordions.

In Paris, a few years after Walther's invention, Viennese and French makers experimented with chromatic free-reeds named *accordion-orgue,* flutina, or *harmonieflute,* accordions with a piano-like keyboard in the right hand. Busson's *accordion-orgue* caught the Parisian public's attention with its single-action reeds and a reservoir bellows that could be pumped, while placed on a stand, with a foot pedal. This exotic free-reed instrument had no bass buttons and a rather soft—but richly nuanced—tone. It marks the piano accordion's beginnings.[9]

Popular demand established a transnational market and the establishment of firms such as Hohner in Germany (1857) and Soprani (1872) and Dallapé in Italy (1876). To succeed, however, the dispersed armies of accordions spreading across Europe needed a command center—and it was Castelfidardo, Italy. By the end of the nineteenth century, most of these instruments were mass-produced by the large companies based in Castelfidardo.

Castelfidardo, located between the Aspio and Musone river valleys, is a scenic Italian hill town of the type that attracts tourists from England, the United States, and the rest of Europe. The town's handful of historic sites and markers evoke the glories of the Risorgimento, the Italian unification movement. There is the Collegiate Church with its onion-shaped bell tower, a Renaissance-style palazzo, and a grandiose (twentieth-century) equestrian monument to the fallen in the Battle of Castelfidardo, in which the town prevailed against the imperialist papal army. The town is also a draw for accordion fans, collectors, and serious players who can afford to commission a fine custom-made accordion from one of the thirty or so remaining family-owned factories or to make a once-in-lifetime pilgrimage. Not far from the grandiose statue is a monument visiting accordionists probably regard as equally significant: a bust of Paolo Soprani, founder of the accordion industry in Italy, who began his distinguished career by pirating the Demian.[10] His brothers Settimo and Paschale then began producing their own accordions in the wine cellar of the family's farm, expanding to an outbuilding on the farm. The first accordions were sold in the fairs and marketplaces of the nearby regions, especially Loreto, a meeting point for religious pilgrims, travelers, and traders. Paolo traveled with his products on horseback to the busy city center of Castelfidardo; in 1872 he decided to open a factory in Piazzetta Garibaldi there. When the factory began receiving orders from abroad (France and the United States toward the end of the nineteenth century), Paolo, now in partnership with his sons Luigi and Achille, opened up a new factory on the elegant, tree-lined Avenue Umberto. In 1900, following the Sopranis' success displaying their wares at the Paris Exhibition, they became members of the Academy of Inventors of Brussels and Paris and were received at the Élysée Palace by Emile Loubet, the president of France. As early as 1899, observers noted the accordion's potential to become a more "elevated" instrument in the salons of Europe.[11]

The accordion had arrived—it had risen above its humble rural origins to become the darling of the salons of Europe. But the Italian pioneers of the accordion had even bigger plans for the instrument. The last decade of the nineteenth century saw a rapid growth not only of the Soprani enterprise, which employed as many as four hundred workers, but of other workshops, including the Scandalli brothers in Camerano and Antonio Ranco in Vercelli, whose firm would later help to launch Guido Deiro's virtuoso solo career in the United States. Soprani's brothers branched out to set up their own workshops—Settimo's in Via Cavour, Castelfidardo, and Paschal's in Recanati, which also became a center for accordion manufacture. All these workshops produced the simple, inexpensive 2-bass diatonic accordion, an instrument that enjoyed instant and outstanding success. It was widely copied by scores of accordion firms hoping to cash in on this success.

The production data from the late nineteenth century are astonishing. No other industry had seen such a rapid rise in Italy. According to an exhibition of industry products from the Marche region, the accordion industry employed five hundred workers in fourteen factories.[12] The rosters of accordion factory workers with common last names suggest that the industry relied on entire families working on the factory floors as well as in their home workshops. This tradition afforded the accordion industry a great deal of flexibility, as workers could be hired and fired to meet ever-fluctuating demand. In the first decade of the twentieth century, the Soprani family shifted from fully handmade production to a fully integrated production line, with electricity powering the machinery to fabricate reeds. This allowed the Soprani firm to substantially increase its profit margin in that same decade.[13] The Sopranis celebrated their success by erecting an enormous neoclassical factory building adjacent to the town's center between 1907 and 1909. They were soon joined by dozens of competitors: Enrico and Paolo Guerrini, Piatanesi, Serenelli, and Sante Crucianelli, creating a construction boom along Avenue Umberto—renamed "Dollar Street."[14]

Shortly before the onset of World War I, a major market shift occurred in the industry. In 1907, the data show that only 690 accordions were exported.

In 1913, that figure rose to 14,365—an impressive figure when one takes note of the many accordion-producing nations in competition with Italy: Russia, Czechoslovakia, Germany, and France.[15] The accordion's rise to popularity and its potential in the field of classical music were noted even by Italy's most famous composer, Giuseppe Verdi, who may have put forth a proposal to the Italian National Conservatory for the study of the accordion.[16]

Although Castelfidardo was the center of Italian accordion production, the town of Stradella in Lombardy played a decisive role in the development of the piano accordion tradition. There Mario Dallapé developed an expansive new system for the bass side of the accordion, with 120 bass buttons arranged in six rows of twenty, with each row staggered diagonally from its neighbor, as the bass button chart shows. The first row of twenty buttons nearest the bellows (the counter-bass row) produces tones a major third above the bass tone; the second (the fundamental row) produces the bass tone; the third is the major chord row (indicated with the capital letter M); the fourth is the minor chord row (lowercase m); the fifth is the seventh chord row (7); and the sixth is the diminished row (d). Ten buttons from the bottom of the accordion in the fundamental row is the button producing the note C—often marked by an indentation or an inlaid rhinestone.[17]

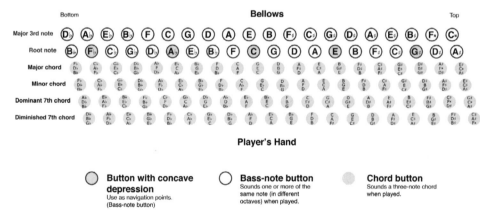

Bass button chart for the Stradella accordion system, developed by Mario Dallapé in Stradella, Italy, in the late nineteenth century. The 120-bass configuration is currently the most common system employed in modern piano accordions. The arrangement of buttons was conceived to give the player's left hand access to the most commonly played bass root notes and chords in Western music (note that C is in the center of the row of root notes, second from top).

We can see, through the Stradella system, why the accordion was so appealing to novice musicians, for the ingenious arrangement of the basses made it so. It was through this system that the developers of the accordion conceived of something that had a universal appeal, at least in Western folk music. The easy harmonic transitions (from major to minor, from tonic to dominant) available through the Stradella system reflected the harmonic progressions of many European and New World folk musical genres, such as the waltz, tango, and mazurka, that were on the rise in Italy and central Europe in the late nineteenth century.

Although the Stradella was not the first piano accordion—that distinction belonged to Busson's *accordion-orgue*—the Stradella system was key to the piano accordion's ultimate popular and commercial success. It allowed Dallapé and all Italian firms to build accordions that had "universal" qualities, at least in Western classical and popular music. It led to the establishment of a common knowledge bank, a kind of musical programming, as something both independent of and important to the folk music repertoire. By providing a bass line, and rhythmic accompaniment, these instruments could take the place of a piano, a bass, or even an entire band. It was the accordion's "one-man band" versatility—and its ability to handle music in any key—that demonstrated its commercial potential and its promise in the field of American popular entertainment. The accordion was now ready to ride a new wave of popular culture sweeping across America of the early twentieth century.

Between 1840 and 1940, one of the most significant population movements occurred between Europe and the Americas. Estimates of the number of Italians who crossed the Atlantic converge at around sixteen million.[18] Among the pioneers of this movement in the early nineteenth century were artisans and craftsmen who perceived demand for their products and services far from Italy. Among these were hundreds of skillful accordion makers, technicians, and salesmen riding the wave of immigration to New York, Chicago, and San Francisco—the cities with large immigrant populations and the key cities in which the American accordion industry established itself. These men hoped to market the accordion not only to fellow Italians but also to immigrants from eastern Europe, Poland, Ireland, Czechoslovakia, and other nations that had experienced the accordion craze in Europe. While many of these nations launched accordion industries of their own during the same period,[19] Italy virtually controlled the export market, particularly in the United States. In the 1940s and 1950s, the factories of Castelfidardo produced 90 percent of the accordions played by Americans.[20] In the earlier age of emigration, the accordion traveled with Italian immigrants throughout the Americas, becoming the defining instrument in a variety of folk and popular musics.

The accordion had practical advantages for Italian immigrants (as it did for other immigrant communities). First, an accordion was more affordable than a piano.[21] It was sturdy, portable, relatively easy to learn to play at least on a basic level, its sound carried very well, and it could be adapted to play a wide range of musical repertoires. With the ease of playing chords with the left hand, the accordion was readily adaptable to a variety of dance rhythms played at social dance events. One account by an Italian historian suggests how the accordion may have been perceived within the Italian diasporan community: "The large Italian populations who had emigrated to the Americas eased their homesickness with the sounds of accordion music. For those forced to leave their place of birth to earn a living in a foreign land, the accordion became a standard part of their luggage, a piece of home that they brought with them."[22] Bugiolacchi's account of accordion-playing immigrants implies that the instrument's appeal was instantaneous and automatic. Yet the Italians' dominance in the field was carefully calculated. Along with other tradesmen and traders—ink vendors from Parma, child street musicians from Genoa, and *figurinai* sellers from Lucca, the musicians and entrepreneurs from Italy were active participants in the mass labor migrations of the late nineteenth and early twentieth centuries.[23] When accordion craftsmen journeyed from Castelfidardo to America to sell their wares, they tested the market, following the routes and methods of other diasporic tradesmen. Accordion factories and retail businesses focused their efforts on cities with large immigrant populations, locating their factories and shops in Italian neighborhoods. Accordion players and enthusiasts came to admire, above all other models, the instruments of Soprani, Serenelli, and Dallapé as the world's finest, citing the quality of their reeds and their workmanship. Italy's leaders eagerly supported the industry in their efforts to advance the nation's productivity and economic prowess.[24] Beginning in the early 1900s, relatives of the Italian accordion makers brought their ingenuity and their passion for accordions to America, establishing the first American outpost of the Italian accordion industry in San Francisco. The ideas and innovations of these immigrants would prove significant for the development of the accordion as a uniquely American instrument.

For most American accordion enthusiasts, 1908 marks the beginning of their history—the first time a piano accordion was performed in the United States and the beginning of the accordion craze. The first two decades of the twentieth century, until America's entry into World War I, marked a prosperous social climate during which the United States demonstrated its political and economic might to the rest of the world. Among America's middle class, optimism prevailed about their economic future as the nation bounded ahead in productivity and economic momentum. This was the climate in which late-nineteenth-century urban Americans witnessed the development of vaudeville, the cultural phenomenon that first brought the accordion to widespread public attention. The vaudeville theaters offered a never-ending variety of acts to a diverse, mobile, working-class and lower-class audience that was increasingly in pursuit of leisure and eager to spend its disposable income on entertainment. It was also during this period that the accordion itself became a constituent of a national American commodity market.[25]

The vaudeville tradition developed from a number of existing musical and nonmusical institutions, especially taverns and saloons in the rough-and-tumble entertainment districts in San Francisco's and New York's seaports. Some of these districts were infamous for prostitution, organized crime rings, kidnappings, and extortions. There was San Francisco's infamous Barbary Coast, a nine-block area of numerous saloons, dance halls, and brothels. Until 1917, when San Francisco's police commission closed down the district, a good accordionist could find regular employment in the Barbary Coast district. The young virtuoso accordionist Angelo Cagnazzo, an immigrant from Italy who became a prominent figure in the accordion industry, played tangos, mazurkas, and fox-trots at Barbary Coast bars and "ten cents a dance" establishments. He later taught Dick Contino, the accordion icon of the 1940s and 1950s.[26]

In an effort to provide "cleaned-up" or more decent entertainment for middle-class audiences, variety and vaudeville theaters opened up in cities across America in the late nineteenth century.[27] Vaudeville's complex formula that drew talent from immigrant ethnic performers, cobbling together dialect songs, slapstick skits, and crass ethnic stereotypes of Jews, Italians, Germans, and Irish, has been well documented by historians. However, vaudeville was also a source of more "elevated" forms of musical entertainment: sentimental songs, light classical music, and "refined" and "cleaned-up" versions of European and American folksongs.[28] In that capacity, music—serious music in particular—was an indispensable, if often overlooked, component of vaudeville. As the vaudevillian memoirist Joe Laurie, Jr., has put it, "from the first days of the honky-tonks to the time when the last exit march was heard at the Palace, music played a very important part in vaudeville."[29]

Vaudeville required a diverse array of musical skills. The musicians in the pit orchestras needed to master cues and sound effects along with classical overtures, marches, and sentimental songs, with little or no rehearsal time. The musical acts that performed onstage had to maintain the audience's attention between the dog act and the acrobats. "Novelty" musical acts featured musicians performing on musical rattles, farm implements, bones, vegetables, gobletphones (water glasses), and bells (handbells, Alpine bells, and sleigh bells). Musical clowns specialized in balloons, saws, washboards, bottles, and "trick violins." Concertina-playing clowns, a phenomenon that originated in London music halls, made occasional appearances on the American vaudeville stage.[30] "Straight" musical acts showcased xylophonists, brass bands, violinists, ragtime pianists, banjo players, and piano accordionists. Accordionists often appeared in ethnic vaudeville sketches featuring Irish, African American, Italian, and Chinese ethnic humor, whether or not accordions were part of a culture's traditional music style. Founded by an aspiring Philippine concert pianist who emigrated to San Francisco, the Chinese act "Ming and Toy" were fixtures on San Francisco's "Chop Suey" circuit in the 1920s and 1930s. Ming (the erstwhile pianist) played piano accordion and ukulele and also juggled.[31]

Whether they were part of "straight" or "novelty" acts, all vaudeville musicians had to face the considerable difficulties in breaking into the business. The vaudeville shows were controlled by a handful of companies (Orpheum and Keith) that controlled regional touring circuits. A performer had the best chance of entering the business through family connections, or joining a "family act," as Anthony Galla-Rini did at the age of seven when he joined his father, John Galla-Rini, a euphonium and guitar player, and two older sisters in their family's musical act. The family also appeared as an accordion quartet. After the sisters left the act, John and Anthony formed a clown duet, Palo and Palet, which Anthony found to be a degrading experience. Anthony attributes to that experience his emerging ambition to shed the trappings of theater and become a respectable solo artist.[32]

The standardized format of most vaudeville shows allowed for only one serious musical act. Theater managers booked all of their acts (musicians included) for fifty-week runs, and available slots were hard to come by. At any given time, thousands of musicians were competing to be the sole musical act in a vaudeville program. Once they had broken into the business, most musicians confronted the fact that they occupied the bottom rungs of a rigidly hierarchical professional world. At the top of the vaudeville hierarchy and pay scale were acrobats, comedy acts, and dancers. Next came musical acts featuring singers, and following those, instrumentalists. Underage musicians with desirable talents could sometimes find themselves indentured by their own families as

Ming and Toy's vaudeville act made regular appearances in San Francisco's "Chop Suey" circuit in the 1920s. "Ming" was the stage name for the Philippine émigré (and classically trained pianist) Jose Paguio.

slave labor. Until he formed his own solo act, Anthony Galla-Rini never saw a dime of compensation from his father, with whom he was required to perform for ten years—until his seventeenth birthday.[33]

Musicians needed to double as stagehands and support personnel. Another famous accordionist who got his start in vaudeville, Lawrence Welk, traveled the Keith circuit. He appeared in the Irish entertainer George T. Kelly's act featuring ethnic stereotypes of Germans and Dutch that were wildly popular with midwestern audiences. As Kelly became increasingly incapacitated by alcoholism, Welk was also expected to move equipment, help with publicity and bookings, and run rehearsals, which later proved to be significant for his later career as a bandleader and producer.[34] Only on very rare occasions would a very prominent musician be the headliner on the vaudeville stage, and only one accordionist, Guido Deiro, was ever featured as a headline act, at New York City's Palace Theater in 1913.

Pietro Frosini with chromatic accordion. (Source: Guido Deiro Archives, Graduate Center, City University of New York)

For most early vaudeville accordionists, the instrument of choice was the chromatic button accordion, a double-action free-reed instrument developed by F. Walther and widely circulated in Europe and America throughout the nineteenth century. Pietro Deiro, Pietro Frosini, Suzette Carsell, and the three Marconi brothers—all luminaries of the piano accordion in vaudeville and beyond—got their start playing the chromatic button accordion and later switched to the piano accordion. Accordion virtuoso Pietro Frosini was one of the early "stars" of the accordion, traveling extensively on the Orpheum circuit and in Europe. He also made the first cylinder recordings of the accordion for Edison, in 1907.

Heralding the movement toward the piano accordion, and the accordion craze in America, was Guido Deiro.

Guido Deiro (1886–1950) experienced the most dramatic rise to success in accordion history, leading him from an existence as a itinerant musician in Europe to the most coveted distinction in the American entertainment world of the time: a vaudeville headline act. Apart from his brother and rival Pietro Deiro (1888–1954; see chapter 2), Guido did more than any other accordion artist to establish a glamorous, high-class image for the instrument. The Italo-American Company's accordion advertisements in the early 1930s proclaimed that Guido Deiro was the "first to introduce the piano accordion on stage, in concert, in records, in radio and film."[35] Guido was not only the first to play piano accordion in America—a distinction also claimed, spuriously, by Pietro—but also the first to become a vaudeville headline act and the first to enjoy a full-time career playing the instrument. His headline-making appearances and his romantic misadventures and marriages to Mae West and four other women offered titillating material for the gossip columns.

Guido Deiro was born to a prosperous family of grocers in the town of Salto Canavese in northern Italy's Piedmont region. The family patriarch, Carlo Deiro, intended for his sons to follow him in the family business and forced them to work "like serfs" in his stores.[36] He strongly disapproved of his sons' interest in the accordion, and nine-year-old Guido had to play his accordion in secret. To escape his overbearing father and the prospect of an arranged marriage, Guido ran away from home at age fourteen and traveled over the Alps to Germany. Toiling in the iron mines near Alsace-Lorraine, he saved enough money to purchase a chromatic system accordion from Ranco Antonio, an early Italian accordion manufacturing firm in Vercelli. The day the new accordion arrived, Guido quit the iron mines and found a position playing resorts in Turin's Lake District, branching out to cafés in Metz and resorts in

Guido Deiro. (Source: Guido Deiro Archives, Graduate Center,
City University of New York)

Switzerland. He also found a teacher, the pianist and accordionist Giovanni
Gagliardi, with whom he worked to develop "a very artistic style of playing
which was original."[37]

As his reputation and stage presence grew, Guido entered into an agree-
ment with Ranco to perform their instruments in various venues in Germany,
Switzerland, and Italy. At some point in his travels, he spotted one of the new
accordions with piano keys in the right hand and decided he had to have such
an instrument. Ranco built him a piano accordion, and Guido gave his three-

row button accordion to his brother Pietro. Inspired by Guido's success in Europe, Pietro—who had immigrated to the town of Cle Ellum, Washington, to work in the coal mines—decided to make the leap to a professional musical career in America. In 1908, two months after Pietro began playing at the Idaho Saloon in Seattle, Guido, having decided to emigrate to America, arrived in that city.

Guido's first appearance in the United States was as a demonstrator of accordions at the Alaskan-Yukon-Pacific Exposition in 1909.[38] This regional world's fair, designed to showcase Seattle as an ambitious port city and the emerging commercial center of the Pacific Coast, featured exhibits built by Alaska, the Canadian Yukon, Japan, and the Philippines.[39] The fair may have provided the ideal moment to highlight the accordion as evidence of American technological and musical ingenuity to the rest of the world—just what the Panama-Pacific Exposition succeeded in doing seven years later, in 1915. Guido surely appreciated the power of the piano accordion as a technological wonder fit for a world's fair, as did his audience at the Pavilion.

On his arrival in Seattle, Guido found a position performing piano accordion as a soloist at the Jackson Saloon, at the salary of $18 per month. He was neither daunted by the prospect of playing for crowds of inebriated miners nor inclined to compromise on his choice of robust, romantic repertoire. "My repertoire consisted of a very large collection of grand opera pieces, including 15 waltzes by the greatest composers in Europe—Waldteufel and Strauss. I played the famous 'Tesoro Mio Waltz' and 'Sharpshooter's March,' the first time it had been played in this country."[40]

Evidently, Deiro proved his talent to be big enough for vaudeville, which was drawing hordes of working-class immigrant audiences in Seattle and San Francisco. Together with an Italian singer, a "Mr. Porcini," Deiro first appeared on vaudeville as half of a duet, the Milano Duo. Dressed in elegant white suits and straw hats, the Duo was booked on the Orpheum circuit, touring Salt Lake City, Spokane, and Seattle. Returning to the City by the Bay, Guido met a Mr. Grauman, father of Sid Grauman, the famous manager of the Chinese Theatre in Hollywood. Grauman suggested that Guido part company with his singer and perform as a solo act. In 1910, the American Theatre in San Francisco booked Guido as "the Premier Piano Accordionist," the first piano accordionist to appear onstage—a designation generally seen as correct by historians and Guido's family members.[41] The program consisted of Suppé's "Poet and Peasant Overture," "Dill Pickles Rag," "My Treasure Waltz," and "I Got a Ring on My Finger." Guido wrote: "There was the time and the place to show what could be done with this instrument. It's now or never, I told myself. . . . My heart was full of melody and I wanted to show the people in the theatre how beautiful that melody was."[42] Around this time as well, Deiro was the first to call the instrument a "piano accordion," a translation from the Italian *armonica systema piano*.[43]

What was so appealing about the piano accordion? From the perspective of the audience, the appearance of the right-hand piano keyboard was novel. From the perspective of the performer, the piano keyboard made rapid-fire virtuoso playing and changing keys easier. And since there was a left-hand accompaniment, a piano accordionist would not have to share the take with a pianist or orchestra musicians. Indeed, Guido's handsome looks, impeccable sartorial style, dynamic stage presence, and rhinestone-bedecked accordion reflecting the stage lights must have made a quite an impression on the audiences. He perhaps went a bit too far in exploiting the novelty value of the accordion by claiming to have built one himself, according to a spurious account by the *Pittsburgh Post*.[44]

In 1913, billed simply as "Deiro," Guido performed at New York City's Palace Theatre, a distinction claimed by no other piano accordionist. Reviewers heralded Guido as "delightful," a "white-flanneled genius," and a "master."[45] They praised Deiro for transforming the piano accordion into an instrument worthy of comparison to the mighty pianos and the organs of the Western classical tradition: "He plays trills, runs, cadenzas, and even glissando effects— high-brow for running the fingers quickly over the white keys—as if he were seated at a big Mason-Steinway, and accomplishes a swell and diminuendo that one has a right to expect only from an organ pumped either electrically or Africanly" (the author probably meant "manually").[46] Some time in 1910–1912, another reviewer said: "Deiro gives to the accordion the sonorousness of the organ and at the same time, the exquisiteness and subtleness of the violin."[47] It is no wonder that critics who had heard the piano accordion before were impressed by the sound of Guido's instrument. This particular one, built by the Guerrini firm in San Francisco, had some unique features that enhanced the player's speed and tone (discussed later).

Like many popular artists of the day, including his brother Pietro, Guido composed his own original works. Beginning in 1916, the accordion publisher Biaggio Quattrociocche began to publish Guido's compositions. He was the author of nearly fifty known pieces: marches, rags, waltzes, mazurkas, quadrilles, and an extended work, *Egypto Fantasia*.[48] Without formal musical training, Guido relied on his publisher to transcribe his performances (live!) to music staff paper. According to some of his fellow accordionists, his genius was his gift for crafting melody. Galla-Rini noted: "Guido had a very fine touch with his hand on the keyboard, so much so, that a simple melody would sound like a sublime inspiration! Someone said, rightly so, that he had a million dollar touch."[49]

Guido used his good looks and charm not only onstage but in real life, not always making the wisest choices. He became known as a womanizer who "could never let a pretty ankle go by without serious consideration."[50] His first wife, seventeen-year-old Julia Tatro, forced him to the altar by threatening him to take him to court for statutory rape (Guido was later arrested on the stage of Chicago's Palace Theater under a warrant for lack of spousal support). His second marriage, the most famous, was to the voluptuous, bawdy stage star Mae West, with whom he appeared as a variety duet.

West abandoned Guido after two years; she wrote in her autobiography that she had had no choice but to leave him, as he was drinking heavily, flying into rages, and threatening her.[51] He had a reputation for lavish and reckless spending—behaviors that no doubt were, like his excessive drinking, triggered by his ever-fragile emotional state. Following the stock market crash of 1929, in which he lost significant investments, he fell into a downward spiral from which he never recovered. After the collapse of vaudeville, Guido failed to

Advertisement for Guido Deiro and Mae West's variety act, late 1920s. (Source: Guido Deiro Archives, Graduate Center, City University of New York)

make a transition to a profitable teaching career as his brother and some of their fellow luminaries in the accordion world had done, although he established a chain of two dozen studio franchises in towns and cities where he performed. These studios and retail businesses did not flourish, perhaps because of the difficulties of running them as an absentee owner (Guido would turn over the management of his studios to an assistant as soon as possible) or because his heart was not in teaching. "Giving lessons is poison for me," he was reported to have said.[52] In 1948 Guido suffered a nervous collapse most likely due to overwork and exhaustion and was hospitalized at a sanitarium in Loma Linda, California, where he died on July 26, 1950. By the time of his death, he had logged hundreds of stage performances and the first accordion performance on film, released by Vitaphone in 1928.[53] He issued 112 three-minute sides for the Columbia record company beginning in 1911; his output included selections from Italian operas; Neapolitan popular songs like "O Sole Mio"; patriotic marches like "Stars and Stripes"; and waltzes, mazurkas, polkas, and dances with ethnic references. He also included his own compositions written in many of these styles.

In 1936, *Accordion World* revisited the rival Deiro brothers' claims to have been the "first" to play the piano accordion. Although Pietro also claimed to be the first to have introduced the piano accordion on stage, in concerts, on radio, and on records, it was Guido's claim that was found to be legitimate.[54]

The exposure and, ultimately, fame bestowed on the Guido and Pietro formed a pivotal moment that launched the piano accordion's ascent in American popular culture and its wide acceptance by the public in vaudeville and beyond.[55] Accordion stars were not the only factor in the piano accordion's rapid rise. Reception from critics suggests that the appeal of the piano keyboard was essential in vaudeville, a medium that emphasized novelty. An admiring 1911 review of a Guido Deiro performance in the *Pittsburgh Post* marveled that the accordion combined the tonal qualities of five distinct instruments: the violin, flute, cello, bass, and piano. "In the hands of a master, it is a wonderful instrument capable of playing the most involved symphonies and at the same time, the simplest harmonies."[56] Indeed, ambitious vaudeville accordionists like the Deiro brothers may have needed to earn public admiration as "real" artists, capable of playing beautiful, "refined" music, or else face scorn from critics who would dismiss them as just one of many novelty acts cluttering vaudeville stages.

The piano accordion may have found favor with vaudeville audiences for a number of reasons. It was well suited for accompanying other instruments and singers. Only the other keyboard instruments, the guitar, and the harp could offer this facility. A piano accordion might be welcome where an orchestra was unreliable or nonexistent. The accordionist could add dramatic visual emphasis to his own performances (and those of others) by playing one of the new eye-catching "theatrical" accordions (discussed later). This was highly significant in the larger halls, where each performer needed to make a visual statement that projected to the back rows. I would like to suggest that accordion players were theatrical performers, not just musicians; they engaged their whole bodies in producing sound and engaging audiences, just as many contemporary pop singers might make use of a microphone or electric guitar for added dramatic effects.

Although they were not clowns or comedians, accordionists made ample use of their instrument's possibilities for visual and sonic expressiveness and for evoking a wide range of orchestral and comic effects that were used well beyond the age of vaudeville. Guido Deiro's *Royal Method for Accordion*, published in 1936, instructs the student on how to reproduce the sounds of not only the violin, the piano, and the organ but also the "laugh."[57] The key factor in accordion performance was the bellows, which received considerable attention in Deiro's method book (and that of his brother Pietro, published in the 1950s). Comprised of eighteen folds, the bellows requires physical agility and strength. Properly handled, it can deliver accents and dynamic and dramatic effects and provide visual interest. Among the notable accordionists to display a high degree of bellows control were Pietro Deiro and Anthony Galla-Rini, whose written descriptions of proper bellows techniques laid the groundwork for accordion pedagogy.

Not all listeners were favorably disposed toward the instrument, and not all critics were prepared to receive it as a welcome addition to the Western classical instrumental tradition. Not all critics heard in the accordion the sound of "chiming bells ringing out in a carillon of joy."[58] A critic for the *Minneapolis Journal* wrote: "a fearful instrument that looks like a cash register, and sounds worse, produces gasps of pleasure at the Orpheum this week. It is called a piano accordion and its behavior is shameless."[59] Such stinging portrayals of the accordion in early reviews must have made a strong impression on its earliest exponents and audiences. I would argue that the "accordion movement" (discussed in the next chapter) constituted an effort to neutralize these criticisms and to elevate accordion culture.

Evidence from photographs, advertisements, and programs shows that at least a half dozen other prominent accordionists joined the Deiros in the vaudeville circuit: the Marconi Brothers, Santo Santucci, Pietro Frosini, Phil Baker, Anthony Galla-Rini, and Lawrence Welk. Accordion playing, like most other forms of "serious" music making, was primarily a male occupation, but female players appeared in vaudeville: Suzette Carsell, Helene Criscio, and the "romantic and delightful Spanish accordionist Opalita." All three played as part of duet acts: Suzette with her sister, Criscio and Opalita with their husbands. Nine-year-old Shirley Temple look-alike Clarice Ralston charmed vaudeville and radio audiences with her accordion playing, dancing, and singing in five languages.[60]

During the vaudeville period and beyond, many accordion bands were organized. The size of these groups ranged from five players to fifty. In 1932, the accordion virtuoso, teacher, and composer Caesar Pezzolo and his forty-one-piece accordion band played at two theaters in San Francisco—one was the Fox, a $5 million building considered one of the world's finest.[61] The members of an accordion band would play four- and five-part arrangements made by their director. Owing to the lack of appropriate material for these bands, conductors found it necessary to arrange most of their own music.[62] An accordion band series published by O. Pagani in 1935 features arrangements of "Dark Eyes," the popular Russian song; "In a Gypsy Tearoom," a fox-trot arranged by Pietro Deiro; "When Irish Eyes Are Smiling"; and "Trieste Overture." As the accordion is a "one-man band" instrument, accordion bands tended to sound like one accordion amplified many times.[63] To add more richness and depth to the sound, accordion bands made use of bass accordions—larger, louder instruments equipped only with a bass section. Accordion bands appearing in the 1920s and 1930s were sponsored by music companies, including Jolly Captain Nick Hope and his Accordion Mates, Edna Berryman's Girl Accordion Band, and the Angeleno Accordion Band.[64]

The City by the Bay proved uniquely hospitable for amateur players and accordion playing as a hobby. The passion for outdoor entertainments in the Bay Area developed in response to the temperate climate and a strong focus on outdoor recreation. The nation's first accordion club was founded in San Francisco in 1916 and continues today. Beginning in the 1920s the club sponsored an annual accordion picnic in Marin County's California Park that attracted over ten thousand people. Prior to the construction of the Golden Gate Bridge in 1936 and the resulting building boom in Marin County, the site offered city dwellers a pastoral retreat by the San Francisco Bay, accessible only by ferry. This event was a draw for not only local accordion enthusiasts but also the local Italian community, whose heritage culture it succeeded in celebrating.[65] The two main events of the day were performances by noted accordionists

(Pietro Deiro and Frank Gaviani), followed by a dance and the raffle of a new $500 Guerrini accordion. Ronald Flynn estimates that the 1933 picnic was attended by over ten thousand people, making the event a touchstone for the city's accordion culture.

The music of accordion performers in the first two decades of the twentieth century reflects the people, cultures, and institutions that shaped their development. The programs of accordion soloists, duets, quartets, and bands shared a common repertoire with one another and with the programs of other instruments: material from Italian opera, sentimental songs, salon music, anthems, and all of the panethnic dance genres (fox-trot, waltz, mazurka, and polka). A key component of accordion performance was the instrumental solo, which was consistently the subject of admiring commentary by critics and audiences. As this kind of showy virtuoso playing was being dropped from the high-status concert, it was finding a welcome reception by popular audiences in the theaters.[66] Accordionists shared in a common language of vaudeville by the turn of the century. Elements of "art" music remained (overtures and operatic selections), along with some elements of ethnic traditional music, such as the Neapolitan song and northern Italian regional music, in the repertoire of Italian accordionists.[67]

Although the accordion's visual and sonic uniqueness had helped it find its place in the entertainment world initially, the piano accordion's status as a novelty instrument faded in the 1920s. The hundreds of surviving theater contracts for the Deiro brothers—and the proliferation of competing vaudeville accordionists—suggest that the instrument had received such wide national exposure that as early as 1928 every American living near a large town or city would have had the opportunity to see or hear a piano accordion. The piano accordion is generally seen to have become widely accepted in the music industry by 1928.[68]

As the 1920s came to a close, the vaudeville theaters began to suffer from competition from other fashionable American forms of entertainment. Accordionists would have to find other venues and other sources of work. They would need to sustain their popularity following the devastating economic collapse of 1929, which shattered many Americans' livelihoods and shook their confidence in the future. Four successors to the vaudeville accordion phenomenon gained momentum in the 1920s and continued to shape accordion culture throughout the Depression years: dance bands, radio, recordings, and the American accordion industry.

ACCORDION IN DANCE BANDS

The introduction of talking pictures in the 1920s helped bring about the end of the vaudeville era. Even before Hollywood and the big screen captured the imaginations of the wider American public, theater owners and managers grasped the fact that showing films could be a more profitable proposition than booking live acts. No more would they need to negotiate with unions and performers or work through the lengthy set of logistics that constituted a vaudeville show, which could consist of dozens of different performers arriving to rehearse and set up at different times of the day.[69] According to Anthony Galla-Rini (and other observers) the closing of New York's Palace Theater in 1932 marked vaudeville's demise. In the late 1930s, 1940s, and 1950s, performers might appear in variety acts in vaudeville-style reviews, and there were various attempts to revive vaudeville. But scholars generally agree that the circuit had ceased to exist by the mid-1930s.[70]

Most vaudevillians, and musicians in particular, faced slim chances of making a successful career transition into the movies. However, many accordionists faced the 1930s with the feeling that their instrument was unique and special and that they belonged to a unique musical fellowship that could offer mutual self-help. In 1934 the magazine *Accordion News*, written and edited by "accordionists, for accordionists," was founded with the intention of providing self-help and career advice beyond the world of theater.[71] The magazine contained employment leads, news about the accordion industry, profiles of players, and many reminiscences of the vaudeville world. There was even an accordion gossip column penned by "Walter Wincher."

For an aspiring accordionist in 1934, nightclub and hotel work could be the key to a regular paycheck—particularly in Chicago and New York. Most of the career advice articles in *Accordion News* (and its post-1936 successor, *Accordion World*) focused on the need to master the new style of music popular with audiences of the day—jazz and Latin music. In his article "The New Four-Piece Combination with Accordion," Russell Brooks noted: "The accordion has found its way into a new type of dance combination; this being the popular four-piece cocktail lounge outfit, now being used by the very finest spots around the country: the Glass Hat Room at the Congress Hotel, the Empire Room in the Palmer House, and Hotel La Salle, all located in Chicago. New York's leading cocktail bars have also gone in for this type of band in a big way."[72] Professional accordionists would often find that the bandleader was in the dark when it came to their instrument, relegating it to the rhythm section without appreciating its versatility. Enoch Light, a former orchestral leader at New York's Hotel McAlpin, said: "the accordion does not belong in the rhythm section. It gives color to other instruments, especially to the sub-tone clarinet or muted trumpet, which sound good with an accordion background."[73] Like vaudeville musical acts, dance bands drew on a wide range of musical forms—ragtime and syncopated music, sentimental songs, ethnic favorites, and so on—but specialized in improvisation and the display of soloistic virtuosity. Musicians had more opportunity to become the focus of a performance and play for discerning adult audiences than they did in vaudeville just by working to improve their skills. But club audiences were more sophisticated than those of vaudeville. "The accordionist should have a perfect knowledge of all the chords, passing tones, blue notes, glissandos. . . . The players that are able to do these things are the ones who will be cashing in on the big money," Light noted.[74]

In the early 1920s, audiences in American cities began to discover an exotic and provocative new genre of music created by Harlem blacks and white Jews on Broadway—jazz. Both black and white audiences and musicians in the 1920s made a distinction between "sweet" and "hot" styles of jazz.[75] "Hot" jazz, with its pronounced syncopations, was seen as exotic, thrilling, and stylish.[76] This new style would be built on the talents of brass and woodwind players, but a few accordionists were eager to make their mark on this dynamic musical subculture. *Accordion World* critic Hilding Bergquist devotes several pages to the best of the "hot" jazz accordionists: Felix Papile, Charlie Magnante, and Anthony Mondy. "Breaks, runs, fill-ins, hair-raising syncopation—thrilling and beautiful; interpretive variations galore! Style that would knock your socks off," he writes of Papile.[77] Although Bergquist said he hoped that aspiring accordionists would extract inspiration from these recordings, hot jazz was—from the perspective of most accordionists, who were white and wanted to work in mainstream show business—a marginal music. It had been driven underground into speakeasies and rent parties by the mainstream audiences who rejected it for fear that jazz music would ignite anarchy and sexual promiscuity. White audiences and bandleaders tended to prefer the smoother, more "refined" sound of sweet jazz, which prevailed in society bands, the groups claiming a musical monopoly in prestigious, whites-only hotel ballrooms and nightclubs aiming to please their upper-class patrons.[78] Bergquist's enthusiasm for hot jazz aside, white accordionists needed to learn a more conventionally pleasing style in order to fit into a society orchestra. In an article for *Accordion News*, bandleader Light described how the accordion needed to contribute to a sweeter and more refined texture by blending with the muted trumpets and strings.[79]

In the 1920s, 1930s, and 1940s, society bandleaders such as Paul Whiteman, Dick Gasparre, Russ Colombo, Erno Rappe, Charlie Previn, Ray Ventura, Joseph Litau, Freddy Martin, Ina Ray Hutton (leader of an all-female band), and Enoch Light hired accordionists to perform regular hotel engagements with their bands.[80] Accordionist Vincent Pirro performed with Paul Whiteman's band in the 1930s.

European bands touring the United States, such as Hakan von Eichwald from Germany and Frankie Witkowski's orchestra from Warsaw, also contributed to public presentations of accordions. The success of these groups—the all-white, high-society bands—helped to launch a number of prominent accordion solo careers, to link them with ideas of Euro-American refinement and legitimate music making, and to set accordionists apart, visually and sonically, from the more "controversial" strains of African- and African-American-influenced jazz. Whether or not white accordionists and their bandleaders harbored racist sentiments, jazz accordionists were a phenomenon of segregated white society bands.

ACCORDION RECORDINGS

In 1878, the introduction of Edison's phonograph was a pivotal moment for accordionists, opening up multiple possibilities for the consumption of their music beyond live theater venues. Home phonographs allowed audiences to bring their favorite stars and musical genres into their parlors. Early recordings of John J. Kimmel on the instrument were made on Zonophone (1904) and Edison cylinders (1906). Victor recorded Kimmel in 1907, followed by several other accordionists; their 1917 catalog shows about seventy accordion items by Guido Deiro, Pietro Deiro, and Pietro Frosini, as well as Kimmel.

In the 1920s, particularly following the establishment of immigration quotas in 1924, ethnic recordings became an important conduit for transmitting memories of the old country and the sounds of the mother tongue. Immigrants from eastern Europe, Italy, and Ireland turned to recording artists who could fulfill their need for inspiration, humor, and edification. The two major recording companies, Victor and Columbia, promoted ethnic or "foreign language" recordings by parceling out such offerings in catalogs devoted to Irish Italian, Polish, German, and Scandinavian recordings.[81] Kimmel, who was of German extraction, was famous for his performances of Irish dance music.

Solo accordion recording artists, whose repertoire was stylistically and culturally diverse, showed the potential to be marketed across ethnic lines and hence be more profitable for the record companies.[82] In 1912, RCA listed Pietro Deiro's recordings of "Stradella Overture" and "Bridal Overture" in catalogs for the Italian, German, and Spanish markets. In 1919, about a hundred of Guido Deiro's recordings for Columbia, ranging from "Dill Pickles Rag" to the Russian song "Dark Eyes," were listed in catalogs for the Italian, Spanish, Mexican, Dutch, Polish, Portuguese, and Latvian American markets.[83]

Deiro's version of the rag "Waiting for the Robert E. Lee" appears as both an ethnic issue ("En Espera" for the Spanish market) as well as in the company's mainstream domestic catalog.[84] The accordionist's eclectic repertoire, its novelty appeal, and its emphasis on light classical repertoire—all features of the vaudeville tradition—continued to shape the musical choices made by artists and repertoire during the early days of recording.

In the later 78 rpm era (the 1930s and 1940s), the accordion was featured mainly in dance orchestras. The dance band phenomenon and the jazz craze were boons to the accordionist's career in the studio; early accordion artists incorporated many jazz and ragtime numbers in their repertoire. The accordion was also a familiar member of ensembles playing "Continental" music, such as French popular song, waltz, and tango, and smoothly arranged polkas and Italian tarantellas. Charles Magnante, possibly one of the most famous exponents of this hybrid repertoire in the 1930s and 1940s, was featured as accordion soloist on more than two dozen albums released by Columbia, Decca, and other labels. His compositions and arrangements stretched across ethnic music, light classical, jazz, and ragtime.[85]

Early recording technology gave accordionists an advantage over other instruments. In a recording studio, sound had to travel through an acoustic horn that then etched the sound waves onto a cylinder or disc. Sound sources that were weak and sounds in the high registers could be difficult to capture on recording. Sound engineers often had difficulty capturing banjos, guitars, mandolins, and other light-textured string instruments and with ensembles playing music with multiple voices or parts.[86] Accordionists proved ideally adaptable to the recording studio. They produced a depth of sound in the middle registers and rich harmonies. Accordionists did their part for the expansion of the new technology, a technology that—like the instrument they played—opened up new possibilities for transforming people's tastes and their recreational choices.

Deprived of the visual dimension afforded by the stage, the Deiros (and successive recording artists) evidently focused on the technical aspects of accordion playing and the ideal of aural perfection. As Pietro Deiro pointed out later in an article for *Etude*, recording and radio artists are judged "solely by what is heard."[87] Indeed, Pietro Deiro, Guido's younger brother, was the first to record on the accordion and the most prolific accordion artist of his day. His output of 147 sides for Victor suggests that he aimed to represent the accordion as a versatile instrument that could represent the popular genres of the day: waltzes, marches, fox-trots, mazurkas, pasodobles, rumbas, Spanish dances, boleros, characteristic dances, and preludes. Pietro composed three concerti for the instrument (his classical compositions are discussed in the next chapter). He recorded over twenty-four polkas of his own composition. The titles of these pieces, "Twinkle Toe Polka," "Polka Bohemienne," "Pasta Fagioli," and "Vivacity Polka," evoke the pleasures of vaudeville and its aim of instant gratification, which these recordings evidently delivered to the living rooms of many delighted American listeners. Deiro's recordings highlight the polka not as a folk dance idiom but as a more "refined" genre. One is struck, however, by Pietro's desire to convey a variety of moods and ideas that can come across in up-tempo duple meter, from the sunny and cheerful "Caresse Polka" and the lyrical "Celestina Polka" to the humorous "Mother's Clock Polka" and the all-too-short "Rhapsody Polka." Several of these pieces were taken from Pietro's method books: *The Master Method for the Piano Accordion* (1937), *Bellow Shake for the Accordion* (1937), and *The Little Accordionist*, volume 3 (1937).[88] By reintroducing his listeners to the polka and encouraging them to play them on accordions, Deiro not only entertained but "elevated" his audience as well.

The introduction of electric recording technology in 1924 expanded the range of what could be captured on recordings. The new condenser microphones could capture the sounds of accordions more effectively, and some of the new aspiring artists attempted to refine their technique in the studio.

THE ACCORDION ON THE AIRWAVES

In the late 1920s, the recording industry began to slip, and radio became a force in the entertainment industry. The economic structure of radio, with its reliance on advertisers, proved more robust than that of records, a consumer product. After 1924 and the closure of immigration, the ethnic recording market was seen as unreliable. Radio also helped to fill a void created by the closure of vaudeville theaters in the 1930s. Like other unemployed vaudevillians, accordionists hoped to showcase their talents on the airwaves. The artists who played these live studio performances needed not only staunch self-confidence in their technique but an elusive talent—connecting with unseen audiences. Pietro Deiro was often heard on the radio, and he devoted a column in *Accordion News* (January 1938) to the art of playing on the air. The radio station KGO hired a staff accordionist, Henry Sinigiani. He performed both with the thirty-five-piece Walter Beba band and with two other accordionists, Johnny Toffoli and Louis Allarra, as a trio.

The popular NBC radio show *Major Bowes' Amateur Hour* staged regular competitions for accordionists and hence was particularly important in exposing them to the kind of virtuosic playing to which they would then aspire. Accordionist Myron Floren, who became a regular on the Lawrence Welk Show, recalled: "One thing I noticed was that accordionists almost always won the competition, and this seemed to further reinforce my love and admiration for the accordion."[89]

The accordionist who appeared most regularly on this show was Charles Magnante, who also held the distinction of being first to play the accordion on the air. He was a Tin Pan Alley song plugger and a busker on the Staten Island Ferry who had played in dance halls as a teenager. One afternoon in 1923, a year when radio was still in its experimental stages, he received a phone call from the musical director of the weekly *Bell Telephone Hour*. Although Magnante did not have a piece prepared and did not know what he was going to play, the announcer told the national audience that Charlie (and another accordionist who would play with him) would "play something of their own." His elaborate, improvised version of "Sweet Sue" launched his long series of appearances on radio and inspired the careers of other accordionists, who turned to him for advice for "making good on the airwaves."[90] In 1938, his regular appearances on the air included the daily *Coca-Cola Show* on WHN, *Lorenzo Jones* weekdays on NBC, *The Schafer Review* Thursdays on NBC, *The Lucky Strike Hit Parade* Saturdays at 10:00 A.M. on WABC, *Major Bowes' Capital Family Hour* Sundays on WEAF, and *Manhattan Merry-Go-Round* on Sundays.[91]

As Magnante's career illustrates, the accordionist could find a promising post-vaudeville niche on the airwaves. The rich sounds of the accordion, its wholesome image, and its versatility could impress audiences in living rooms throughout America, while contributing to the shape of entertainment on the airwaves. All of the performances discussed in this chapter so far—live theatrical shows, recordings, and radio broadcasts—helped to sell the accordions themselves, increasingly seen as products of American know-how and ingenuity.

THE ACCORDION INDUSTRY

San Franciscans played a significant role in the development of accordion culture. The Gold Rush drew hordes of immigrants (as well as native-born Americans) eager for the prospect of instant wealth. The Fisherman's Wharf district is a lasting symbol of the Italian influence on the city, as is North Beach's Little Italy district, where many Italian immigrants had settled after 1849. From the beginning of the 1900s to the 1950s, the city of San Francisco was home to eight accordion manufacturers, most of them in North Beach. Their names and dates of operation were as follows.[92]

Louis Miller	1883–1917
Galleazzi & Sons	1896–1944
Guerrini Company	1903–68
Paul Greub	1924–75
Colombo & Sons	1927–?
Standard	1933–36
Pacific	1945–54
Cirelli	1946–present

In 2008, I visited the site of the Guerrini factory at 277–279 Columbus Avenue and Broadway. A visitor to that location in 1954 might have picked up the scent of glue and celluloid in a busy accordion workshop with a dozen craftsmen at work. In 2008, I smelled pan-fried noodles. The building had been torn down, and the address no longer existed. On that site, I found a Chinese restaurant, one of many in that area. The expansion of San Francisco's Chinese population—as well as the expansion of the city's financial district into North Beach—had forced accordion makers (along with many other shopkeepers and small manufacturers) to relocate. Many accordion makers moved to the Mission District.[93] Paul Guerrini once worked for the San Francisco firm Galleazzi & Sons. In 1903, he started his own factory, the Guerrini Company. In 1907, he sold the business to Pasquale Petromilli and Colombo Piatanesi, who operated the Guerrini firm. The company employed thirty-nine workers, all from Italy. Craftsmen would come to the United States for two years, return to Italy for six months, and return again. Guerrini ultimately returned to Italy, where his descendants continue to manufacture accordions in Castelfidardo.

Indeed, a driving force behind the early accordion industry in both Italy and America was a network of skilled craftsmen who grew up in their families' accordion businesses and married within these families.[94] Emil Baldoni, a brother-in-law to John Piatanesi (Colombo's son), was a master accordion craftsman in New York City who has over the years been connected to all the accordion companies in that city: Ace, Bell, Pancordion, and Titano; he is now the principal of Baldoni Accordions, based in Milwaukee. The strong family connections underpinning the accordion business helped to establish a unique pattern of innovation and secrecy. Although many manufacturers attempted to conceal their innovations or to restrict their spread through patents, ideas spread quickly through the close family ties that accordion manufacturers shared.[95]

The first piano accordions made in the United States were manufactured by the Guerrini Company in 1908.[96] The models shown in the Guerrini catalogs of the 1910s and 1920s reflect an obsession with novelty and "features." A catalog of the late 1920s introduced the treble switch—or reed coupler—on Model No. 26, "an instrument of refined elegance," listed at $575. This switch allowed the player to play in the first, second, third, and fourth octaves, "to obtain four different tonalities," without weighing down the player with additional keyboards (the early accordions had as many as three rows of piano keys). The catalog describes No. 26 as follows: "A player may use it without fear of his being compelled to stretch his arms awkwardly or to waste an excessive amount of energy, which might impair the complete enjoyment of the artistic effects. This latest innovation is especially useful to ladies, to youngsters who have not acquired their full strength, to grown persons of a delicate constitution and those with arms shorter than the average."[97]

Having reduced the size and weight of the piano accordion without limiting the player's range, the Guerrini Company developed refinements in the sound. Vincent Cirelli, an octogenarian accordion repair technician who worked on the first Guerrinis at the tender age of eleven, credits the firm with inventing the tone chamber (*cassotto*), a cavity in the internal structure of the accordion through which the sound from selected sets of reeds must pass. The tone chamber gives the accordion a tone Cirelli describes as more blended, refined, and mellow.[98]

The construction of the reed blocks, which hold the reeds inside the accordion, was an ongoing challenge for early accordion makers. Like the cases, fashioned of African mahogany, the reed blocks had traditionally been made of wood, but a less expensive three-ply veneer. Guerrini, Colombo, and other American makers developed reed blocks made of more lightweight aluminum beginning in the 1920s. These reed blocks could be molded or die cast in lieu of wood fabrication processes.[99]

A look through Guerrini's catalogs from the 1920s confirms that these innovations were available to consumers willing to spend $400–800 on one of their thirty models. The choice of case designs and colors beyond the traditional black and white dazzle the modern eye, accustomed to black and white accordions. Model No. 22 ($525) was finished in green celluloid; No. 16 in white mother of pearl, with silver and blue ornamentation; model 14 in lavender. In addition to the standard Stradella 120-bass models, Guerrini offered 140-bass models and switches in the bass—the first accordions to offer such features. Noted Guerrini Company employee Henry Sinigiani stated that Guerrini "could put things on an accordion that no one else could think of. When you bought a Guerrini accordion, it was like buying a Steinway piano."[100]

Of Guerrini's many admiring customers, no two were as significant for shaping the company's high-class reputation as the vaudevillian virtuoso brothers Pietro and Guido Deiro. Ten years after Guido appeared as a performer and demonstrator of Guerrini accordions at the 1916 Panama-Pacific Exposition in San Diego, Guerrini crafted for him a custom 140-bass model, adorned with gold flowers and an eagle insignia (on display at the World of Accordions Museum in Superior, Wisconsin). This accordion, built in 1926, was equipped with several new features: a left-hand mute operated by the left-hand thumb that opens or closes a set of round portholes on the back panel. Mutes would have been ideal for accompanying singers and suppressing some of the volume that could potentially cover a solo voice—exactly what Guido needed to bear in mind as he began his vaudeville career as part of a duet with singers. At either end of the bass panel, Guido had access to two air-release buttons so that he could take in or blow out extra air through the bellows. A Guerrini accordion designed for Pietro Deiro was equipped with an even more accessible brass air-bar, making it possible to reach the air release from any point on the left-hand button board. These buttons provided the potential for more coordination and control of the bellows, a fundamental of modern accordion performance.[101]

Although no sales figures survive from this period, there is evidence to suggest that the endorsements of two major artists, Guido and Pietro Deiro, encouraged further innovation and competition among accordion manufacturers. When Petromilli and Piatanesi dissolved their partnership in 1927, Piatanesi started a new factory with his son in North Beach—the Colombo factory—and acquired a building. He attempted to compete with Petromilli by incorporating some of his former partner's ideas into his own designs. For example, the treble switches introduced by Guerrini appeared on Colombo accordions and were available in various types and positions: the hinged lever type, atop the keyboard; a position atop the cover plate; and a third type forming a fingerboard in front of the keyboard. The latter two are operated by a finger.[102] The palm shift, a half-inch protrusion from behind the keyboard that could be depressed by the palm without removing fingers from playing position, eventually replaced the thumb slide shift in the Colombo accordions of the 1920s.[103]

Colombo "X" accordions were possibly among the earliest to incorporate five treble reed banks: two at midrange, one that extended the range an octave higher, another that extended an octave lower, and a quint-reed bank. The quint reeds offered an added fifth interval on one shift, and an octave and a fifth on another shift. Because it was not possible for the player to know the number of reed banks engaged without sounding tones, the addition of a retrofit device with an electric bulb indicated whether the accordion was set to play with or without the lowest octave. The catalogs advertised the indicator light as "of great value to the accordionist in radio, vaudeville, or orchestral work."[104] Colombo advertised their new system of welding as a "major structural innovation" in the accordion, following Guerrini's push toward more lightweight instruments. "This in itself is a major improvement since it lightens the weight of our new instrument about three pounds or more. Because of these new methods, our late model is very easily managed and its response is quick and accurate."[105]

The opening of the Standard Accordion Company in 1933 added a third major manufacturer to San Francisco's North Beach accordion district. Their (1930s) catalogs feature models designed for broadcasting (the "Radio Model Supreme") and the dance orchestra ("the Cosimo Model, designed to stand hard usage and handling"). Standard Accordion reintroduced features and options that had been patented in the 1920s, such as the indicator light. No doubt the most unusual model introduced by Standard was the 1935 harp-shaped keyboard, which offered a visually striking variation on the piano accordion's traditional straight keyboard: the keys gradually decrease in size from the bottom to the top. The smaller keys at the top helped to decrease the instrument's weight but required hours of practice for the player to adapt to it. The data shows that only six of them were sold, and the company was out of business by 1937. But during their four years of operation, they served prominent players in San Francisco's dance hall scene: Gino Enrico, Peter Comparino, Romy Avivano, Virginia Deromeri, and Angelo Cagnazzo—of Barbary Coast fame.

As the piano accordion caught on with consumers, the accordion industry expanded eastward to Chicago and New York City. With accordion retail stores and businesses crowding Mulberry and Grand Streets on the Lower East Side of Manhattan, New York's Little Italy became an "accordion district" in the 1930s. Excelsior and Acme accordions were made in New York as well. The "vaudeville style" persisted in accordion designs through the late 1930s. Manufacturers tried to outdo each other. Accordions from the period, embedded with abalone, rhinestones, and colorful semiprecious stones, were designed for maximum visual impact on theater stages, where they might catch the light (and the attention of viewers in the back rows).

Accordion design in the early twentieth century was a constant struggle to balance aesthetic concerns with the functional requirements of the instrument. Ornamenting accordions added bulk and weight. The new designs added bulk and weight to the accordions, which weighed twenty-five to thirty pounds. For a working accordionist who regularly performed standing up, this could result in extreme discomfort or even injury (the average height and weight of a man in 1900 in the United States was five feet nine inches and 160 pounds). Manufacturers tried to offer a solution. Engineering the keyboard to conform to the natural curves of the human body, Petosa, Scandalli, Hohner, and a handful of other accordion companies in the 1920s and 1930s developed instruments with curved keyboards—perhaps demonstrating that the accordion, with its reputation for clunkiness and bulk, could be a truly "ergonomic" musical instrument.[106] Expensive to produce, these models failed to find a market, and manufacturers abandoned them. Tastes would change as well.

Some players of chromatic accordions, which prevailed in the vaudeville scene through the 1910s, were taken with the novel look of the piano accordion but were reluctant to learn the new system or to sacrifice the range of notes offered by the chromatic system. These players could opt for an unusual new model of chromatic button accordion. Its right-hand button board was adorned with squared-off shanks that were made to resemble piano keys. These instruments were advertised as "imitation piano accordions." Pietro Frosini may have invented the idea when he glued a dummy piano keyboard over the buttons on the left side of his chromatic accordion to make vaudeville audiences think they were seeing a performance of the more novel, hence more desirable piano accordion.

All of the accordion factories in San Francisco shared several significant features that helped to shape the industry from its beginnings: they (1) specialized in high-end, custom-built accordions; (2) relied on pre-mass-production techniques—each accordion was made by a single craftsman from start to finish; and (3) sought out input from well-recognized local accordion artists, who were featured in their ads.[107] San Francisco's industry catered to artists, not the everyday consumer; the city's manufacturers were focused on "theatrical accordions," not on the everyday player. Had it not been for the city's accordion club, an Italian community that was so admiring of the accordion, and a favorable year-round climate for outdoor events, the accordion might have had a more limited reach in the Bay Area and beyond.

I have discussed the function of the accordion in Italy's manufacturing industry. Bugiolacchi argues that the accordion was promoted as a symbol of Italy's ambition to industrialize, highlighting local common sense, ingenuity, and know-how.[108] There is evidence to suggest that San Franciscans may have perceived the accordion similarly in the wake of the devastating 1906 earthquake. Just nine years later, San Francisco staged the 1915 Panama-Pacific International Exposition, celebrating the opening of the Panama Canal and demonstrating to more than eighteen million visitors that it remained "the city that knew how."[109] Just as the building of the canal was seen as a Herculean feat, so was the construction of the Exposition, with its three hundred thousand cubic yards of landfill reclaiming land from the San Francisco Bay. The Exposition featured an actual Ford assembly line, which turned out over four thousand cars; the Machinery Palace; and various displays of technology from diesel engines to typewriters to moving picture machines. Guido Deiro was said to have demonstrated Guerrini accordions at that company's booth, along with over a dozen accordionists from the vaudeville circuit.[110]

Although the accordion had been introduced to San Franciscans seven years earlier, this fair was the first public occasion at which the instrument was presented as evidence of American engineering and manufacturing know-how.

While San Francisco's entrepreneurs developed high-end—and exotic—accordions in the 1910s and 1920s, they were not inclined to produce accessible, affordable instruments for the mass market. The accordion in San Francisco became a quintessential vaudeville instrument, offering social capital to its immigrant audience and players. After the Great Depression hit in 1929, the industry began making different kinds of accordions, and the locus of the industry shifted from the cosmopolitan City by the Bay to America's heartland (a story continued in the next chapter).

In 1934 the editor of *Accordion News*, the new monthly magazine "of accordionists, by accordionists, and for accordionists," wrote optimistically about the potential of "accordion culture" to thrive.[111] The accordion not only had survived the collapse of vaudeville and the Depression but also had become an integral part of mainstream popular culture. American factories had an "ever-increasing amount of business," because the new models were serviceable to the everyday player.[112] The accordion was regularly featured on radio broadcasts, and great artists of the day, such as the Deiro Brothers, Anthony Galla-Rini,

Charles Magnante, and Pietro Frosini, had recording contracts and lucrative deals with accordion companies whose products they endorsed. A network of accordion schools, bands, and clubs was thriving throughout the United States, and "social events in connection with them become continually more interesting and important." As the editor observed, the accordion world was strengthened by the unique fraternal ties developing around the instrument and "the three great interlocking branches of the profession, the accordionist, the manufacturer, and the publisher."[113]

For over fifty years, the accordion factories of Italy had provided instruments for domestic and public performances of popular music. The new American firms challenged that hegemony by first providing high-end artists with models such as those crafted by Guerrini and Colombo in San Francisco. The Chicago and New York firms—Italo-American, Iorio, and Excelsior—departed from this model by mass-producing accordions for amateur players. The popularity of radio and the increasing taste for musical recordings intensified interest in the accordion. One of the unintended effects of this early twentieth-century accordion recording boom was that it served to preserve a canon of work that accordion virtuosi in subsequent decades could emulate and reinterpret. In the area of accordion music, the popular music industry, at first fueled by vaudeville, did not displace amateur and recreational performance—a type of displacement that was a familiar pattern in mainstream America for other instruments—but absorbed the energy of the club and band movement. Although the accordion phenomenon may have been fueled at first by demand for novelty, it reached new audiences and found new modes of transmission beyond the vaudeville circuit in the late 1920s. The decline of vaudeville, the advent of the electric microphone, the immigration quotas of 1924, and the renewed significance of ethnic musical recordings all contributed to the development of accordion culture as a reflection of the changing sensibilities of American audiences.

During this formative era, the older diatonic button boxes and chromatic accordions declined in popularity among Americans. The "theatrical" piano accordions advertised by the San Francisco firms had their heyday. Colombo, Standard, and Guerrini had competition, from the Midwest and the East Coast, from newer accordion firms who wanted to cash in on the vaudeville market and the trend toward flashy, expensive instruments. After 1935, accordion makers—led by Excelsior in New York City—focused exclusively on manufacturing uniform-looking, unadorned black-and-white piano accordions. During this period, the piano accordion displaced the chromatic button accordion in popular culture, receiving its designation as "the accordion" and its current status as a visual and sonic icon. Ironically, this status was bestowed on it by generations of immigrant Americans whose forebears in Ireland, Italy and eastern Europe had played the diatonic button accordion. While some writers have highlighted the nostalgic yearnings associated with accordion playing in immigrant communities, the "standardization" of the accordion could be seen to reflect a different and opposing idea: the "assimilationist" aspirations of white ethnic Americans observed during the first decades of the twentieth century. Indeed, the accordion filtered into public consciousness at the turn of the century as a result not of its traditional ethnic associations but of its visibility in commercial popular entertainments of the day. It is fair to say, as one observer of the period did later, that in spite of its popularity in the first decades of the twentieth century the accordion was generally shunned by serious musicians. Accordion music was confined to vaudeville and variety shows, dance halls, and ethnic folk contexts. Accordion concert artists and radio "staff accordionists" would play transcriptions of popular classics or original compositions by Pietro Frosini and Pietro Deiro and Italian-American favorites. It was music that existed in popular entertainment and was very rarely performed as part of formal concert programs.[114]

Intent on changing this perception, a rear guard of accordion teachers, performers, and publishers increasingly emphasized a more elevated accordion repertoire. Accordion music compositions from the turn of the century, and onward, came to be seen not as a fad or an expression of ethnic heritage but as part of the timeless heritage of Western classical music. This repertoire served as a canon for the accordion movement, led by virtuoso performing artists. Another concern was improving the design of the piano accordion and seeking more uniformity in keyboard design and tuning. The sober, dignified accordion artists of the 1940s and 1950s, sporting their sleek black and white Excelsiors and Titanos, bear only a superficial resemblance to the popular and flashy vaudeville performers of the 1910s and 1920s. The accordion's ties to old Europe, to Italian heritage, and to ethnic folk music were severed—at least in the mainstream accordion world.

CHAPTER TWO

*S*QUEEZEBOX *B*ACH

The Classical Accordion

THE APRIL 18, 1939, Carnegie Hall Accordion Concert featuring Magnante's quartet was "the biggest single event to occur in the world of the accordion."[1] *Cue* printed a tantalizing advance notice of this concert, which was covered by a half dozen critics in the mainstream media.

> For no very good reason, the piano accordion is usually associated, in the minds of many, with college reunions, trade association dinners, and barrooms. Charles Magnante has made up his mind that this shameful misconception must stop, and he's going to fire the opening gun in Carnegie Hall next Tuesday night. With his quartet, he'll fill the old hall with the lilting strains of pretty nearly everything from Johann Sebastian Bach to George Gershwin. It's the Bach that Mr. Magnante's proudest of, and the particular composition that he's elected to try his hand at is no less than the celebrated *Toccata and Fugue in D Minor*, specially arranged by himself for accordion quartet.[2]

As one of the first recitals featuring the accordion in a major classical music venue, Magnante's concert reflected a significant shift from the familiar, everyday contexts of earlier accordion performances: theaters, barrooms, and hotel ballrooms. Magnante's concert offered the earliest presentations of the accordion by formally dressed *artistes* performing classical repertoire onstage. These presentations were characterized by the selection of repertoire considered appropriate for the audience and the accordion (Bach, Mendelssohn, Mozart) while incorporating composers who were recognized symbols of American music (Gershwin). Beginning in the 1900s when Guido Deiro had performed opera transcriptions for coal miners, accordionists had begun to entertain a new set of ideologies about what the accordion should do. Their efforts intensified in the 1930s and reached a fever pitch in the 1950s. The accordion needed to claim its place, accordion advocates argued, a legitimate "position." It aspired to a better repertoire, better audiences, and improved instruments. By the 1950s, dozens of "accordion conservatories" were schooling aspiring accordion virtuosi in proper repertoire and technique; the accordion was offered as a major at several colleges and universities. Accordion bands renamed themselves "accordion symphony orchestras," expanded their ranks and repertoire; some went on tour. Some accordionists managed to make full-time careers as teachers and recitalists while directing their own accordion studios, rising like phoenixes from the ashes of the vaudeville tradition. As the accordion surged in sales and profitability in American culture (discussed in the next chapter), accordion artists responded with ambivalence, constantly seeking strategies to distance themselves from the masses and establish legitimacy for their instrument.

A year before Magnante's concert, the American Accordionists Association (AAA) was formed and made it its aim to engage in "activities for the advancement of the accordion, without pecuniary profit," to "hold competitions and to promote the study and improvement of the accordion," and to "publish literature to be of service to accordionists."[3] While such appeals seem intuitively obvious nearly seventy-five years later, they highlight the accordion's independence during much of the nineteenth and twentieth centuries, confirming that its advocates viewed their interests as distinct from those of the mainstream music world. Although the call for widespread cooperation in the accordion field was not entirely successful, such self-conscious organizing activities were needed to legitimize the idea of a community of accordionists. Seen in its context (1938), the AAA's mission statement was daring. It aimed to do no less than bring about a sea change in attitudes toward the accordion in America over the course of the twentieth century.

The era between 1938 and 1960 represented a zenith of prestige for the accordion movement and the period when the accordion became more recognized as a serious instrument in American culture. This chapter examines the ideologies and ideas connected to the effort to improve both the instrument and its perception by the classical music world. Inspired by the image of Magnante and his quartet invading Carnegie Hall, many foot soldiers of the accordion were inspired to take up the fight and claim their place in the important venues that had hitherto remained accordion-free zones. These free-reed soldiers were largely unified in their efforts to bring the accordion into the mainstream of musical culture, but their internal unity did not translate into unity with the culture as a whole; close examination of their rhetoric reveals discontinuities between their idea of the accordion and the idea that persisted in mainstream society.

Some who have addressed this particular set of issues refer to the "classical accordion" or the "Classical Free-Reed" (the name of an established website and online journal on this topic).[4] The accordion advocates of the day never employed such terms. Although they did not shy away from expressing their opinions about "good," "serious," and "proper" music, they did not compartmentalize repertoire in the categories familiar to us today (i.e., Western art music, European art music). They would not have embraced the concept of "classical" (long-lasting, worthy of being considered a classic), because they perceived the classics as part of their living, contemporary cultural heritage. Most early accordion advocates did not place any particular value on contemporary composers or original music for the accordion. Both light classical and popular selections were mixed together without any apparent regard for the distinctions between "highbrow" and "lowbrow" art that authors such as Lawrence Levine have described.[5] "Popular" mainstream accordionists gave "classical" concerts with a popular flavor. For example, on May 15, 1960, as part of the Sano Accordion Symphony concert at Town Hall, New York, accordion virtuoso Myron Floren (of *Lawrence Welk Show* fame) and the Symphony performed a newly commissioned work by a contemporary composer (William Grant Still) along with a hodgepodge of accordion orchestra transcriptions of works by Debussy, Khachaturian, Sir Arthur Sullivan, and Gershwin and the popular standard "Lady of Spain," a program that would appear lightweight by contemporary standards.

Indeed, the accordion's value to society rested in its expression of mainstream values and its embrace of music that would appeal to all. The program of advancement proposed by accordion advocates revolved around not so much new repertoire, or "great" repertoire, or a new style of playing, as a shift in aesthetics. They set out to break down barriers, stereotypes, and misconceptions in order to shine the spotlight on the "improved" accordion. In order to do this, they had to shift the accordion's image away from both its urban and cosmopolitan vaudevillian connotation and move its geographical centers to the Midwest and the East Coast.

In the 1930s, the loci of the accordion industrial complex—teaching and sales—shifted from San Francisco to Chicago and New York City. Chicago was a center for band instrument manufacture. One indication of Chicago's fast-growing accordion niche was a fast-multiplying network of accordion schools—fifteen were listed in *Accordion World*'s 1945 directory—and hard-driving teacher-dealer figures such as Dave Biasco, Leo Piersanti, and Ben Matusek. At Piersanti's accordion school in the 1920s, the first in Chicago, students could choose instruction in either Italian or English, using Piersanti's own method books. Piersanti was also the exclusive Excelsior dealer in the Chicago area. Not to be outdone by these smaller entrepreneurs, the Rudolph Wurlitzer Company set up a school and retail establishment outside Chicago in Oak Park and took an especially aggressive approach to teaching and selling accordions, hiring Magnante as an artist-consultant and demonstrator of them.[6] In the 1930s, their standard policy was to move a new student up to a 120-bass accordion after the fifth lesson. With this approach, Wurlitzer had figured out the key to selling accordions by the hundreds.[7] Accordion schools also sold instruments, often as part of a lesson package. Many studios contracted with an accordion manufacturer to produce inexpensive instruments branded with the school's name. The instruments were sold to students at the school, at a reduced rate, benefiting the school as well, which received free advertising (on the front of the accordion).

The most admired accordions of this period (1920s–1930s) were made in New York City by the Iorio and Excelsior companies. Two Iorio brothers, Augusto and Amedeo, makers of organs in Rome, founded the Iorio Accordion Company in 1907 in Manhattan, using the capital they had earned playing as two-thirds of an accordion trio in France in the 1900s. It is believed that they manufactured the first piano accordions in New York City. Like the San Francisco and Chicago manufacturers, Iorio experimented with new designs and features: a double tone chamber, invisible treble and bass shifts, aluminum plate shift mechanisms, and a slanting right-hand keyboard "placed at a scientific angle to meet the natural position of the player's arm and hand."[8] According to a 1935 review of the Baby Grand Philharmonica, Iorio also introduced a two-section bellows, which made it easier to produce tremolo effects.[9] Iorio also experimented with moving the keyboard toward the center of the body by about two inches, for better balance and handling.[10]

Excelsior, like Iorio and Italo-American, sought to make the instrument easier to play. For example, Excelsior developed the "master switch"—a device used for coupling all the reeds on the accordion's treble side—after designs by Pietro Deiro, an Excelsior artist. Following this, other accordion companies began to offer the master switch. Flynn notes: "this is a good example of how improvements came about in the early days and how inventions were incorporated quickly by the other major accordion manufacturers."[11] Excelsior's most visible contribution to the accordion—the one with the most far-reaching implications for the everyday consumer—was the newly streamlined look it designed for the instrument in the 1930s. With the new design, their marketing strategies diversified, as they attempted to continue high-end instrument production while aspiring toward mass production. Excelsior Accordions (note the elite-sounding Latin name) was an important force, not only with the exceptionally high standards of quality it set for the industry but also with its drive to promote the accordion. Their factory, offices, and showrooms were located at 337 Sixth Avenue in Greenwich Village. After World War II, Excelsior opened a completely new and modern plant in Castelfidardo. Excelsior, like other accordion companies, reached out to accordion artists and capitalized on their prestigious names—anointing accordion artist spokesmen. Of the twelve founding members of the AAA, accordion virtuosi all, seven were "Excelsior artists," including Charles Magnante.

In the mid-1930s, Excelsior broke with the vaudevillian tradition of crafting highly ornamented, expensive accordions for artists, seeking a uniform design that would be more practical to mass-produce while remaining desirable in middle- and upper-class social contexts. Excelsior believed that it had its finger

Black and white Excelsior accordion, c. 1930s.

CHARLES MAGNANTE

Excelsiola

The same rhythmic verve and singing tone that is the Magnante hallmark can be yours with this recording model Magnante *Excelsiola*. Designed to Charles Magnante's own specifications, it incorporates the exclusive Excelsior *Sound Chamber*. Forty-one treble keys, ten treble tone selectors, six automatic bass shifts, 4/5 sets of reeds, two sets of reeds inside *Sound Chamber*, two outside.

MODEL M Acoustical **$1350**
MODEL ME Convertible Electronic . . . **$1500**

Charlie Magnante, Excelsior artist. Excelsior brochure, 1957.

on the pulse of what the accordion community needed. The future of the accordion, as one of the company's enthusiastic observers from the accordion world pointed out, was not in vaudeville or theater but "in the drawing room, atop its bigger brother, the grand piano."[12] Therefore, it needed to have a more dignified appearance, minus the "showy, garish, and dance-hall glitter of the accordion."[13] *Accordion World* reported how the expert designers of Excelsior accordions, in their search for an appropriate modern design for the accordion, "combed piano showrooms and the keyboard instrument exhibits of the Metropolitan Museum of Art in New York." Their efforts resulted in a new kind of accordion.

These sleek, black-and-white Excelsiors went by various names: the Concert Grand, the Symphony Grand, and the Baby Grand. All were seen as *the* instruments that made the accordion synonymous with good taste, elegance, and class. "With its quiet, simple, but thoroughly artistic and beautiful lines . . . it will fit appropriately with dignity in a symphony orchestra as well as in the most fastidiously furnished and fashionable drawing room or salon of the refined home. No doubt that people of wealth, education and refinement will show a new interest in the accordion."[14] The company took special care to portray such people in their advertisements. Some Excelsior ads in accordion

On board the liner, U.S.S. United States

Excelsior brochure, c. 1957.

magazines showed formally attired audiences, such as couples in evening wear in hotel ballrooms and other elegant settings. In a 1957 promotional flyer a couple aboard a cruise ship listen raptly to the sounds of a strolling Excelsior artist, clad in a white dinner jacket. Could this woman's admiration of the accordionist be more than musical? The ad seems to suggest that the accordion might be an instrument of seduction.

Despite the elitist cast of Excelsior's advertising, the Concert Grand and Symphony Grand demonstrated the accordion's potential to reach a more mainstream audience. Its new, streamlined design, stripped of ornament and the earlier hodgepodge of European-Italian-baroque-Greco-Roman visual references so that it resembled a machine more than an objet d'art, was geared to the more austere and conservative social and economic climate of the 1930s. With its clean lines and black-and-white palette, the new accordion could appear more down-to-earth and functional—in short, more "American." More traditional European accordion companies made accordions that looked pretty; Excelsior made accordions that looked efficient. This new design was widely copied by other post–World War I Italian and American accordion firms.

A related accordion marketing strategy, equally important for potential customers' perceptions of the accordion's elevated status, was to promote it as an efficient, technologically advanced product of American ingenuity. American accordion manufacturers saw themselves as innovators, likening innovation to improvement. The 1930s and 1940s witnessed a surge in accordion-related patents and new designs to improve the accordion's performance and the ease of learning to play it. In the early 1940s, the Texan accordionist-inventor John H. Reuther developed an "improved piano keyboard" for the treble side of the accordion, arranging the black keys in groups of twos and threes in between the white notes (instead of above them, as on the piano keyboard). Because the fingering for all twelve major scales and twelve minor scales would be identical, Reuther called his invention the "uniform keyboard." No doubt some studio owners were intrigued by Reuther's claims that the uniform system could cut down on the study time required to learn scales on the piano keyboard by half and help students progress more rapidly to a full-sized accordion. At least one studio was enthusiastic enough about Reuther's invention to commission a line of uniform-keyboard accordions to promote to students.

More switches—the mechanical levers that effect changes in reed coupling— were added to the accordion, enabling the player to produce more combinations of reed sets. Manufacturers began to indicate these combinations by the use of switch symbols.[15] Accordion reed combinations are conventionally described

Robotti "uniform keyboard" piano accordions designed by
the Houston inventor John Reuther.

in terms of vocal ranges and dynamics (soprano, alto, tenor bass, soft bass, soft tenor, etc.). The switches are more commonly indicated with the names of other musical instruments such as Oboe, Clarinet, Violin, Bassoon, Bandoneon, and so on. Indeed, one chief virtue of the "refined" accordion was its ability to represent the textures of the symphony orchestra.

Crucial for the development of the "symphonic" aesthetic was the development of a better quality of the tone produced by the reeds. "Duraluminum" reeds made of Swedish blue steel were advertised in many models of accordions. The delicate nature of accordion reeds and their sensitivity to moisture and humidity prompted a slew of claims to innovation: "Acmaloy Reeds," for example, were "unconditionally guaranteed"; "Directone reeds" promised "tremendous carrying power."

One problem for manufacturers was that most of these innovations were hidden; they took place on the inside of the instrument, involving subtle changes in the reeds and tongues beyond the understanding of the ordinary player.

So advertisers had to refer to other more familiar technologies. "Television may be around the corner," says an ad for the Butti accordion, "but the Butti Television Grand is here." Clocks and cars, symbols of efficiency and speed, appeared alongside accordions in many Excelsior ads, claiming that the company's products were "As Modern as Tomorrow." New designs suggested that the mechanical qualities of accordions were becoming fetishized. Switches and screws were no longer concealed by elaborate grille plates. The cases became sleeker, and Excelsior's black-and-white design giving the accordion the look of a mini-piano became iconic. As the accordion acquired its more uniform appearance it gained potential for more efficient production, cheaper materials, and more profitability.

Indeed, the visual analogy between accordions and machines was not lost on a reporter at the 1936 Music Trades Convention in Chicago. John Reuther wrote of Excelsior's "modernistic" exhibit of its new models: "The color scheme was black and white, the walls being covered with white satin for a striking contrast against the black accordions. The instrument rests upon fixtures of cut glass and chromium. Their slogan for the new instrument is 'As modern as tomorrow' and after hearing the demonstration, I think it quite apropos."[16]

The new look of the accordion helped to emphasize, at least visually, the "technological" aspects of the accordion that the manufacturers wanted to sell to their customers. Accordion companies promoted their products as the fruits of American technology. Manufacturers in Italy and the United States competed with one another to develop the most efficient switching devices and the lightest construction. Superlatives abound not only in ads for high-end Excelsiors ("Years Ahead in Performance and Styling") but in ads for instruments of all price ranges: The Finest. The Most Exquisite. Master Craftsmanship. Thrilling. The Best. The Best and Nothing But the Best. The Greatest Development in Accordion History.

While Excelsior and other advertisers were prepared to offer "scientific" evidence for their improvements, careful scrutiny of these advertisements and the instruments they promoted fail to substantiate most of these claims for superiority. Accordion manufacturers remained beholden to the idea of progress, coupled with an energetic entrepreneurial strategy. Accordions begat accordions: ladies' sized accordions, bass accordions (for accordion band and orchestra performance), and student accordions.

In the 1940s, the culture of the accordion became stratified. Student accordions (12-bass models) were plain and unornamented. "Ladies' accordions" had a piano keyboard with slightly narrower keys (less than one-eighth inch).

"Professional" accordions were designed for club date musicians (hotel and nightclub jobs). Top-of-the line "artists' models," a throwback to vaudevillian kitsch, received the full ornamental treatment, with elaborate mother-of-pearl inlays, intricate flower and plant designs, and the artist's name emblazoned on the grille with rhinestones. These instruments represented the accordion as an "aspirational" instrument, the object of the customer's desire to be admired in the shop window before purchasing an entry-level accordion in a much lower price range. Excelsior, aware that its instruments were too expensive for the average American, attempted to lure customers in with its lower-priced Accordiana line.

Accordion artists of this era advocated the industry's technological and artistic innovations, which they believed were needed in order to raise the accordion to a level of artistic perfection. Some accordion reformers argued that the standard Stradella bass accordion had become a "stumbling block" to their efforts to develop and improve the instrument. "The reason why the accordion can never reach the heights that many wishful thinkers among accordion enthusiasts dream about . . . lie(s) mainly in the bass side of the instrument where the shortcomings are so tremendous that the greatest geniuses could not overcome them in attempting to interpret great music."[17] Since the Stradella bass system was designed as a shortcut system for easily reaching the I, IV, and V chords in the common major keys, and this chord bass pattern is used in many traditional waltzes and polkas, as well as rock 'n' roll and blues, we can easily interpret his statement to mean that the author feared that the accordion could actually discourage players from moving on to better music. In the same magazine, Willard Palmer's "Open Letter to Accordion Manufacturers" asserted the serious accordionist's need for a larger bass keyboard, with an additional two octaves of usable range for the left hand, so that "all of Bach's organ works will be possible for the accordion."[18]

In the 1940s, a few American accordionists began pressuring accordion manufacturers to redesign the accordion to enable the performer to create independent melodic lines on the left-hand side and to build chords in any inversion apart from the major, minor, dominant seventh, and diminished seventh chords available from the preset chord buttons. The result was the introduction of the free-bass system accordion in the United States. The term "free-bass system" refers to a variety of left-hand manual systems, some of which had been available since the turn of the century, when some manufacturers added three rows of chromatically ordered single notes next to the standard bass. American accordionists traveling abroad for international competitions in the 1950s had found, much to their astonishment, that the free-bass accordion was widely available in Europe as a serious instrument for study and that there was a much larger modern repertoire for it than existed in America.[19] During the 1960s and 1970s, several of these accordionists offered their input into the manufacture of free-bass accordions for Americans. The free-bass system developed by John Serry, Sr., featured dual keyboards for the left hand and incorporated two sets of reeds tuned in octaves, providing a range of tones exceeding three and a half octaves. These were designed for independent access for the thumb and remaining fingers of the performer's left hand. Giulietti and Titano began developing accordions that offered both the free-bass system and two rows of bass buttons laid out according to the traditional Stradella system. These accordions, known as "converter" accordions, were widely adopted by classical accordionists. However, as accordion teacher and Accordion Teachers Guild past president Joan Sommers has pointed out, these instruments only offered the player access to two octaves of single tones without having to make use of the switches. The Europeans favored the chromatic-system free bass, which offered a three-octave range, giving the accordionist unprecedented contrapuntal facility and access to any work in the standard keyboard literature, without the need for transcription.

For Sommers, this discovery was both empowering and disheartening. An accordionist mastering the chromatic system could play the same repertoire as a pianist or organist, demonstrating once and for all the instrument's legitimacy. But Sommers also realized that few American teachers and students were likely to commit themselves to learning the free-bass system, not only because of the difficulty and complexity of the instrument but also because of the overbearing influence of the static, conservative accordion industry in America. "The main distributors of instruments in America would not bring in anything but the Stradella instrument. There are a lot of oldtime accordionists who didn't know the free bass, and don't want to learn it or teach it; they didn't know how to sell it."[20] She believes Americans should have been more resistant to industry pressure and adopted the improved free-bass accordion, which would have given them more access to a complex, advanced classical repertoire as well as credibility in the performance and competition circuit.[21]

It is important to bear in mind that changes in accordion design, construction, and timbre, though presented by their advocates as "improvements," have been highly contested since the introduction of the free-bass system in the late 1940s. To adherents of the traditional Stradella accordion system for the piano accordion, the circle-of-fifths arrangement could represent a masterwork of design and scope not to be tampered with. For the accordion industry, the Stradella accordion was their bread and butter. Beginning students could master a polka tune or waltz on the Stradella accordion in a few lessons, because only one hand position and two or three chord buttons were required to produce a simple oompah accompaniment using the I and the V chords.

Mastering the free-bass system, on the other hand, requires a more sophisticated music-theoretical toolkit. The player must make use of single tones to construct chords and harmonic progressions. Advocates of free-bass accordions were, in a sense, advocates for more advanced knowledge of music theory and technique for accordionists and a vision of the accordion as an instrument for "schooled" artists. When free-bass advocates in the Confédération International des Accordéonistes (International Accordionists Association) introduced a motion to require all entrants in the Coupe Mondiale, the international accordion competition, to play free-bass accordion, it was roundly defeated—a victory for the Stradella accordion and the mainstream vision of the accordion. Indeed, the accordion industry and the production of accordions for the American market were too intimately tied to an established network of teachers, performers, and entrepreneurs to sustain too much innovation, as the following analysis of the accordion studio system will show.

THE STUDIO SYSTEM

Mainstream American conservatories and music departments had been developing for decades, affiliated with major colleges and universities and created and sustained by networks of patrons, critics, and community members. By contrast, accordion studios cropped up as an extension of accordion teachers' commercial interests—packages of musical instruction and promotions. These teachers did not only provide lessons; they scheduled and promoted recitals, arranged repertoire, conducted accordion ensembles, and sold music, instruments, and lesson packages (an accordion often came with six months of lessons). Anticipating that the profitable days of vaudeville would soon come to an end, both Guido and Pietro Deiro established the first accordion teaching studios in 1928 (in San Francisco and New York, respectively). Guido Deiro promoted his chain of accordion studios on the West Coast.

Guido would choose a town and give a concert at a local theater, generating publicity and an audience. He would announce during the concert the opening of a new Guido Deiro accordion studio in town and sign up new students afterward. After a few weeks, when the studio was running, Guido would turn

Guido Deiro studio. (Source: Guido Deiro Archives, Graduate Center,
City University of New York)

over the roster of students and the retail business to a local teacher. He continued this practice until the late 1930s, when most of his business ventures
fizzled out.[22]

The individual responsible for the national spread of the accordion studio
and the phenomenon's longevity was Guido's younger brother, Pietro Deiro Sr.
His "Accordion Headquarters" at 48 Greenwich Avenue in Manhattan housed a
stable of dozens of professional accordion teachers. Eventually he established a
large chain of Pietro Deiro accordion studios along the East Coast that became
the platform for his immense success in the accordion business.

Realizing that his students required more sheet music for accordion, Pietro
founded his own music publishing company, Accordion Music Publishing
Company (AMPCO), later known as Pietro Deiro Publications, and his own
record label, AMPCO Records. It became the largest publisher of accordion
music and method books in the United States, building a catalog of over ten
thousand works for accordion in classical, jazz, and popular styles. Deiro also

Pietro Deiro's studio and retail store (aka "Accordion Headquarters") on Greenwich Avenue in Manhattan. (Source: Guido Deiro Archives, Graduate Center, City University of New York)

wrote and published numerous method books, including popular adaptations of Czerny's and Hanon's piano methods for accordion.

Pietro parlayed his advice to students into his own newsletters (the *Pietro Musicordion*) and in columns for mainstream music magazines such as *Etude* and *Metronome*. His success in promoting the accordion gained the attention of the Italian manufacturing community, who presented him with a parchment scroll and gold plaque. Pietro encouraged his students to admire him as a mythical figure. He had a plaster bust of himself produced to sell to students as collector's items, and he even minted "Pietro Deiro coins." As noted, both scholars and members of the Deiro family doubt that Pietro deserves credit as the "first" to play piano accordion in America. However, he is seen by many as a supremely influential father figure, a "Daddy of the Accordion," an image he carefully cultivated early in his career. Pietro's business model was widely imitated by many other accordionist-entrepreneurs, many of whom were his own students. Jacob Neupauer, who served as an assistant director of Pietro Deiro's accordion studio in Allentown, Pennsylvania, has noted that a competent accordion teacher could open a studio and within three months expect to have forty students. Teachers made commissions on the sales of instruments in addition to their income from giving lessons. Young children began on inexpensive 12-bass accordions. After a certain number of lessons, the teachers were urged to sell their parents a forty-eight-bass accordion. By the time a child reached the age of ten, he or she was expected to adopt the full-sized 120-bass accordion. As commissions on instruments (which cost $100–300) were 10–20 percent and studios could hope to sell at least two instruments to a single family with one accordion student in the home, the accordion business encouraged aggressive marketing. Many accordion students were first drawn to the instrument by such teachers selling their wares door-to-door and providing dazzling demonstrations.[23] Sometimes the teachers offered on-the-spot tests assessing the children's musical abilities as a come-on to the parents to buy instrument-and-lesson packages. The accordion studio business was so profitable that teachers employed by a studio would open their own studios as soon as they were able to come up with rent for a storefront. Arguably, the studio system provided the economic momentum behind the accordion movement. In 1953, a peak year for the accordion, 250,000 accordions were sold in the United States—comparable to the sales of all the band instruments combined.[24]

The accordion studio movement did not generate the same momentum in all regions of the country. Accordion businesses were concentrated on the East Coast and West Coast (the San Francisco Bay Area, New York state, and

Pietro Deiro coin. (Source: Guido Deiro Archives, Graduate Center, City University of New York)

New Jersey, with large cities like Los Angeles, New York, and Washington, D.C., taking the lead). The working-class ethnic heartlands of western New York state, Ohio, Wisconsin, and Michigan saw heavy enrollments of young students in accordion studios, even in small towns such as Batavia, New York, where Roxy and Nelly Caccamise's Accordion Studio was established as late as the 1960s.

Accordion studios were apparently entirely absent from most of the southern states, that is, Mississippi, Alabama, Tennessee, Louisiana, and South Carolina. Accordion studios seem not to have emerged in either white or African-American communities in the South. Old-line Anglo-Americans (upper-class whites) do not appear ever to have been drawn to the accordion in any significant number. Indeed, despite the aristocratic cast of Excelsior ads, the accordion phenomenon appears to have been limited to white ethnic middle-class and working-class America.

Roxy and Nelly Caccamise's accordion studio in Batavia, New York, was one of many across the country that organized accordion bands for its students. By 1960 the guitar was available as an instrument of instruction.

In the 1950s and 1960s most accordion studios closed down or became places of instruction for other instruments, leaving spotty ethnographic evidence of the studio phenomenon. However, one surviving accordion studio in New Jersey, Acme Accordions, provides a valuable snapshot of accordion studio culture from the period. Owner Stanley Darrow, born in Camden, began his accordion career as a performer and door-to-door accordion salesman and teacher. Together with his then wife, Sherrie, also an accordionist, he founded two accordion studios in central New Jersey. Darrow's intent was to groom outstanding performers and enter them in competitions in Europe. Each year, Darrow himself takes a six-week tour of Europe, playing live concerts and radio broadcasts. Wishing also to enhance the profile of the accordion in the academic world, Darrow founded the American Accordion Musicological Society (AAMS), which sponsors symposia on scholarly topics. In 1960 the Darrows founded the Westmont Philharmonic Accordion Orchestra, which has 150 members and continues to rehearse weekly.

Today, over 125 students take lessons with Darrow and his current wife, Joanna Arnold, at the Acme Accordion School in Westmont, New Jersey. The pair are described in trade publications as accordion "greats," and Arnold has played with the Philadelphia Orchestra. Owing mainly to Arnold's efforts in promoting the business, the Acme Accordion Studio thrives, to my knowledge, as the country's only full-service, full-time accordion studio, offering lessons, performance opportunities, instrument sales and repairs, and in the words of one student, "a nurturing environment for accordionists—a 1950s accordion bubble."

ACCORDION PUBLISHING

For an instrument that was relatively new to the music world, teachers and students required new music method books and arrangements. In 1911, shortly after Guido Deiro's appearance on the vaudeville stage, Octavo Pagani, a young Italian nobleman and army lieutenant, resigned his commission and emigrated to New York City. In search of a profitable business (and possessing capital from his brothers' savings), he opened the firm O. Pagani Music Dealers in New York.[25] He advertised in newspapers all over the United States and developed a mail order music business alongside his storefront on Bleecker Street in the West Village. In 1918, Pagani met Pietro Deiro, who was at the time receiving wide acclaim as an accordion artist, and realized the possibilities for creating a piano accordion catalog. Pagani urged Pietro to write a piano accordion method book; in 1919, Pietro's book was put on the market. It sold over sixty thousand copies.[26] The Pagani piano accordion library expanded with the definitive method books *The Jazz Accordionist*, *The Virtuoso Accordionist*, and the accordionist's answer to piano virtuoso Karl Czerny's famous method book, *The Accordion School of Velocity*. By 1933, 75 percent of Pagani's business was devoted to accordion music.[27] When accordion artists began to demand arrangements of copyrighted material that could only be obtained by paying large royalties, Pagani obliged. Hence arrangements of popular numbers such as "St. Louis Blues," "Nola," "Ah, Sweet Mystery of Life," and others were arranged and published especially for the accordionist. Pagani's early success helped to spur on the field of accordion publishing in the 1930s and enhance the instrument's prestige value by improving its available repertoire. A significant issue was the lack of music for the accordion, beyond transcriptions. Pagani was joined by a wave of competitors eager to make their mark in the accordion publishing field with works composed by virtuoso accordionists: Pietro Frosini, Charlie Magnante, Fox DiBella, and Biaggio Quattrociocche all emerged in New York City offering method books and sheet music for accordion and other instruments. Recognizing that his many students needed appropriate repertoire, Pietro Deiro established AMPCO, later known simply as Pietro Deiro Publications. The company published hundreds of works composed and arranged for accordion by Deiro. By the 1930s, some of these new publishing houses were hiring demonstrators to promote their products in store fronts, helping to create more on-the-ground exposure for the accordion.

The business strategies and cultural tastes of the powers behind the accordion world—teachers, manufacturers, and publishers—controlled the nature of the music played and heard in the accordion world. As might be expected in the climate of the post-Depression era, independent accordion studios looked for ways to capitalize on the accordion's appeal and expand their business: publishing music, method books, and introducing opportunities for group and solo recitals. At the recommendation of Anthony Galla-Rini, accordion studio owners incorporated graded accordion bands into their curricula.[28] These bands made use of arrangements in three or four parts, and often made use of bass accordion. Many studios organized two bands: an auditioned group for playing challenging material and another open to all who played accordion. As little material existed for accordion bands, the studio owners were expected to arrange their own, and conduct.[29]

As accordionists struggled to identify their instrument with high musical culture at midcentury, a significant distinction between "good" music and its less prestigious counterpart resided in the fact that good music was written down and performed by literate, schooled musicians and taught by "professionals." In the early days of the accordion studio movement, we find a diverse array of method books for the accordion, developed by individual accordion teachers for their own students.[30] These are widely inconsistent in their approaches. Few of them address accordion-specific issues, such as handling of the bellows; they often assume that the student has prior knowledge of music theory or of other instruments such as the piano. Although accordion teachers in the 1930s and 1940s complained that their field was plagued by poor standards of accordion instruction—Pietro Deiro and other studio owners were infamous for hiring piano teachers to teach accordion—little effort was made in the early days of the accordion movement to promote a single, consistent method for the instrument.

The situation changed dramatically in the early 1950s when two accordion virtuosi, Willard Palmer and Bill Hughes of Houston, developed a set of method books that integrated accordion technique, music theory and note reading, and repertoire. The result was the Palmer-Hughes Method for Accordion. Consisting of ten graded volumes, the series remains in print today. It made ample use of illustrations to capture the younger player's attention. These images provide valuable insights into how the accordion industry perceived its audience (or wished it to be perceived) as white, Anglo, and upper middle class. The inside cover of volume 7 shows a preppily dressed accordionist serenading a bobby-soxed female listener; on the page presenting the tune "Relative Samba," an elegantly dressed family dances to the sounds of the accordion in their living room.[31]

The industry's aspirations to disseminate the accordion among elite audiences may have been misguided. "We used to snicker at these pictures," says William Schimmel, who grew up playing the Palmer-Hughes method. "None of us working-class German, Italian, and Jewish kids who played the accordion dressed like that." Although the books' repertoire of polkas, marches and waltzes—designed for a "balanced musical diet"—quickly became dated, Palmer-Hughes became the most widely selling accordion method book on the market. By 1961, there were over sixty-five Palmer accordion method books in print, amounting to sales of over eight million volumes.[32]

One of the most widely discussed pedagogical issues after 1950—a topic frequently covered in accordion magazines—was bellows technique. Polka players and practitioners of related folk accordion styles push and pull the bellows dynamically, often extending all eighteen folds for dramatic effect. This feat

"Relative Samba," illustration and music in the popular Palmer-Hughes Method for Accordion series by the renowned teachers and performers Willard Palmer and Bill Hughes.

requires a great deal of upper-body strength—particularly while performing standing up, the convention for polka and other dance band accordionists. Accordion teachers in the 1940s and 1950s wished to impose the standards of smooth, consistent bellowsing on their students; they considered the techniques of polka players crude and low-class.[33] In the methods promoted by mainstream accordion teachers, controlling the bellows was key. "Classical" accordionists performed sitting down with the bellows braced on the inside of the left thigh for control. Accordion bellows technique was compared to developing bowing technique on a violin and proper breathing in singing. The beginning player was taught to open the bellows in a "fan"-shaped motion and never to change the direction of the bellows while sounding a tone. More advanced players moved on to consideration of bellows technique as part of the musical aesthetic of the accordion, placing bellows changes where a singer would take a breath and calibrating the direction and strength of the changes. Indeed, accordion virtuosi Pietro Frosini, Pietro Deiro, and Albert D'Auberge devoted entire method books to bellows techniques.[34]

Despite the preponderance of spontaneous improvisations and memorization in accordion-based folk styles, proponents of "good" accordion music depended on notated arrangements that allowed faithful realization of the piece from the printed score in the Western classical tradition. By the 1950s, popular dance numbers like "Lady of Spain," if rendered by literate musicians like Myron Floren, could be considered "high class." The formal harmonic structures of most published accordion pieces—solo, small ensemble, and accordion orchestra music—were smoothed-over renditions of dance tunes, popular tunes, "folk" songs, and jazz and ragtime tunes. But accordion advocates insisted that the worth of their instrument rested on the existence of formally notated music—in large quantities. The establishment of accordion publishing companies became a key part of their mission to find a place for the accordion in the music world.

Published music was part of a controlled capitalist system of production, consumption, and reproduction. The accordion publishing industry and the accordion magazines promoted their notion of musical literacy, offering arrangements of small-scale classical repertoire for accordion. Most of these pieces were arranged for solo instruments. The publishers also offered ensemble pieces arranged in four or five accordion parts, for accordion bands and orchestras, emulating standard orchestral arrangements. The publishers introduced, at the recommendation of the AAA, a standard notation for the accordion. According to the conventions established by the so-called AAA notation, the bass clef is divided into upper and lower "zones." Notes in the lower zone, below the middle line in the stave, are single bass tones; notes in the upper zone are chords. Major chords are indicated by the capital letter M above the note or by nothing, as major is the "default" chord. Minor chords are indicated by a lowercase m, dominant seventh chords by the number 7, and diminished chords by "dim"; these symbols are shown between the clefs.[35] In addition to the conventional keyboard fingering indications in the bass, an underscore below the note—for example, 1, 2, 3, and so on—indicates that it is fingered on the counter-bass row.

In the 1940s and 1950s, accordion music appears to have progressed in three different directions, indicative of Americans' tastes and attitudes toward "other" styles of music. Different forms of "folk" music—a recontextualized repertoire that we might call "refolklorized" music—rose to prominence in the accordion world. Many accordion advocates were émigrés from Europe and had performed their local and national ethnic dance tunes at social dances, family gatherings, and religious events featuring the accordion in ensembles with other instruments. However, they did not feel confident that such material could stand on its own as the basis for a "good" accordion repertoire. It needed to be cultivated, improved, and "properly arranged." Arranging and performing such folk genres as the polka on the piano accordion was by no means a "natural" or logical extension of the immigrant tradition. Pietro and Guido Deiro successfully performed this repertoire in vaudeville, recorded it during the early days of sound recording, and helped to spread the appeal of this popular music, through the record companies' ethnic music catalogs, to listeners of many nationalities—creating new patterns of reception and consumption of folk music.

A significant feature of "refolklorized" music is that it was arranged, notated, and presented alongside classical music. As mentioned earlier, an eclectic mix of classical, operatic and folk music characterized the repertoire of vaudevillian accordionists. Italian-American accordionists, like Italian singers, regarded opera as part of their cultural patrimony rather than a rarified, distant, elevated art form and regularly performed transcriptions and arrangements of operatic arias and overtures. Guido's regular appearances at Italian-American clubs and Italian-American war veterans' association meetings in the 1920s routinely featured these kinds of offerings.[36] Operatic numbers and the classics mixed liberally with Italian folksongs, waltzes, and polkas, and there is no evidence to suggest that the performers or the audiences valued some of these genres more than others.

In the 1940s, however, discourse surrounding folk music in the upper echelons of the accordion world began to take on a pointed, polemic quality. Accordion publishers and teachers denigrated folk music and the players who performed it as musically illiterate and inept. Guardians of proper music for the accordion condemned rehashings of folk and popular tunes. Anthony Galla-Rini wrote: "musical tastes having been of a deplorably low standard in the past, such musical banalities as 'Sharpshooters March' and 'Beer Barrel Polka' should not be played in public, or given as lesson assignments."[37]

Accordion advocates, however, had to contend with their constituents' ethnic and cultural diversity. Most players of the accordion were white ethnics—first and second generation immigrants from Germany, Italy, Russia, and eastern Europe—who perceived their families' musical traditions as assets, not liabilities, in the study of the accordion. Pietro Deiro attempted to bring the skills of "trained" accordionists and composers to the task of arranging folk music for a series of AMPCO publications highlighting national and ethnic folk music styles for accordion. In the introduction to his *Ukrainian Folksongs and Dances* (PD #870), edited by Michael Storr, Deiro wrote: "we feel that in Mr. Storr we have the finest Ukrainian performer and accordionist to compile and arrange such a collection . . . the many years of his experience plus his authoritative background made him the logical choice to arrange and compile this book, retaining the authenticity and melodic qualities of Ukrainian Folk Music."[38] Likewise, AMPCO offered volumes of Lithuanian, Spanish, French, Italian, and Scandinavian songs for the accordion—totaling about two hundred published collections of folk music. *Music, Scandinavian Style* was edited by the prominent Swedish/Finnish accordion artist Walter Ericksson, who composed, arranged, and performed for virtually every Scandinavian musical group in the tristate New York area. The cover depicts Ericksson himself in a chef's toque, preparing a traditional smorgasbord—an apt metaphor for the banquet of ethnic musical delights awaiting the piano accordionist.

The vast majority of the music published by AMPCO and its successor, Pietro Deiro Publications, is characterized by simple meters (2/4, 6/8), even phrasings, and the keys that are easiest to play on the accordion: C, G, D, and A, with their minors. The style of accordion music published between 1938 and 1960 remained virtually consistent, utilizing the basic chordal capabilities of the left hand with its unchanging alternating bass pattern (single tone and chord). Accordionists generally played root position chords, with their fourth or third left-hand finger firmly placed on the note C (roughly in the center of the bass button board and indicated with an indentation or jewel on the button). Generally, they played single tone on the strong beat and the chord tone on the off beats (the ubiquitous "oompah" rhythm). Arrangers for the accordion rarely ventured beyond I, IV, and V harmonies. Mastering the bass side of the accordion is the biggest challenge for the student, and reproducing such repetitious harmonies was a quick and painless way of training the accordionist's left hand. The right hand generally played melody (single tones), but harmonies in thirds were often added, especially in "Italian" and French music. Accordionists who play such arrangements (and they still do today), describe this music as fun to play—instant gratification for the accordion—but not as music worthy of their admiration and respect.

Deiro's publications, as well as the contents of accordion magazines of the day, also reflected an emerging interest in jazz and contemporary popular music.

Cover of *Music, Scandinavian Style*, compiled by the Scandinavian-American accordion virtuoso and bandleader Walter Ericksson, a collection in Pietro Deiro Publications' Dollar Line.

Improvised music was generally not part of the pedagogical agenda for accordion teachers, whose goal appeared to be replication of preexisting compositional models. In an effort to keep up with the times, Deiro created, with the help of jazz artists like Art Van Damme and accompanying LP recordings, moderately challenging works in a jazz style, encouraging performers to develop their own jazz riffs and providing blank pages for that purpose. Simple swing rhythms and formulaic approaches to building jazz harmonies (adding the sixth to a triad, for example) placed such pieces safely outside the "dangerous" world of hot jazz and squarely within the comfort zone of the white, middle-class suburban audience with a beginning to intermediate skill set. A "good" accordionist was seen not only as having the ability to play the notes (i.e., pushing the correct buttons and keys) but also as demonstrating expressive playing—the key to which was correct handling of the bellows.

Very little of this published repertoire, jazz or folk, was intended to function as social dance or ritual music; it was meant as light concert fare and teaching repertoire.[39] The basic conventions employed in arranging the music and its simplified presentation reinforced accordion leaders' thinking about the accordion: while the accordion was challenging to play well, it could be made accessible to beginners with dumbed-down music and basic techniques. Pietro Deiro's simplified arrangements are seen in a critical light by many classical accordionists, a reflection of his arch-conservatism and even his musical ineptitude. Of his "original" published compositions in a classical style, few were actually composed by Deiro himself.[40] Pietro, like many of his contemporaries who played the vaudeville circuit, was not formally trained and had to hire musically educated ghostwriters, such as Alfred D'Auberge and Frank Henri Klickmann, to compose his classical scores. This pair, skilled in writing for various instruments, composition, and theory, were responsible for most of Pietro's "original" works. It was only with the help of these formally trained artists (and his gift for self-promotion) that Pietro was able to claim his place in history as "Daddy of the Accordion" and the "Paderewski of the accordion," a reputation that has been seen as exaggerated and by some accounts, fraudulent.[41] Yet Pietro's compositions were widely performed by accordionists in America and abroad, with symphony orchestra, and these performances no doubt increased the accordion's visibility on the concert stage.

An important direction accordion music took at this time was what we may recognize as the "classical accordion." From the early days of the accordion in the first decade of the twentieth century, when Guido Deiro played opera transcriptions, its advocates had committed themselves to creating and promoting what they considered "good" music—music that not only entertained its audiences and players but also enlightened and uplifted them.[42] Admired accordion advocates like Galla-Rini recognized masterpieces by Bach, Mozart, Tchaikovsky, Mendelssohn, and others as elevating and inspiring classics of prime importance for developing the accordionists' talents and proving their readiness for the concert hall. Galla-Rini noted: "there will always be the need for a number of skillfully-transcribed arrangements of good music, most carefully selected—this to prove the musical legitimacy of the instrument."[43] The accordion's associations with the decadent culture of saloons and brothels and the lowbrow culture of vaudeville were problematic. Accordion advocates had to accommodate opposing musical tastes, embracing the classics because of their status but programming popular novelty numbers and folk tunes because of their appeal across the board to their audiences and the less developed tastes of beginning students. Therefore, the repertoires of both accordion professionals and amateurs were highly eclectic: transcriptions and arrangements of works ranging from Beethoven, Brahms, and Bach, solo and symphonic works to thousands of waltzes, mazurkas, schottisches, and polkas. Jazz standards and ragtime numbers continued to appear on both amateur and professional programs, as well as the well-worn "Lady of Spain." Accordion magazines suggested programming lighter popular numbers as encores for concerts and for holding students' interest but emphasized the need to program only "good" music.

One aftermath of the death of vaudeville and the rise of new performance contexts was a new generation of accordion players who did not emerge from the traditional contexts of vaudeville, saloons and theaters. These players—a balanced mix of male and female artists and teachers—became the pioneers of an improved accordion. This new generation of accordionists, both male and female, had to fight against the image of the dashing, cigar-smoking Italian male virtuoso: images of Pietro Frosini lighting a cigar with a $10 bill and the womanizing Guido Deiro did not suit their personalities or performance contexts. They had to earn the trust and respect of the middle-class families who were willing to entrust them with their children and their money. The image of the accordion world that is revealed in accordion band and competition programs from the 1940s and 1950s is one of a middle-class, proper society of schoolteachers, serious-minded and conservatively attired. Photographic documentation of AAA dinners and fundraising events shows that 20 or 30 percent of the accordion world's leaders and teachers were women, and many were in their twenties and thirties. Most were from middle-class professional families; they were college graduates, and some held advanced degrees. They were self-conscious daughters of the middle class whose worldview and musical tastes provided the underpinning for the belief that they had the duty and the ability to transform the traditional power relationships that had hindered their advancement. Some advanced their careers by seeking older male teachers as mentors, or through their spouses, but some—as Elsie Bennett and Helmi Harrington—did not.[44] They subscribed to ideals that were becoming widespread among women in the musical world. Their aspirations to become equal members of the accordion world would not be fulfilled until the 1980s and 1990s.

In the 1950s, national and international competitions emerged in the accordion world, advocated by those who desired a more virtuosic approach to performance and the pursuit of high standards in general. Faithe Deffner, an accordion manufacturer and promoter and the publisher of *Accord*, explained why competition should remain a core value of the accordion community: "Competition is known to bring out the best in us, to set goals and create standards. History verifies that societies which eliminate competition invariably slip into mediocrity."[45]

In 1958 the AAA held a series of contests known as the Accordion Olympics; over ten thousand contestants entered. The champion, Don Lipovac, represented the United States in the 1958 Coupe Mondiale, the world competition sponsored by the International Confederation of Accordionists, an event that was promoted as part of the Worlds Fair celebrations in Brussels. The AAA sponsored contests at the local and national level, as they still do today. Events like these, as well as competitions on the local level, promised long-term benefits for accordion studios whose students participated in them. Students on the competitive track stayed enrolled longer, practiced harder, and purchased more expensive instruments. Discussing the characteristics of accordion "champions" in *Accordion World*, Mickey Bisilia noted that contests "are very important to the student. It keeps the interest of all concerned at a very high pitch. In summing up the makings of a champion, I would say that it is a four-way deal: 1st—a talented student. 2nd—a competent, interested teacher. 3d—parental cooperation; 4th—a fine instrument."[46]

Competition standards became so embedded in the accordion world that some observers lamented that virtuosic showmanship was being emphasized over artistry.[47] Indeed, competitions were never a simple matter of identifying the "best" accordionist according to "objective" criteria. Competitions have profound implications for the nature of the music that is performed and the character of a music culture.[48] Competition judges, who set standards and control deviations from the norm, come to the fore and exert their influence. Competition culture encouraged creation of "art music" for accordion. The AAA commissioned composers to write challenging, virtuosic "test pieces."[49] The social organization of accordion competition culture privileges the pursuit of individual self-esteem and the transmission of core values (which, as Deffner pointed out, include losing graciously). It enables certain performers to achieve "greatness" by becoming "champions" and gives the winners the power to represent and speak for the accordion community. These winners frequently go on to become competition adjudicators, a role that carries unique status within the accordion world.[50] As this culture developed, the relevance of competition, and its ill side effects, were (and continue to be) debated by accordion advocates. Yet accordion studio and conservatory directors acknowledged the financial benefits they expected from encouraging their students to participate in competitions that would motivate them to continue with lessons and purchase better instruments.[51]

Ensuring that accordion players of all abilities—not just at the competition level—had a forum for performance, accordion clubs became popular, welcoming players of all abilities. These clubs, some formed by teachers and studio owners for their students, were associated with urban and community cultural life. Members usually met once a month, giving performances, meeting friends, sometimes raising funds—and certainly socializing. There were (and still are) accordion clubs in most major American cities: Boston; Oakland, California; San Francisco; Washington, D.C.; Los Angeles; Houston; Minneapolis; and Chicago, with some cities, such as Houston, having two or three. A natural offshoot of such clubs were accordion bands, which often performed with other instruments, such as guitar, strings, percussion, and guest vocalists.

In the 1940s, symphonic accordion ensembles rose to prominence: the New York Accordion Symphony, the Springfield Accordion Orchestra (Massachusetts), the Duluth Accordionaires (Minnesota), the Houston Accordion Symphony (later known as the Palmer-Hughes Accordion Symphony), and the Philadelphia Accordion Orchestra (PAO). They followed the example of the Hohner Symphony Accordion Orchestra, formed in Trossingen, Germany, in 1931. Not to be confused with accordion bands, which were smaller and played lighter repertoire, these large free-reed orchestras, made up of fifty to a hundred members, aimed to convince their listeners of the viability of the accordion in the serious music field by presenting popular and classical works.[52]

As the founder of one of the first such ensembles in the United States, the New York Accordion Symphony, Joseph Biviano is considered to be the father of the accordion symphony movement in the United States, even though much of his career in the 1940s and 1950s revolved around session music engagements and repertoire that some of his colleagues would have considered lowbrow, such as "Pizza Party" and "More Beer."

Jacob C. Neupauer and his orchestra, the PAO, took an ambitious approach to the accordion orchestra, creating an ensemble that circulated at the top echelons of the professional music world. Born to a Slovak-American family in 1917 and active with his local Slovak Catholic church choir, Neupauer performed accordion on local and national radio broadcasts at the age of twelve. After mastering a variety of instruments and earning his Ph.D. in music (from Combs College in Philadelphia), Neupauer went on to direct a variety of musical ensembles, including the Philaccordion Concert Quartet and the Neupauer Symphonic Group. Committed to improving the visibility of the accordion in the music world, Neupauer founded the PAO as an independently owned and operated nonprofit group. It was primarily comprised of students from Neupauer's conservatory: thirty-two accordions, harp, double bass, timpani, and two trumpets.

For thirty years, this orchestra concertized on major concert stages throughout the eastern states, from Pennsylvania's coal regions to Washington, D.C., including the Philadelphia Academy of Music, Philadelphia Town Hall, and Atlantic City's Convention Hall. The PAO offered subscription concerts at the University of Pennsylvania Museum Auditorium. They appeared for twenty-four consecutive years on all of the piers in New Jersey. On February 9, 1958, the PAO presented a concert performance of the first act of Verdi's *La Traviata*, featuring the full cast of the American Opera Guild. On April 1, 1962, the PAO performed the first act of Smetana's *Bartered Bride* with the Meistersingers,

The Philadelphia Accordion Orchestra with its conductor, Jacob C. Neupauer.

a one-hundred-voice choir. Neupauer often spoke from the podium before concerts, discussing the merits of the accordion. Initially high-minded in his efforts, Neupauer adapted with ease to his unexpected role as a showman. "I became a promoter without realizing it," he commented.[53] Neupauer recalls capacity crowds at most of his events, thanks to the blocks of tickets purchased by accordion studios for their students; "we had busloads coming in from Allentown and Camden." These concerts also drew in a reliable contingent of novelty seekers, audiences who found the idea of an accordion orchestra so amusing that they requested photographs to show off to their friends.[54]

The significance of the PAO and other accordion orchestras, such as the New York Accordion Orchestra and the Palmer Hughes Accordion Symphony, was the momentum they gave to the accordion world's official vision of the "classical" accordion. This musical direction, while generally consistent with Pietro Deiro's vision, better expressed the desire to improve the accordion. The individual most responsible for this direction was Anthony-Galla-Rini, who (as told in chapter 2) broke away as a youth from his father's vaudeville act to make a career as a professional classical accordionist. As a self-supporting seventeen-year-old who had no way of financing a college or conservatory education, Galla-Rini studied music theory on his own, purchasing recordings of great artists and composers such as Rachmaninoff, Heifetz, and Paderewski. In the early 1930s, Galla-Rini established himself as an accordion teacher and studio owner in San Francisco, publishing his own method books and arrangements. Sponsored by Wurlitzer, he joined the staff of the National Music Camp at Interlochen, Michigan, as an accordion instructor. Determined to introduce the accordion on the concert platform, Galla-Rini composed two accordion concertos, one of them for the free-bass accordion. He has been featured on numerous solo and orchestral recordings, arranging hundreds of transcriptions from orchestral work for accordion ensembles, orchestras, soloists, and students. One significant project Galla-Rini undertook was altering the standard pitch combinations used on the bass side of the accordion. He had objected, among other accordionists, to the use of the fifth in the preset chord combinations for the dominant and diminished seventh chords, which he felt would lead to incorrect harmonies. At his suggestion, the omission of the fifth became standard in the Stradella system. Departing from the "short-hand" notation adopted by the AAA, he also insisted that the exact pitches of all the left-hand chords be notated, as well as the exact pitches of all five sets of reeds in the left hand. Galla-Rini's insistence on this more detailed, complex notation system called for a higher level of musical knowledge on the part of accordionists. his controversial proposal led to a rift within the AAA board and Galla-Rini's abrupt exit in 1941 to establish the Accordion Teachers Guild.[55]

Galla-Rini led a vocal contingent of accordionists who believed that the accordion should be more accepted in conservatories and college music departments. Since the 1920s, when it had been established by the Deiro brothers, the accordion studio system had existed in its own profit-driven subculture, separate from the academic music world. Some studios aspired to become "conservatories," offering full courses of study including theory, composition, piano, and other instruments of the orchestra. Jacob Neupauer was a former colleague of Pietro Deiro and established his own Accordion Conservatory in Philadelphia in 1948. At Neupauer's conservatory, the accordion could be used as a major instrument toward a two-year diploma course, the equivalent of a trade school or community college degree. The Conservatory preparatory course was designed for high-school-aged music students who wanted to prepare for entrance to a music school or liberal arts college. The Accordion Conservatory's legitimate status (accredited by the National Association of Schools of Music) enabled William Schimmel, a Neupauer graduate, to transfer all the credits he earned at Neupauer to the Juilliard School of Music, where he enrolled as a piano and composition major. Indeed, in a recent interview, Neupauer suggested that Schimmel deserved credit for "introducing the accordion to Juilliard."[56]

But Juilliard did not accept the accordion as a major instrument, nor did the other elite musical conservatories of the East Coast. Schimmel recalled of his time at Juilliard in the 1960s that it was expected that playing the accordion (like the mandolin, banjo, and saxophone) was to be pursued in venues outside an academic setting, such as club dates. New accordion majors and programs (master's and doctoral programs) came about outside the august musical institutions of the East Coast, the result of efforts by accordion teachers and performers who were able to persuade deans to accept their instrument. At Combs College, Butler University (Indianapolis), VanderCook College of Music (Chicago), the University of Missouri at Kansas City (UMKC), the University of Houston, and the Lamont School of Music (University of Denver), the accordion could be used as a major instrument toward a degree. Of these UMKC was (and remains) the only institution where the highest academic music performance degree, the Doctor of Musical Arts, could be earned in accordion performance, and it is the nation's only academic music department or school of music that treats the accordion as a major instrument, retaining a full-time accordionist on its faculty.[57] It supports a community accordion orchestra that regularly enters competitions and travels on concert tours in Europe, Australia, and New Zealand. In addition, UMKC's program places a great deal of emphasis on orchestral and chamber music and opportunities to play alongside other instruments.

Joan Sommers launched UMKC's four-year program for accordion performance majors in 1960 and has served as its chair since them. One problem she faced in persuading her fellow faculty and administrators of the accordion's legitimacy was the lack of repertoire for the instrument.[58] As noted, the AAA's distinguished founders aimed to "publish literature to be of service to accordionists," but contention remained about the kind of literature that should be published. A vocal contingent of prominent accordion advocates, such as Galla-Rini and Willard Palmer, had agreed that transcribing and arranging the classics was a legitimate undertaking for accordionists, while remaining completely indifferent to contemporary music.[59] Few had challenged that indifference until a new generation of professional players and teachers had moved up the ranks. These individuals had never been part of the accordion's vaudevillian social context, and they were formally educated. This newer generation became the pioneers of a new vision of the accordion that was more attuned to the classical contemporary music scene.

In "The Emancipation of the Accordion," an article for *Accordion and Guitar World,* twenty-three-year-old accordion virtuoso and Columbia University graduate Carmelo Pino argued that the accordion, in order to become an instrument recognized in the classical music world needed quality, original musical literature, not simply transcriptions. "Transcriptions for the most part sound second-hand to one familiar with the original version. For the purposes of firmly establishing a place for the accordion in the art world the transcription will not do. The answer to our problem lies in the direction of serious compositions specifically for the accordion and which will sound best when played on that instrument. When the accordion has in its catalog a library of original music acceptable to the music public in general, and music critics particularly, our goal will have been achieved."[60] Pino, who later built a full-time career as a performer, teacher, and music professor in the Washington metropolitan area, was neither a reformer nor an activist. But he may have seen his vision realized in the work of a fellow student at Columbia, Elsie Bennett.

In the mid-1940s, Bennett (nee Blum), a promising young accordionist in her twenties, arrived in New York from Michigan to study music at Columbia. Her aim was to complete her master's degree at Teachers College, with the accordion as her major instrument. As Columbia had no accordionist on the faculty, she had to look outside the College for a qualified instructor. The virtuoso Joseph Biviano was available for such an arrangement, and he was given an adjunct appointment at Columbia. The next hurdle for Bennett was to prepare a master's degree recital for the accordion representing all major musical style periods. To represent the baroque, classical, and Romantic periods, Bennett had her pick of numerous transcriptions of Bach, Mozart, and Tchaikovsky, as well as newly composed works—such as Deiro's accordion concertos—in a Romantic idiom. However, when seeking accordion repertoire from the twentieth century, Bennett found only a handful of ensemble works that included the accordion: Virgil Thomson's enigmatic opera *Four Saints in Three Acts* and a brief interlude in the tavern scene of Alban Berg's *Wozzeck*.[61] Alarmed by this absence, Bennett approached her composition teacher, the American avant-garde composer Otto Luening. Luening, a pioneer of electronic and magnetic tape music in the 1950s and 1960s, was not familiar with the accordion, but Bennett rallied him to her side. Luening insisted to Bennett that if the accordion were ever to gain in prestige in the classical music world, it would need original literature by reputable contemporary composers—not a repertoire of transcriptions by dead masters. Furthermore, instructing Bennett in the culture of the New York City music world, Luening insisted that these composers would need financial incentives to compose for the accordion; he later joined the roster of distinguished composers receiving commissions from the AAA.[62]

By 1953, newly graduated from Columbia and having started her own accordion studio in Brooklyn, Bennett joined the board of the AAA and began researching American composers who could be approached for commissions. She soon found Magnante, Galla-Rini, and the conservative camp of elder male leaders of the AAA to be vehemently opposed to the idea of commissioning new works, and perhaps even dismissive of this young woman's zealous persistence.[63] Not to be discouraged, Bennett invited Luening to speak at an AAA meeting about the importance of supporting new music for the accordion. Apparently, his arguments must have been convincing; the AAA board agreed to establish the Composers' Commissioning Committee, with Bennett as chair. She continued to hold that position and act as the accordion world's composer-liaison of sorts for thirty more years, well into her seventies.

In *Accordion World,* Bennett reflected on her mission of commissioning music for the accordion:

> In the art of music, one of the finest examples of growth and change has been the development of the accordion from a "popular" fun instrument to the status of a

standard "serious" instrument in orchestra or band and of a solo instrument worthy of the greatest talent. Today, great accordion virtuosos, using the magnificent instruments that have been developed—and which they have helped to perfect—are recognized as serious musical artists. One drawback to full development of the accordion was the dearth of original compositions in which it was either solo instrument or part of an ensemble. As a new instrument, the accordion lacked the great background of composition that abounds for the piano, violin, etc. There were no accordions when the great symphonies and concertos of the past were written.[64]

The unique distinction of becoming the first American composer to receive a commission to write for the accordion belongs to Paul Creston. Creston, born Giuseppe Guttoveggio to Italian immigrant parents in 1906 (d. 1985), was a strategic choice for the AAA. Creston was one of the most widely performed American composers in the 1940s and 1950s and the recipient of a Guggenheim Fellowship. At the time Bennett approached him, his conservative and lushly neo-Romantic music had fallen out of favor with the American public; he was working as a church organist in New York City and welcomed the offer of a commission for the accordion. Having worked with unconventional orchestral combinations featuring the marimba, the saxophone, and the trombone, Creston was drawn to unusual instruments and sound combinations. He told Bennett, "the accordion has always fascinated me, due perhaps to its power and its ability to reproduce *sforzando* and *piano*, which is in the realm of the bass. From the accordion's system of (Stradella) basses, one can gain unusual harmonic effects by combining the basses with what the right hand can do."[65] Creston's working-class Italian roots and his early musical experiences as a theater organist had likely given him favorable exposure to the accordion. The Sano Accordion Company provided him with an instrument, and Bennett herself taught him how to play it.

The result of these efforts, Creston's Prelude and Dance, op. 69, satisfied the AAA on several levels. It was exuberant and dramatic, filled with virtuosic challenges for an accomplished player. Second, the writing was idiomatic to the instrument—an important feature, given the AAA's desire to showcase works that would not transcribe successfully to other instruments or ensembles. Third, the piece fit the mold of "traditional" accordion works and hence could appease the conservative AAA board. Robert McMahan, a board member who was active on the Commissioning Committee, wrote: "the piece is definitely a light classic, with its merry-go-round quality and abstract, punctuated left-hand oom-pah-pahs in the Dance."[66] The piece was premiered by the accordion virtuoso Carmen Carrozza in Carnegie Hall on May 18, 1958, as part of a festive joint concert featuring Anthony Galla-Rini, Charles Magnante, and other accordion virtuosi. Creston went on to receive three more commissions from the AAA between 1958 and 1968, including his Concerto for Accordion and Orchestra, which is seen as one of the all-important works of the accordion classical repertoire.[67]

Bennett's successful association with Creston provided a kind of template for the AAA's future commissioning efforts. Bennett would begin each commissioning cycle by "targeting" composers whose reputation and fame would be an asset to the AAA. Next, she would write to these composers, sometimes following up with personal visits. If a composer expressed interest, she would provide sample scores, information about the accordion, for example a bass chart, and sometimes an instrument for his use. She also provided the composer with a personal accordionist-mentor and collaborator; that role was most often filled by accordion virtuoso Carmen Carrozza. The commissioned works were usually premiered by Carrozza in New York (Carnegie Hall and Town Hall), and received brief notices in the *New York Times* and *Herald Tribune*.[68] The majority of the scores were later published by one of the accordion publishing companies: Pietro Deiro, Jr., O. Pagani, or Ernest Deffner.

Among Bennett's most ambitious and successful efforts was the William Grant Still commission in 1960. Still remains a legendary figure in twentieth-century American music: the first African American to conduct a major American symphony orchestra, the first to have a symphony of his own (his first symphony) performed by a leading orchestra, the Los Angeles Symphony Orchestra, the first to have an opera performed by a major opera company (the New York City Opera). Bennett first wrote to Still in early 1959, sending him information about the workings of the accordion, along with a copy of Creston's Prelude and Dance. Still, the recipient of a Guggenheim fellowship and well remunerated for his Hollywood film scores, could hardly have been an easy target for a modest commission from an accordion association. In addition, Still was, according to his daughter Judith Still Headlee, "tired and discouraged and less optimistic, and unlikely to indulge himself in learning new instruments such as the accordion." Bennett persisted in her usual fashion. In a letter responding to Bennett on March 12 of the same year, Still wrote that he had reviewed her materials and he was very impressed with the accordion's apparent capabilities. Bennett then arranged for a visit from the West Coast's (and possibly America's) most famed accordionist, Myron Floren of the Lawrence Welk Orchestra and television program. Still's daughter has a faint recollection of their meeting: "I came downstairs one afternoon and found some gentleman in the living room, demonstrating the accordion. He was instructing my father in the instrument."[69] Evidently, Floren was quite pleased with Still's *Aria,* reporting to Bennett that he found it beautiful, with many interesting color changes. It was premiered on May 15, 1960, as part of the Sano Accordion Symphony concert at Town Hall. Participating were Eugene Ettore, a virtuoso accordionist and the accordion symphony's conductor. Floren and the orchestra performed the *Aria,* as well as a hodgepodge of accordion orchestra transcriptions by Debussy, Khachaturian, Sir Arthur Sullivan, and Ferde Grofe, and "Lady of Spain," which Floren had helped to make ubiquitous. Bennett requested that he perform her own composition *Four Nocturnes,* and he did.

The Still composition, followed by its successful premiere, was seen as a coup for the AAA. The work went on to enjoy exposure in at least a half dozen performances at mainstream New York venues.[70] Robert Young McMahan, who has performed (and recorded) the piece, writes favorably about it as both a fine example of Still's style and a well-crafted work for accordion.[71] Bennett and the AAA followed up on *Aria*'s success by asking Still for another accordion solo. The goal of this commission, as Bennett put it in a letter she wrote to Still on February 21, 1965, was "to write a simple piece that could be used for teaching purposes."

The contract was sent to Still the following summer, on July 5, 1966; the resulting piece, indeed easier technically, was entitled "Lilt." It joins other commissions for intermediate-level pieces that the AAA made around the same time. According to the AAA's contract records, "Lilt" was its twenty-ninth commission. An article in the fall 1968 issue of *Accordion Horizons* announced the publication of "Lilt" by Pietro Deiro, Jr., and the fact that it had been chosen as a test piece for both the AAA Eastern Cup and New York State regional competitions that year. In addition, Still is quoted as describing his new piece as a "jaunty, good-humored little tune with an easy, infectious rhythm." As may be expected for a student-level composition, it is melodically, harmonically, and formally simpler and more "popular" in nature than the weightier Aria. Both works are highly valued today by accordionists.

According to conversations with AAA board members, Bennett deserves credit for over fifty commissioned works for accordion in diverse idioms, genres, and instrumental combinations. A list of these works appears on the AAA's website.[72] Many of them represent well-known names in American music at midcentury: Lukas Foss, Ernst Krenek, Elie Siegmeister, Alexander Tcherepnin, and David Diamond (pictured with Bennett).

Elsie Bennett with American composer David Diamond, 1950s.

In the accordion world Bennett is regarded as a legendary figure, a zealous Joan of Arc type who overcame her humble musical background to become a giant in the accordion world. Her musical tastes and her understanding of the contemporary music world were seen as unsophisticated, even naïve. Mc-Mahan recalled that Bennett was so unfamiliar with the contemporary music scene that she had to search for names of American composers in reference works like *The New Grove Encyclopedia of Music and Musicians* and Baker's *Biographical Dictionary of Musicians*. Once Bennett found these composers and established a connection with them, by mail or in person, she was relentless. Energetic, charming, and well-liked by the composers she "adopted," Bennett often established lifelong friendships with them, dispatching cards on their birthdays each year. Indeed, she displayed sophistication in both her interpersonal dealings with composers who were regarded as celebrities and her knowledge of the issues surrounding composition for the accordion. To do so, she had to overcome resistance from the AAA's older male leadership, whose values and attitudes regarding women reflected their old-world origins.[73]

Most composers of a certain stature whom Bennett approached either turned down the commissions or simply ignored the AAA's solicitations. These composers included Marc Blitzstein, William Schuman, Darius Milhaud, Paul Hindemith, Heitor Villa-Lobos, Carlos Chavez, Aaron Copland, Roger Sessions, Samuel Barber, Vincent Persichetti, Giancarlo Menotti, and Luigi Dallapiccola. Stravinsky's constant confidant Robert Craft had to protect the maestro from Bennett when she chased them down a Manhattan street in hot pursuit of a Stravinsky masterpiece for accordion. According to some accounts, a taxicab provided Stravinsky with his escape route.[74] Correspondence between Bennett and the composers she identified for possible commissions supports the notion put forth by some AAA advocates that the instrument faced an "uphill climb" to recognition. One reason for this (as discussed earlier) was the instrument's lowbrow, trivial reputation in the art musical world. Even a radically innovative composer like Henry Cowell, commissioned by the AAA to write his *Iridescent Rondo* for accordion, produced a work with an "all-over effect like a vaudevillian novelty."[75] In fact, Cowell had heard Pietro Deiro perform onstage numerous times in his youth.[76] When Bennett eventually persuaded Otto Luening to write a piece for the accordion, he chose to create a "flashy, etude-like, *moto perpetuo* solo based largely on the chromatic scale and supported by simple diatonic harmonies." McMahan believes that Luening, although well disposed toward the accordion, simply could not get past the old vaudevillian stereotypes of the instrument.

An even more significant stumbling block was the instrument's complete lack of a profile in the classical music world. As Bennett and others had pointed out, the accordion had been invented too late for Bach, Mozart, and Beethoven to have written for it.[77] Even the most erudite and accomplished American composers lacked familiarity with it, particularly the bass side. But even if the accordion lacked a past, composers could be educated about it as the "instrument of the future," McMahan said,[78] if only the AAA would work tirelessly to "bring the accordion to the attention of the ablest people now composing music." The correspondence Bennett kept up with composers is evidence that the AAA succeeded in its efforts to bring greater public attention to the instrument. Cowell declared that he was impressed by the accordion's tone and dynamics. Virgil Thomson, reflecting on his commissioned work, the Concerto for Accordion and Orchestra, wrote of the accordion's "terrific accents" and "the way it can snarl."[79]

Although Bennett deserves credit for bringing into being what most American accordionists acknowledge as their twentieth-century repertoire, the character of this repertoire as commissioned by the AAA reflects a conservative eighteenth- and nineteenth-century cast. Most of the commissioned works, as McMahan has pointed out, make use of classical form such as the rondo and sonata; adhere generally to the conventions of traditional tonality; and showcase the accordion as a virtuosic instrument in the tradition of nineteenth-century Romanticism.[80] A notable exception is Ernst Krenek's *Toccata for Accordion*, the twentieth commissioned work of the AAA, recognized as the first atonal work in the series of commissions. This work had to wait five years for its premiere performance in 1967, by McMahan himself, then a young composition student at the Peabody Institute. (The piece figures significantly in McMahan's own development as a musician-composer and his own quest for the accordion's legitimacy).[81] It is clear from the evidence provided by discussions with AAA board members and the scores themselves that new music was a controversial subject within the AAA. Only within the past twenty years has the AAA (at McMahan's urging) undertaken to commission works by composers exploring the potential of avant-garde compositional techniques for the accordion.[82]

CONCLUSION

A wave of new respect for the accordion, fueled by postwar prosperity, consumer culture, and a renewed enthusiasm for technology, spread through America in the 1940s and 1950s. Growing out of the vaudeville tradition, a sustained interest in light classical and cultivated folk music percolated in the accordion world, taking hold in specific geographical regions—the East Coast, West Coast, and Midwest. A favorable response from composers, although limited, provided a cultural confirmation that the accordion was ready for the art world. The arguments made by accordion world enthusiasts also laid the groundwork for controversy and debate. Leaders like Pietro Deiro and Anthony Galla-Rini had hoped that through the incorporation of certain styles and sounds of respectability, the accordion could come to be embraced by a more elevated class of players and listeners, but they had merely found new ways to use the accordion to recycle watered-down versions of the classics. In the popular dance music that Pietro Deiro promoted and published, the accordion was presented as lighthearted entertainment, with a palatable dose of "folk." Although manufacturers liked to present the accordion as progressive and modern, the "classical accordion" was awash in transcribed masterpieces and watered-down pops numbers for much of the first half of the twentieth century.

By the 1950s, Americans no longer viewed the accordion as a vehicle for barrooms and polkas; it had been transformed into an instrument worthy of artists. Although most vaudeville accordionists were self-taught and few could read music, the accordion world adopted new ideas of musical literacy. The accordion's bassetti system was reformed (modestly) to reflect certain harmonic formations that were seen as correct. As for accordionists who aspired to become professionals and virtuosi, a small, select group of academic programs and "elevated accordion studios" (conservatories) accommodated their needs. The accordion was presented as appropriate for academic study in several institutions of higher learning, most notably UMKC. The "squeezebox" was accepted in polite surroundings: recital halls, colleges, and middle-class living rooms. The accordion's ethnic associations were far from dead, however; some of the people who took up the accordion were attracted to it because of its ethnic connotations and the possibilities offered by Pietro Deiro's publications of appealing, easy-to-play ethnic numbers. And the accordion craze of the 1940s and 1950s was an early, unofficial flirtation with commodified folk music, a phenomenon that helped to set the conditions for the accordion's revival in the 1990s (discussed later).

Ultimately, the idea of the "classical" accordion was not the idea of the accordion that proved the most significant. Most mid-twentieth-century players did not believe that the accordion had to be elevated or promoted to an "official" slot. The overwhelming idea was that the accordion was an instrument for everyone, and as such it had an important role to play in mainstream social life and the construction of middlebrow American values. That role will be explored in the next chapter.

Early accordion, c. 1816, attributed to Friedrich Lohner, Nuremburg, Germany. Swedish handwriting inside original case reads "at the end of the 1820s, Johannes Dillner, former priest at Ostra Ryd, received this accordion from Countess Brahe at Rydbolom as a gift and it was the first one or one of the first brought to Sweden and cost 40 Rdr." (Photo by Henry Doktorski)

Eight-key accordion, 1820s. Early accordions appeared in a variety of key configurations and sizes, some preceding the Demian; others were unauthorized copies of the Demian. (Photo by Henry Doktorski; Source: World of Accordions Museum, Superior, Wisconsin)

Dallape accordion, late 1800s.
(Photo by Henry Doktorski)

Paolo Soprani diatonic
accordion, late 1800s.
(Source: Alex & Bell
Accordion Museum,
New York)

Beaver diatonic accordion, made in Germany, 1906.
(Source: Alex & Bell Accordion Museum, New York)

Ficosecco diatonic accordion, made in Italy, 1921.
(Source: Alex & Bell Accordion Museum, New York)

Butti accordion, 1920s. Accordion manufacturers of the 1920s
and 1930s embellished grilles with rhinestones and semiprecious stones, designed to catch the lights on the vaudeville stage.
(Source: Alex & Bell Accordion Museum, New York)

Galanti accordion, 1920s. (Source: Alex & Bell
Accordion Museum, New York)

White pearled Excelsior accordion, 1930s. (Source: Alex & Bell Accordion Museum, New York)

Italo-American accordion, made in Chicago, 1920s. (Photo by Henry Doktorski; Source: World of Accordions Museum, Superior, Wisconsin)

Petosa accordion with "ergonomic" curved keyboard, 1936.

Hohner Accordions' contribution to the curved
keyboard trend, 1930s. (Source: Alex & Bell
Accordion Museum, New York)

Frontalini accordion, 1930s. (Source: Alex & Bell Accordion Museum, New York)

The streamlined look of Titano and Frontalini accordions from the late 1930s and beyond reflect the industry's trend away from highly ornamented vaudeville models. (Source: Alex & Bell Accordion Museum, New York)

Dave's Accordion Studio on Glendale Avenue, Los Angeles. Like many other studio operators offering accordion instruction in the 1960s, the owner probably added the guitar with the expectation that the Beatles and their ilk were a passing fad. Of the hundreds of accordion studios that once operated, only one, Acme Accordions in Westmont, New Jersey, remains.

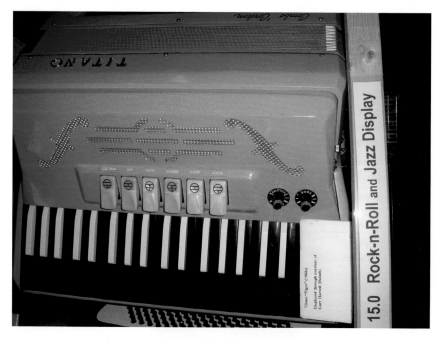

Tiger Combo accordion coated in a high-shine "Fiat Orange" finish, on display at the World of Accordions Museum in Superior, Wisconsin. (Photo by Marion Jacobson)

Brave Combo. Carl Finch, accordion and vocals; "Little Jack Melody," bass guitar; Arjuna Contreras, drums; Jeffrey Barnes, saxophone; Danny O'Brien, trumpet. (Photo by Jane Finch)

Accordion Tribe recording in Lars Hollmer's "Chicken House" studio in Uppsala, Sweden, 2001. Left to right: Accordionists Otto Lechner, Austria; the late Lars Hollmer, Sweden; Guy Klucevsek (with hat), United States; Maria Kalaniemi, Finland; Bratko Bibic, Slovenia. (Photo by Bengt Alm)

Two-time Grammy Award–winning alternative rock duo They Might Be Giants (John Linnell, accordion, John Flansburgh, guitar). They have since expanded their guitar-and-accordion-plus-backing-tracks format to recruit a supporting band. (Photo by Jayme Thornton)

Accordionist and vocalist Heidi Wohlwend, aka "Doodles La Rue" of the eclectic blues trio Five Cent Coffee.

(Photo by Martin Cooper)

Those Darn Accordions, 2008, reconfigured as a professional touring band. From left to right: Susie Davis, Lewis Wallace, Paul Rogers, Suzanne Garramone, Michael Messer, and Carri Abrahms. (Photo by Jim Merithew)

The city clears the streets for a morning accordion parade leading to La Plaza Park at the Cotati Accordion Festival in 2008. (Photo by Patti Davi)

Two young dancers improvise during Alex Meixner's performance on the main stage at the 2008 Cotati festival. (Photo by Patti Davi)

An accordion band organized by the Golden State Accordion Club performs midcentury-style accordion band arrangements and popular standards in the club's tent at the 2008 Cotati festival. (Photo by Patti Davi)

Dick Contino, now an elder statesmen of the accordion, headlines at the 2008 Cotati festival.

Smythe's Accordions, a retail business in Oakland, California, displays its wares at the 2008 Cotati festival. (Photo by Patti Davi)

At the midpoint of the Cotati Accordion Festival in 2011, festival organizers invite anyone with an accordion up to the main stage to participate in a group performance of "Lady of Spain," whether or not they know the song or can play the accordion. A little girl holding a toy accordion joins in. Past "Lady of Spain-A-Ring" audience participation events have drawn as many as 100 "accordionists." (Photo by Patti Davi)

Bronze statue of Cotati festival founder Jim Boggio in La Plaza Park.
(Photo by Patti Davi)

Tex-Czech band
Czechaholics with
accordionist Mark
Hermes (Photo by
Marion Jacobson)

An accordion band organized by Shelia Lee for the 2010 Accordion Kings and Queens festival in Houston, highlighting the piano accordion in an event that focuses primarily on Tex-Mex and Cajun music and the button accordion.

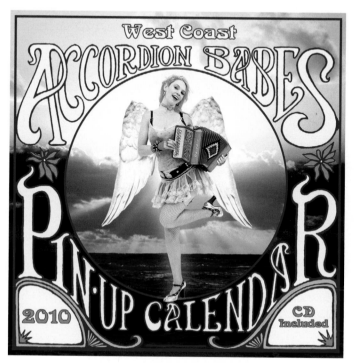

Accordion Babes 2010 Pin-up Calendar cover image featuring Renee de la Prade, button accordionist and bandleader of the Bay Area Celtic/Cajun fusion band Culann's Hounds.

Fannie Mae, accordionist and bandleader of Below the Salt, an indie band from Port Townsend, Washington. (Photo by Shannon Conyers)

The Grauman Collection

Items from Joan Grauman's accordion memorabilia collection, displayed and sold at accordion conventions and festivals.

Frank "the Great Morgani" Lima entertains as an accordion-playing Vatican Swiss guard (note papal miter in foreground) at the Food & Wine Festival in Capitola, California. (Photo courtesy Frank Lima)

*J*QUEEZEBOX *R*OCK

The Rise and Fall
of the Accordion in
American Popular Culture

THE PERSPECTIVE I HAVE TAKEN on accordion advocates in the previous chapter may have created the impression that the accordion's place in American mainstream culture was secure. Ensconced in the cultured musical institutions, the accordion would continue to develop as a concert instrument, safe from the influences of ethnic music and the vicissitudes of popular taste. Such was the highbrow vision for the accordion. However, events in American culture of the 1940s, 1950s, and 1960s intervened dramatically in the life of the accordion, transforming it in subtle and profound ways. The first section of this chapter chronicles the response of the accordion world to the events of World War II, the postwar transformation of the accordion, and issues of expansion and conflict that arose during this time within accordion culture. I introduce two postwar accordion celebrities, Dick Contino and Myron Floren, and describe how their musical identities offered opposing identities for the accordion. I look at the various treatments of the accordion in popular culture, which include, among other things, the accordion world's flirtation with the teen idol image and rock and the accordion's increasingly endangered status in television and popular culture in the age of rock 'n' roll.

Accordion advocates experienced a moment of panic over the status of the industry during World War II. In October 1942, the editor of *Accordion World* protested the shutdown of musical instrument factories and the halt of imports from Europe as a senseless act of political posturing, resulting in "foolish deprivations": "Are we deprived of accordions in order to make sure we do not blow out the flames of war with a puff from an accordion bellows? A mere carload of metal would keep the country supplied with accordions for a year."[1] He argued that the production of musical instruments, and the accordion in particular, not only created jobs and businesses for Americans but was an activity that should be seen as patriotic.

Accordionists felt the need to defend the accordion during a war, in a climate of scarcity, military mobilization, and patriotism. *Accordion World* published articles portraying accordionists as loyal Americans, buyers of war bonds, and supporters of the war effort. The accordion itself was portrayed as a utilitarian tool of that effort. In June 1944, the magazine proudly noted, "USO Camp Shows continues its drive to sign up more and more accordionists for work in American camps and naval bases. As the [Allied] Invasion [of Normandy] drives ahead, there will be greater need than ever for this most mobile of accompaniments."[2] In a 1944 series of articles *Accordion World* chronicled the adventures of Jerry Cummings, an accordionist who played for troops and naval forces in out-of-the-way and dangerous places such as Jerusalem, Cairo, and the Australian bush.[3] As the voice of the accordion industrial complex, *Accordion World* published patriotic proclamations and encouraged serving the war effort. Accordion clubs were encouraged to support their members in military service and to keep in touch with members overseas. The magazine also published advice on accordion repairs during a time "when your present instrument must suffice for the duration."[4]

Accordionists, as an industry and a profession, attempted to contribute sufficiently to the war effort that they would not be asked to sacrifice further. Resolutions were passed at meetings of retailers, such as the Merchants Association of Ohio, in which minimum allotments of materials were requested in order to meet "student and professional demand, so that music can continue to do its share in the war effort."[5] Accordionists and ensembles with accordions touring army posts in the 1940s were a hit with servicemen from America's heartland. They entertained the troops with their local and regional folk styles of music (polka and waltz) as well as jazz and popular music. Notable accordionists who served in the armed forces and who built distinguished careers included Manny Quartucci (drafted into the army in 1942), Charles Nunzio (enlisted in the navy in 1942), Mort Herald, and Carmelo Pino, who enlisted and served as a naval officer during the Korean War. The career of African-American accordionist Graham W. Jackson is an outstanding example of what military service could do for one's musical career in the 1940s. A graduate of Hampton University and a high school music teacher in Atlanta, Jackson (also an organist and pianist) found opportunities as an accordionist and musician that might have otherwise been closed to African Americans in the South by enlisting in the U.S. Navy in 1942. Jackson's numerous citations and his success in helping to raise over $3 million in war bonds earned him national attention and, ultimately, seven opportunities to perform in the White House. No doubt Jackson's patriotism and military record, as well as his musical talents, were significant in building his reputation while helping him cross racial barriers.[6]

Radio and recordings disseminated the accordion to mass audiences during and after the war. In the late 1930s, Decca, Columbia, and Victor produced 78 rpm recordings of swing and jazz accordionists. Radio stations featured regular broadcasts of "staff accordionists," sometimes as often as six mornings a week, as in the case of Pietro Frosini. Accordionists with regular radio slots included Joe Biviano, Charles Magnante, and Pietro Deiro. In the early 1940s, accordionists could be heard performing daily on five New York stations (WOR, NBC, CBS, WOV, and WINS). Charles Nunzio recalls performing, on average, thirty-five radio appearances per week in the 1930s and 1940s.[7] Ethnic radio stations featured accordionists in musical styles reflecting their audiences' tastes. Paul Szenher, the accordionist in Eddie Gronet's polka combo, performed twice weekly on American House's Polish-language program on WWRL Brooklyn. He also made records with a jazz combo for Apollo. In the Midwest, feed companies sponsored programs that featured the region's ethnic musics, including accordionists. *Accordion World* was the glue holding together the national movement. The monthly publication carried news about competitions and conventions, arrangements, news from the clubs, gossip, and columns by key figures in the mainstream musical world, such as Sigmund Spaeth, who advocated accordion instruction in public schools.[8] Ambitious accordion studios expanded after the war—particularly in the Midwest—and generated students, instrument sales, and performances, which further popularized the accordion. In Milwaukee, over thirty-six accordion schools flourished. The Twin Cities area was home to the Traficante empire of accordion studios and retail operations; its flagship studio in Minneapolis had seventeen accordion teachers on the payroll. Returning soldiers became a new target market sector for the instrument. GIs returned with accordions purchased—and enjoyed—in France, Italy, and Germany. Quite a few outstanding Hohner instruments had been seized from Nazi soldiers and brought home as spoils of war. Accordion studios (and other music studios) welcomed a wave of GIs seeking music instruction under the Veterans' Bill of Rights.[9] Very young students, another untapped market, became a focus of the studio movement. In the accordion-minded city of Chicago, Central Academy's "Musical Fairyland," launched in 1947, was hailed as a model of instruction for ages five to eight. Students learned music theory and accordion technique in group games and reward-based activities, such as earning "merit money" for correct bellowsing. In 1950s, the Academy's enrollment varied between one thousand and eleven hundred students. Imagine each of all twenty-two teachers on staff giving two recitals a year and preparing their students for annual competitions (Central Academy regularly entered the AAA Festival each year) and multiply that level of activity by hundreds of accordion studios in dozens of American cities to ascertain the impact of accordion clubs, bands, and accordion orchestras on daily life in the United States, and to understand the wide range of community-based contexts (apart from the ethnic accordion-centered musical enclaves discussed in the next chapter) that accordionists could avail themselves of for performing.

In the 1940s, discourse surrounding folk music in the upper echelons of the accordion world began to take on a pointed, polemic quality. The increasing seriousness of accordion playing (as discussed in the previous chapter) inspired key figures in the accordion world to campaign against slights against the instrument and to counter the perpetuation of its ethnic image. Accordion publishers and teachers denigrated folk music and the players who performed it as musically illiterate and inept. Guardians of proper music for the accordion had condemned rehashings of folk and popular tunes (as discussed in the previous chapter). Accordion playing was due for some housecleaning if it was to have a shot at mainstream acceptance. After the crises and shortages of World War II, the accordion world turned its attention aggressively once again toward making its organized, official voice heard, as it had in the 1930s when the AAA was formed. Unfortunately, the industry had to contend with new and unanticipated challenges in the 1950s, when rock 'n' roll dominated the conversation as a new and unpredictable influence on American popular tastes and musical instrument choice. As the rock 'n' roll craze took root in the 1950s, accordion sales declined. From the industry's perspective, the situation became dire, forcing a reconsideration of the idea of the accordion as an instrument for all Americans, a principal theme in advertising campaigns of the 1930s and 1940s. In part, the industry framed the challenge in terms of a tactical offensive. A major dispute within the accordion world centered on conflicting perceptions of the accordion as artistic pursuit, of the accordion as "amateur" leisure pursuit, and of its "proper" repertoire. These disparate views, in turn, reflected the tensions among three different social and cultural agendas held by three groups within the elitist accordion industrial complex: Lawrence Welk's middle-aged fans, affluent audiences, and younger audiences. This conflict shaped the three groups' opposed notions of the role of vernacular musics, including rock 'n' roll. One individual who wished to influence the image of the accordion was Dick Contino—who, at least early on his career, appeared to be the accordion star of the industry's postwar dreams.

DICK CONTINO: VALENTINO OF THE ACCORDION

Dick Contino, with his performances on radio and television, did more to fix an image of accordion playing in the popular imagination than did any other artist or group. These performances transformed a teen accordionist into a national icon and held out hopes for steady employment—if not stardom— for accordionists during the late 1940s and 1950s. Born to Italian parents in Fresno, Contino learned the accordion from his father, a butcher. He traveled to San Francisco for weekly lessons with Angelo Cagnazzo—an entertainer in the city's "Barbary Coast" saloons, as noted earlier. In 1947, having dropped out of college, Contino worked as a delivery boy in his father's shop while devoting his spare time to practice on the accordion. It was then that Contino first developed his ambition of appearing as a soloist on a national broadcast and gaining greater recognition for the instrument, as his website describes.[10] To provide Contino with more opportunities in the entertainment world, the family decided to move to Los Angeles, and there he successfully auditioned his way into the musicians' union.

Meanwhile, the admired bandleader and impresario Horace Heidt was emerging from retirement to launch a new radio show, *The Original Youth Opportunity Program.* The basic premise of the show was to allow talented youth to perform before the public, who would act as judges of their performances. Heidt felt that young people who lived outside Los Angeles or New York deserved an "equal opportunity" to find an audience. In a departure from the typical Hollywood premiere of a new program, Heidt located his premiere in a "typical American town"—Fresno, Dick Contino's hometown.[11] Heidt heard Contino audition at the musicians' union headquarters and selected him to be one of four contestants to appear on the initial Philip Morris broadcast to compete for the $5,000 grand prize.

Contino's debut performance drew a dramatic response from the audience and the press: "It was on the otherwise calm night of December 7, 1946 when Dick gave his rendition of 'Lady of Spain' and the bobby-sox audience stomped, clapped, and yelled with frenzy, declaring him the winner by a margin of a full 30 points on the applause meter, thereby awarding him the first prize of $250."[12]

Dick Contino, c. 1941. (Courtesy Dick Contino)

Thirteen weeks of competition ensued, culminating in the quarter finals in Manhattan, broadcast live on NBC. When Contino played his rendition of "Flight of the Bumble Bee," the chorus of screams from teenaged female fans in the audience caused the applause meter to register the highest mark of the evening. Contino responded to the audience's excitement in the manner of a seasoned celebrity. "Raising his arms like a triumphant prize fighter, the young man basked in the adulation of his fans."[13] With his victory in the quarter finals, Contino earned the right to tour with Horace Heidt's orchestra as a guest star, appearing in live performances three or four times a week. He also gained additional exposure by appearing on Heidt's weekly Sunday radio broadcasts.

Contino's months on the road with Heidt solidified his craft as a crowd-pleasing performing artist. Heidt became Contino's mentor, coaching him in the stagecraft of performing before crowds of female bobby-soxers: "Contino absorbed each of the elements—the brief hesitation during a song; the way of involving the audience as part of the performance, with his customary zeal. Heidt was pleased as he watched his protégé perfect the ways of commanding a crowd."[14] The audience always responded consistently to his alluring stage moves. "Contino flashed his smile, shook his head and swayed his hips. With every move, the girls in the crowd swooned. At the number's close, many in the audience leapt to their feet and cheered."[15] It was during that period that Heidt dubbed Contino the "Valentino of the Accordion."[16]

An important component of Contino's success was his reliance on "standards," songs that were recognizable to most members of his audience, performed in a lighthearted style with fast tempos and plenty of runs, passagework, and arpeggios displaying the performer's dexterity. The wildly popular *Major Bowes' Amateur Hour* had accustomed listeners to virtuoso performances on the accordion in this particular style. Like listeners to Bowes's program, Contino's audiences were racially and culturally diverse. While his biographer, Bob Bove, points out that bobby-soxers were certainly the most vocal members of the audience, Contino had older listeners as well. Ostensibly, Contino's repertoire was calculated to please the masses, not just the highbrow accordion enthusiasts.

Heidt worked closely with Contino to prepare charts for tunes such as "Return to Sorrento," "Canadian Capers," and his signature piece, "Lady of Spain." Each of these numbers was reworked with virtuoso passages aimed at showcasing Contino's "distinctive" style of performing (if one takes Bove's description at face value). Two years after his debut in Fresno, Contino went on to Horace Heidt's Grand Finals in Washington, D.C., winning the first prize of $5,000.

Contino's winning song, "Lady of Spain," proved to be significant to his career and to the accordion world in ways he could never have imagined. The song, written by four seasoned London songwriters (Robert Hargreaves, Errell Reaves, Tolchard Evans, and Stanley J. Damerell) seemed poised for a short shelf life as an English novelty hit.[17] It was written in pasodoble rhythm, with a 9/8 meter, and was evidently intended as part of a series of lighthearted tributes to Iberian beauties (hence "Lady of Madrid" and "Lady of Barcelona," published in London's "Tin Pan Alley" popular music district on the Charing Cross Road in the 1930s). "Lady of Spain" developed a life of its own. It crossed the Atlantic (sans the Ladies of Madrid and Barcelona) in the 1930s, when some American accordionists began playing it as their "Spanish" number. One of the earliest photographic records of Lawrence Welk shows him in his vaudevillian touring days in Spanish costume for "Lady of Spain." In

Contino's winning performance of the song, he adds bellows shakes and sudden modulation from C to Db. He continued with the same arrangement in his over forty appearances playing the song on the *Ed Sullivan Show,* which transformed "Lady" into an iconic song. It was after his first appearance on the show that hundreds of Dick Contino fan clubs began to appear across the country. His growing popularity convinced him to leave Heidt's organization and form his own troupe, which performed in theaters in Chicago, Kansas City, Pittsburgh, and Milwaukee. Infuriated by Contino's departure, which he did not approve, Heidt retaliated by suing his protégé for breach of his seven-year contract, a matter that was ultimately settled in court.

More serious troubles for Contino ensued when he was to be inducted into the military in 1951. Distressed by the prospect of being away from his family (and no doubt the interruption of his career), suffering what he later referred to as a series of anxiety attacks, he left his barracks. His desertion and subsequent indictment by a military court produced one of the choicest scandals of the year in American entertainment. Immediately on completing his six-month jail sentence at McNeil Island, he was again drafted. Completing his basic training as an infantry rifleman, he entered the service with a unique restriction: while on active duty, he would not be allowed to play the accordion—the source of his insubordination and a potential distraction from his patriotic duties.

Shortly before he was to be shipped to a frontline unit in Korea, a military official familiar with Contino's talents intervened to change the orders: he was to head a Special Service Entertainment Unit that would perform for troops. After entertaining soldiers for two years with his repertoire of standards, Contino received his honorable discharge in 1954, ready to move on with his musical career and public appearances. But he found that he had fallen out of favor with the American public. After several months struggling unsuccessfully to find bookings in major clubs and theaters, he met Frank Sinatra, who offered him an engagement at the Mocambo, one of the premier show clubs in Hollywood and a gathering place for producers, directors, and stars (as well as a haunt for Los Angeles' most notorious underworld figures). It was there that Contino met and married actress and Hollywood beauty Leigh Snowden, who helped him jump-start a very brief career in movies.[18]

In 1954 Contino moved his growing family to Las Vegas, where he performed regularly at small clubs, struggling to regain name recognition. In 1955 he came up with the idea of presenting himself to the public as the "Liberace of the Accordion." His intention to challenge Liberace to a musical duel received a brief write-up in the *Pittsburgh Post,* but there is no evidence that such a competition actually took place.[19] Around the same time, Contino discovered that his military record was a serious liability. At his live performances in Vegas, he was often heckled by inebriated audiences who called him a "draft-dodging bum" and a "Dago slacker." Snowden began bringing Contino's discharge papers to gigs to display in his defense, but this seemed to have little effect on audiences' negative reactions. He was unable to obtain bookings at the larger clubs he desired in Las Vegas. Throughout the 1960s, his anguish over his reputation escalated into regular drinking and gambling binges.

In the 1950s, Contino enviously witnessed the admiration that accordionist Myron Floren received from audiences on Lawrence Welk's television show. Contino hoped that he too could become a favorite with television audiences. Following his discharge from the army, he had appeared on the *Ed Sullivan Show*, introduced as "Staff Sergeant Dick Contino." Although Sullivan had publicly acknowledged his military service, Contino found that stories about his draft-dodging continued to circulate. In the 1960s, the General Artists Company approached him about putting together a band for a new television show. After he had invested considerable time and resources into developing arrangements, costumes, and props, the sponsor (Singer Sewing Machines) withdrew, citing concerns about the fallout from his draft-dodging reputation.[20] Shortly thereafter he had a chance to explain himself before the American public while appearing on the *Joey Bishop Show* (ABC's competitor to the *Johnny Carson Show*). During the interview, Contino launched into the draft controversy without masking the anger and resentment that had been building up in him over the years. "I was waving my arms and gesturing," he recalls, "trying to say, in essence, 'what do you want from me?' I served my time in the Army and paid for any mistakes that might have been made. I did what was right for my country." Bishop did not invite him back on the show, later explaining to Contino, "you just can't come on national television and tell off the American people."[21] Contino had to wait twenty-five years for his comeback as an accordion elder statesman, one of the unexpected developments in the life of the accordion that I will discuss in chapter 6.

THE MIDDLE CLASS EMBRACES THE ACCORDION: WELK AND FLOREN

The accordion, as Lawrence Welk's instrument, became visible to a broad middle-class audience in a way that had not been possible for the violin, the piano, and band instruments.

Lawrence Welk, 1950s.

In his biography, Myron Floren credits Welk's show with keeping the accordion in the forefront of popular culture. "Over the years the Welk Show featured Charles Magnante, Art Van Damme, Bill Palmer, Bill Hughes, Frank Marocco, Johnny LaPadula, Frank Yankovic and many others. The show also popularized the beautiful instrument loved by accordion aficionados everywhere, and it paved the way for so many talented young artists who are well known today, perhaps even famous, because of opportunities afforded through the efforts of Lawrence Welk."[22]

Accordion-playing country and western star and bandleader Peewee King, who also had his own television show for a time, primarily reached audiences in the South and the Midwest. Dick Contino had the greatest appeal to audiences when he was a young artist, before the draft evasion scandal tarnished his reputation. Less tied to the history of working-class music and culture than Contino and King, and profoundly influenced by the conformity of 1950s popular culture, Lawrence Welk and his colleague Myron Floren were poised to be embraced by the white middle class as leading cultural icons in the age of television.

Welk's core audience occupied a significant position in U.S. history. As the first generation of people with money to spend following World War II, they had the power to reject the values of youth culture and to seek out cultural alternatives to rock 'n' roll. In an age of unprecedented consumer affluence, they looked for meaning and value in the symbols and signs of their collective middle-class identity. In a culture that celebrated the "organization man," they pursued musical experiences that were perceived as authentic, because they represented an idealized past. The accordion itself had become a middle-class status symbol. Middle-class fascination with the accordion had been prefigured in the visibility of accordionists in society bands and the widespread interest in arrangements of jazz standards in "swing" style (discussed in chapter 2). Artists such as Guido and Pietro Deiro, Peewee King, Frankie Yankovic, and Dick Contino utilized the traditional idioms of local and regional folk music, adapting and arranging such material for accordion. Like King, whose refined arrangements of "hillbilly" songs created his signature Western swing sound, Welk utilized the legacies of Dixieland jazz, country, and even rock 'n' roll while disregarding the ethnic or rebellious nature of these idioms and their potential to create an oppositional discourse.

Nothing better illustrates the idea of the accordion as an American icon better than the personal histories of Welk and Floren. Welk's biographers portray him as an immigrant who overcame his language barrier to become a beloved American entertainer. The son of Alsatian parents, Welk grew up in North Dakota, where he worked alongside his brothers on his father's farm. While a child, he spoke German at home. A popular myth about him, encouraged by his son Larry, was that he spoke no English until he was twenty-one. In reality, Welk learned English in grade school and even took diction lessons in the 1950s, evidently intent on becoming accent free (he maintained, perhaps intentionally, a slight lilt in his voice, creating the impression that speaking English was awkward for him). He derived his musical inspiration from recordings of Bix Beiderbecke and later white Dixieland jazz artists, who reinterpreted the music of pioneering black New Orleans jazz artists for white fans. Touring throughout the Upper Midwest and Texas on the Keith vaudeville circuit, Welk adapted and arranged traditional styles of music to contemporary audiences, developing his skills as a bandleader and performer. His wholesome image, impeccably tailored suits, and knack for involving the audience in his shows had a powerful appeal to middle-class audiences. He specialized in dance numbers and sweet jazz, continuing to avoid hot jazz and rock 'n' roll.

In the 1940s, Welk built a reputation as one of the nation's most visible society bandleaders, particularly in the midwestern cities. The band performed a ten-year stint at the Trianon Ballroom in Chicago, regularly drawing crowds of seven thousand. His orchestra also performed frequently at the Roosevelt Hotel in New York. The term "champagne music" was derived from an engagement at the William Penn Hotel in Pittsburgh, when a dancer referred to Welk's band's sound as "light and bubbly as champagne." In 1944 and 1945, Welk and the orchestra appeared in many motion picture "soundies." In 1951, Welk settled in Los Angeles and began producing *The Lawrence Welk Show* on KTLA in Los Angeles, where it was broadcast live from the Aragon Ballroom in Santa Monica. After becoming a local hit, the show was picked up by the ABC network in the spring of 1955, with Dodge as a sponsor. Welk and each of his band members received a new car; his family continued to receive a new model each year, ensuring his lifelong loyalty to Dodge.

During its first year on the air, the Welk hour instituted several regular features. Adding a visual dimension to Welk's "champagne music" tag line, the production crew engineered a "bubble machine" that spewed streams of large soap bubbles across the bandstand. Whenever the orchestra played a polka or waltz, Welk himself would dance with one of the female vocalists, known as "Champagne Ladies." Welk always reserved one number for himself, soloing on the accordion. Trumpetist-singer Rocky Rockwell always performed at least one novelty number.

These features of his show became so routinized that comedian Stan Freberg lampooned them in his recording *Wunnerful, Wunnerful!* In Freberg's version of the *Lawrence Welk Show,* the bandleader orders "Champagne Lady" Alice Lon to stop polka dancing on his accordion, which can be heard shattering. The bubble machine goes haywire and floats the entire Aragon Ballroom out to sea, where it is later discovered in ruins. The accordion part (as arranged by Billy May, player unknown) was purposefully played "badly" with dissonant chords blasting at full volume. Ever responsive to his audience, Welk was said to have responded to the satire in subsequent seasons of his show, using the bubble machine less often and scaling back on his accordion solos.

Welk's program had a policy of playing well-known songs from previous years so that the audience would hear only numbers with which they were familiar. Rarely, in the television show's early days, the band would play tunes from the current *Billboard* Top 100 charts, but strictly as novelty numbers—for example Elvis Presley's "Don't Be Cruel" sung by band member Bob Lido, wearing fake Presley-style sideburns. The repertoire of the *Lawrence Welk Show,* like his live band performances, never deviated from popular standards, polkas, and novelty tunes, delivered in smooth arrangements. Welk's insistence on wholesome entertainment led him to be conservative in his musical tastes and exert full control over the repertoire and performances. The show was regularly pilloried by critics who referred to his music as corny, old hat,

Mickey Mouse, and the "squarest music this side of Euclid." As one reviewer put it, Welk's show should satisfy those who are looking for "nice, clean Rotarian entertainment."[23]

The *Lawrence Welk Show* featured contemporary music alongside the classics, transforming songs by the Everly Brothers, Paul Williams, the Beatles, and even Frank Zappa into "champagne" music by stripping away syncopations and other rhythmic irregularities and adding thick string, woodwind, and free-reed textures. From 1960 through 1965, the Lawrence Welk orchestra had twelve records on the *Billboard* Top 100 charts, with "Calcutta" reaching the top-selling position, a unique accomplishment for a big band during the rock 'n' roll era. By the 1970s, Welk had adopted the full range of contemporary music styles: country, Latin, jazz, and even psychedelic rock to the iconic big band format. Never seen as a virtuoso or star player, his presentations of a "family" culture on television and his performances—as bandleader and accordion—had powerful appeal for middle-class audiences eager to drown out the noise generated by rock 'n' roll culture.

Like Welk, Myron Floren became popular for his playing, affable personality, and reliably solid and unaffected middle-class image. As a child of Norwegian farmers in a rural area near Roslyn, South Dakota, he practiced on a $10 accordion given to him by his father, playing waltzes, polkas, and schottisches. With this repertoire, he was well prepared to entertain his audience of Scandinavian immigrants at fairs and community events. Floren has recalled: "I would play polkas and mazurkas if the crowd was mostly Polish; for Norwegians and Swedes, I would play waltzes and schottisches."[24] Years later, when working on the *Lawrence Welk Show,* Floren noted that he adopted Welk's credo: "play what the people want to hear, and they will always listen." Meanwhile, he was developing elevated musical tastes and inclinations beyond the *Billboard* Top 100. He listened to the Metropolitan Opera broadcasts, jazz, and country and western. He taught himself how to transcribe piano literature for the accordion. He also listened to the regular broadcasts of radio "staff accordionists": Frosini, Magnante, and Nunzio. These artists, as we have seen, played a diverse, eclectic repertoire of standards, light classics, and ethnic music.

Floren enrolled in Augustana College in South Dakota with a major in English and minor in music, playing bass viol in the college orchestra. Although the conductor had coolly informed Myron that there was no musical literature for the accordion, he soon found opportunities to play on a local radio broadcast sponsored by a harness company. He also canvassed Sioux Falls in search of accordion students. He took a special interest in teaching, apparently, developing his own methodology for an instrument for which the pedagogical literature was still spotty. He also appeared on local radio stations.

Patriotic and eager to follow in the footsteps of army accordionists, Floren had a childhood history of heart disease that earned him a 4-F disqualification from military service. He needed to find another route to beginning a professional music career, and did so by performing country and western music in a band known as the Buckeye Four. Floren might have remained a "regional" accordionist, known primarily in the Upper Midwest, had he not attended a dance in St. Louis where the Lawrence Welk orchestra was playing. When Welk recognized Floren in the audience, he invited him onstage to play a number with his band. Floren's choice of song turned out to be "Lady of Spain," the song popularized by Dick Contino. Hearing the overwhelming response from the audience, Welk hired Floren as a permanent member of his band. "Lady of Spain" became Floren's trademark song, as it had been for Contino, and he played it regularly on the *Lawrence Welk Show*, albeit in a more toned-down, less virtuosic style. Floren's regular presentations of the song helped make the song an icon, no doubt inspiring Eddie Fisher to reintroduce "Lady of Spain" to American audiences as a vocal number, making it number 6 on the *Billboard* charts.

Although the formally educated Floren was seen as a superior accordion player to Welk, and his style was more conservatory than cornball, the two men developed a close working relationship. As Welk scaled back his own solo performances, he increasingly allowed Myron to display his virtuosity. Occasionally the two appeared as an accordion duet. Over the next thirty-two years, Myron became one of the most visible members of the Welk orchestra and the Welk organization itself. It began with the band's migration to California, along with concert dates on the road. It continued with his exposure to television, first on local broadcasts from the Aragon Ballroom and later on the ABC network and numerous recordings with Welk and his orchestra.

During his time on the show, Floren served as an assistant conductor. He even took over some of Welk's duties as artistic director and was frequently called on to settle disputes within Welk's musical "family."

In every detail, Floren embodied the ideals of the middle-class culture and the popular image of the assimilated immigrant—he was often introduced on the show as the "Happy Norwegian." Floren's meticulous (trained) playing style and his accidental (and highly public) rise to stardom reinforced the belief that anyone who was willing to work hard could become an artist. His emergence as a leader in Welk's rigidly hierarchical organization elevated hard work and self-restraint over sensuality, emotion, and other unconventional artistic standards (better personified by Contino). Floren's congeniality and refusal to indulge in excess, like Welk's, reflected the values of middle-aged people anticipating a bright future. His stage image (as well as that presented on his album covers) conveyed innocence, charm, and congeniality.[25]

But Floren and Contino and Welk all had a faint sense forged in their childhood years of the significance of their past, the cultures of early Dixieland jazz, and the energetic rhythms of the polka. All three players' musical backgrounds were shaped by the cultures of their immigrant childhood: in the lives of Floren and Welk the European and Scandinavian popular dance repertoire had provided their foundation in music making and entertaining a crowd; in Contino's life it was Italian popular song. As a bandleader, Welk relied more heavily on techniques originating in Dixieland, honed and refined by the big band sound—call-and-response technique, bending notes, and a lush orchestral sound. Despite Welk's and Floren's pretense at solidarity with America's immigrant working class, they manifested the accordion industrial complex's ambivalent embrace of "folk culture" (and polka culture) and disdain for anything polluted by African-American culture. Their staunch adherence to the Top 100 repertoire and their repetition of certain "standards" without regard for individual style or originality and their leanings toward the schmaltzy tainted all accordionists by association.

The middle-class musical "backlash" propagated by Lawrence Welk on television had staying power. In 1971, ABC canceled the *Lawrence Welk Show,* then sponsored by Geritol, citing the need to attract a younger audience. Welk immediately arranged for his show to continue on as a syndicated program on 250 stations across the country, until the final original show was produced in 1982. Perhaps self-conscious about his mediocre performance skills, Welk chose to step aside and feature Floren, the "trained" accordionist. Floren could better represent the ideal of the skilled virtuoso artist without running afoul of the family culture propagated on the program. Recognition for the instrument was growing not through Welk but through Contino and Floren—a recognition spread powerfully through "Lady of Spain," a popular song that placed aspirations to virtuosity within the context of 1930s and 1940s big band music. Contino, in his impassioned, virtuosic, and self-absorbed renderings of "Lady," tried to tie the song to his image of himself as an accordion icon, whereas Floren's more restrained performances harnessed the song to a distinctly middle-class pursuit of pleasure in moderation. In the end, Floren's vision of the song—and the accordion—won out, forever closing the door to an accordion teen idol.

Instead of slim, sexy accordionists, images of out-of-touch, square, and stale accordionists had conquered television by way of the *Lawrence Welk Show*. Not even Contino and his network of fan clubs could counter that image; Contino's hit, "Lady of Spain," was seen as overexposed and as a touchstone of mediocre accordion culture. Perhaps this is one reason why some professional accordionists today refuse to play "Lady of Spain."[26]

As the rock 'n' roll craze took root in the 1950s, declining sales of the accordion presented a dire situation, at least from the industry perspective. The idea of the accordion as an instrument for all Americans, a principal theme in the advertising campaigns of the 1930s and 1940s, clearly needed reconsideration. In part, the industry framed the challenge in terms of a tactical offensive. A major dispute between the accordion industrial complex and the mainstream accordion world centered on conflicting perceptions of the accordion as an artistic pursuit, the accordion as an "amateur" leisure pursuit, and the accordion's "proper" repertoire. These disparate views, in turn, reflected the tensions between the social and cultural agendas of Lawrence Welk's middle-aged, affluent audiences, the teen audience, and the accordion "old guard." This conflict shaped the three groups' opposed notions of the role of vernacular musics, including rock 'n' roll.

Beginning in the 1950s, the commercial success of rock 'n' roll and indications of changing popular tastes sent conflicting messages to accordion advocates. In 1954 Bill Haley and the Comets recorded "Rock Around the Clock," arguably the first rock 'n' roll hit and the moment of rock 'n' roll's arrival on the international scene.[27] The original formation of Haley's group, the Saddlemen, featured an accordion.[28] As a country swing band, that group seemed to prefigure the ability of the accordion to transition to the rock band, or at least open up new professional opportunities in teen styles. In the 1958 film *The Girl Can't Help It*, an obscure rock band known as The Three Chuckles, featuring keyboardist-accordionist Teddy Randazzo, made an appearance. The handsome profile and athletic style of accordion virtuoso Dick Contino are incarnate in Randazzo's performance. Randazzo not only is agile in the backbend, dancing with an accordion on his chest, but also appears radiantly confident in his virile rock idol image. Here was strong evidence to suggest that an accordion-playing rock star could soon appear on the scene to replace the disgraced Dick Contino—and that accordion makers could potentially make a killing selling instruments to teens.

However, there were more ominous signals on the horizon. In 1955 Americans bought 120,000 accordions (a figure comparable to the sale of all the brass instruments purchased by public schools). By 1958 the total number of accordions sold dropped to 92,000. What must have seemed particularly alarming, especially to music dealers who were members of the National Association of Music Merchants (and would have tracked such information in the Association's annual reports), was the steady rise in guitar sales: from 250,000 in 1955 to 700,000 in 1963. In 1964, a very bleak year for the accordion world, guitar sales topped one million, and accordion sales dropped down to fifty thousand, half the figure reported for the console organ. In Castelfidardo, seventeen accordion factories closed down between 1960 and 1963.[29]

One might assume from my previous discussion of the accordion industry's activities that accordion advocates would have launched a well-organized offensive against the decline of their instrument. Yet, while searching back issues of *Accordion World* for any official response to the rock 'n' roll phenomenon or the Beatles invasion from 1957 to 1963, I found no mention of either, only a handful of articles by teachers urging students to adhere to their studies of classical repertoire and technique. Yet the display ads placed by accordion studios in the backs of the magazines offered students instruction in rock 'n' roll music.

As the organized voice of the accordion world was keeping watch over the "proper" repertoire and technique of accordion students, it was failing to respond to the concerns of its constituents over a wide range of issues from accordion repertoire to image to affordability. Music producers were moving increasingly toward the guitar and keyboards, which were seen as more flexible and easier to integrate with the texture of rock 'n' roll bands. The Playboys' producer, Snuff Garrett, later spoke about the use of the accordion in that band and other rock 'n' roll bands of the period, many of which he produced. "The accordion was really for novelty effect," he said. "In the industry, we called it a 'color' instrument, like the autoharp or the whistle sounds we used. The accordion could really cut through the band. I was always trying to 'hide' John's sound." Garrett's aim, as he explained, was for the guitar sound to predominate in the band. "I have a lot of respect for what Lawrence Welk did," said Garrett, "but there was no way the accordion could touch the guitar . . . or even the keyboard." Indeed, Garrett's remarks seem to suggest that the accordion was no longer admired as the ultimate versatile, one-man-band instrument; on the contrary, its dense, distinctive texture was a noisy intrusion on the ensemble texture of the rock band.

One factor that may have impeded the accordion's use in rock 'n' roll was its ubiquity, particularly on radio and television. Because the accordion had been used so much in dance and pop orchestras for shows in the 1940s and 1950s, its sound may have become relegated in the public's mind to music that was featureless "background" music with hardly a personality of its own—particularly not one that would appeal to youth.[30]

The accordion became associated, like the dance bands in which it appeared, with staid "establishment music." And, of course, there was the *Lawrence Welk Show,* which, during its national run on ABC from 1955 to 1971, displayed the accordion week after week in its most stereotypical commercialized forms.

Another factor in the accordion's disappearance from the popular music mainstream may have been its weight and size. Not every piano accordion had 41 treble keys and 120 bass keys. Teddy Randazzo appears to be playing a compact, twenty-one-pound 72-bass model in his movie. But classical teachers would have discouraged their students from buying smaller instruments because they lacked the full keyboard and a full array or register shifts that were called for in arrangements of classical music for accordion. Moreover, one can easily understand why, in a tight and competitive market, accordion dealers would have steered customers toward larger instruments, which were more expensive and profitable. In the accordion distributors' catalogs from the 1930s, 1940s, and 1950s, only piano accordions, and then only full-sized ones (41-treble and 120-bass), appear with any regularity.

Yet we know from unofficial accounts that full-sized accordions could hurt players' self-images, not just their lower backs. I recently spoke with players who grew up playing the accordion in the 1950s and 1960s about how they perceived the possibility of playing rock 'n' roll as accordionists. Most of them stopped playing the accordion and switched to other electric keyboard instruments such as the Hammond organ (introduced in 1936), which was "much better for banging out staccato chords."[31] They perceived the accordion as "old school" and outmoded and the associations with ethnic and folk music as unwelcome baggage. Hans Stucki, an Ohio-born accordionist-turned-keyboardist for The Angry, has recalled: "I wanted to play 'real rock and roll music'—enough already with the Swiss . . . the Gospel, the accordion contests."[32] Another player who was accomplished at the accordion and grew up in the accordion "competition scene" discussed the impact of popular music trends in his choice to abandon the accordion:

> As the Beatles and similar groups consumed our imaginations in 1964, I gave up
> the accordion. I never saw a group with an accordion at the time—not as I recall,
> anyway—not even Gary Lewis and the Playboys, whom I liked very much via airplay,

but don't remember seeing on television. It was only sometime after their heyday
that I learned they had had an accordion player (or Cordovox?) in their group. I
was aware, however, of the thin, reedy Farfisa organ sound so popular among garage bands of those same years. And I liked it. Bud I don't think I ever consciously
connected it with the accordion sound that apparently fueled it in the first place.
When I was about twelve I got a guitar for Christmas. Nothing could stop me from
practicing. The guitar was it for me.[33]

A number of former accordion players I interviewed, all of whom happened
to be male, indicated that the instrument made them uncomfortable with their
onstage profile. "The accordion had the wrong image. It made you look fat or
pregnant. It wasn't much help in getting the girls, which is what rock music
was all about anyway."[34] Indeed, there is plenty of anecdotal evidence from
the 1960s—and abundant images of skinny Beatles and Rolling Stones toting
featherweight Fenders—that suggests that many players of the accordion experienced a disjuncture between their chosen instrument and the commercial
interests and values behind their new favorite music.

The spotty evidence from accordion magazines suggests, interestingly, that
accordion's staunch guardians of propriety did everything they could in their
power to enforce these distinctions. Some alarmist accordion teachers noted
the dangerous influences of rock 'n' roll: "A careful analysis reveals that Rock
'n' Roll has a hypnotic influence on its participants while on the dance floor
and is the germ of nervous energy and unrest led by hopped-up rhythm and
doped-up music resulting in gang warfare, riots, broken furniture and broken
limbs, plus crime and rape of every nature and description known to our law
enforcement authorities."[35]

The proposal for "keeping rock 'n' roll under control," as the title of a 1957
article in *Accordion World* put it, was twofold: first, stronger policing at dances,
and second, steering accordion students toward "correct" choices in popular
songs to play. "A pupil with a family 'jive' background after six or eight weeks
can begin to be prepared for 'Old Smokey,' 'Whatever Will Be Will Be,' and
'Love Me Tender.' Then he advances in ability, he can be introduced to simplified arrangements of 'Neapolitan Nights,' or 'O Sole Mio' or semi-classics
with a definite melodic appeal."[36] The best way to appreciate the accordion
world's dramatic hostility and indifference to rock is to compare its reception of rock with that of *Guitar World*, which merged with *Accordion World*
in 1958 to form *Accordion and Guitar World*. While the guitar section (in the
front of the magazine) urged readers to "embrace rock, become a hep teacher
[*sic*] and watch your popularity grow," the accordion section remained silent

on the issue.[37] Accordion enthusiasts hoped that rock 'n' roll would only be a passing fad that would eventually lead students back to the classics. As the accordion advocate Elsie Bennett put it, "one of the finest examples of growth and change has been the development of the accordion from a 'popular' fun instrument to the status of standard 'serious' instrument in orchestra or band and of a solo instrument worthy of the greatest musical talent."[38]

It is difficult to tell how many accordionists shared Bennett's optimism and how many were more inclined to agree with an anguished comment from a distinguished accordion maker: "*that* music trend put a bullet hole through the accordion!" Either way, only a few accordion advocates felt empowered to take action in the face of increasing incursions from rock 'n' roll and the electric guitar.[39]

The accordion industry, at least in the early 1960s, appeared to offer a few concessions to rock musicians and fans by producing a variety of compact, easily portable, and inexpensive free-reed instruments. The Chicago Musical Instrument Company made and marketed Farfisa electronic organs in the United States. That company also introduced a new instrument called the Cordovox, an accordion wired to an organ generator. The instrument is seen by accordion players as useful but as producing an inferior sound. The voices range from "fuzzy" brass-like sounds to "reedy" oboe-like sounds. The vibrato can sound sharper and more pronounced than on most Italian-made accordions, but some musicians can use this to great effect.

While demonstrating this instrument to his customers at a Pasadena music store, a young musician named John R. West was tapped to be the keyboard player for Gary Lewis and the Playboys, who regularly made the Top Ten list in the mid-1960s. When the band appeared on *Hullaballoo*, a teen dance show, West's Cordovox appeared to be snapped shut. He was simply playing electronically without moving the bellows, and the resulting sound was a tinny, faint organ-like timbre, never evoking the rich texture of the accordion reeds. (The emcee interviewing the band made a remark about the lazy accordion player.)

As the formally organized accordion world became increasingly contentious and unable to represent its constituency with a unified voice, one accordion company hatched a unique plan to try to "include" the accordion in the mainstream world of rock. Ernest Deffner, the head of Deffner Associates in Mineola, New York (on Long Island) had been in the accordion business since 1934 and had been making more than 30 percent of the U.S. volume in accordion sales). Ernest's wife, Faithe Deffner, who worked in publicity, became one of the first in the accordion industry to identify the need to reach out to a

Advertisement placed in various accordion and music trade magazines by Deffner Associates, Mineola, New York, 1960s.

younger market and was responsible for a crafting a number of advertisements that proclaimed "Accordions Are In" and showed young people playing the accordion in combos.

One of Deffner's companies, Pancordion, maker of instruments for Myron Floren and Lawrence Welk, designed the Tiger Combo accordion and had it built in Italy. But Deffner also owned the Titano accordion line, and because the two accordion firms had exclusive dealer franchises in the United States and dealt with accordion schools, Titano made a version of the Tiger Combo for their dealers called the Combo 'Cordion.[40]

Tiger Combo advertisement.

These instruments, offered to the public very briefly in the 1960s alongside other "improved" instruments, were part of an effort to make the accordion more popular and, as such, represent a dramatic departure from the familiar strategy of promoting the accordion as a way to introduce people to classical music and redirect their interest in folk music toward classical technique. Both were similarly conceived and presented as the "Rockordion" in advertising materials. The following excerpt from a press release, written by Faithe Deffner (who took over the business following Ernest's death) demonstrates the firm's aim to appeal to insecure adolescents like Michael and Hans: "For the mod youngster who digs the rock, folk, and Mersey beat of the swinging '60s, a Combo 'Cordion called Tiger is stalking the scene. You're the swinger with Tiger Combo. Combo 'Cordion is excitement."[41] In another advertisement, a combo of young men in Beatles-style slim pants are evidently a rock band fronted by an accordion. If Deffner's press release for the Tiger failed to send the message that this was not Lawrence Welk's accordion, her "Make the Scene with Tiger" ad campaign did. These ads, which appeared in *Accordion World* in the mid-1960s, show a line drawing of four young men clad in Beatles-style slim pants, with the accordionist playing lead. This Tiger Combo 'Cordion was available at $150, including a colorful carrying case.[42]

These accordions were neither new nor unique in their size and technology. The Tiger was equipped with two regular sets of reeds and a microphone hookup. Some of its design features, however, were novel. To break the mold of uniform black-and-white accordions, the Tiger was sprayed with a multicoat color finish and lacquered in a choice of three Fiat colors: Sun, Blue Moon, and Fire.[43]

"Make the Scene with Tiger" advertisement
for the Tiger Combo 'Cordion.

Enhancing the visual impact of the high-gloss auto paint and its trendy sports-car-like image was a slanted keyboard—to allow the audience to see the accordion player's "flying fingers." Calling attention to the activity on the keyboard was the reverse color scheme: white "black notes" and black natural keys. What most distinguished the Tiger from other acoustic and electric accordions was an extra set of reeds, tuned a fifth above, intended to be used to perform the current popular music: "a quint reed activated on three of the instrument's six treble registers, providing piercing lead or swinging chords in the audio colors which are presently flipping teen age [sic] record fans."[44]

Following the last known 1967 advertisements, we lack documentation on the fate of the Tiger accordion. Would there be more such instruments? An American Idol–style star search? Of recordings and radio broadcasts there seem to be none. What were the makers' intentions for the "Rockordion"? Was this simply an attention-getting label or a grand plan to transform the accordion into a leading instrument in the American rock band? One issue that has surfaced among players commenting on the Tiger years later was the peculiarity of playing with the quint reeds. The addition of the fifth added a dense chordal texture that seemed out of touch with rock music. "When you played 'Love Is Blue' using simple thirds, the quint reeds automatically formed block chords. Great for Elvis's late ballad style, but not rock 'n' roll."[45]

Tigers simply appear to evaporate after a brief moment on the scene, much as Dick Contino did in the wake of his desertion scandal.[46] Willard Palmer, who worked with Faithe and Ernest Deffner, was best known to his public (and remembered in his obituary by Deffner) as the founder of the accordion program at the University of Houston and the coauthor of the ten-volume *Palmer-Hughes Accordion Course*, developed in partnership with Bill Hughes.[47] If Palmer was ever seen in public promoting the Tiger, the record does not show it. Palmer was in his forties—an elder statesman where rock was concerned—at the time the Tiger was introduced. Elsewhere, echoing Bennett's view of popular music, Deffner attributed the failure of the Tiger to the shortsightedness of accordion teachers. "The program didn't succeed because accordion teachers saw rock as a passing fad. They disliked the music and refused to teach it to their students."[48] Ultimately the Tiger accordion, developed as an inexpensive, entry-level instrument, failed to receive the backing of its own constituency. Ralph Stricker, who was involved in developing electronic accordions in the 1960s and 1970s, notes that the Tiger could not be seen by professional players as a "serious" instrument: its 72-bass keyboard did not have the range and its reeds did not have the quality expected from a "professional" instrument.[49]

By 1965 the accordion itself was in the midst of what many perceived to be a terminal state of decline within the general music scene—as becomes clear from accounts in the mass media and impressions from former players. One writer notes: "It was in the early 1960s, with the rise of rock 'n' roll, that Western teenagers came to view the squeezebox as the embodiment of everything that was hackneyed, dorky and terminally kitsch about their parents' culture."[50]

One indication that the accordion movement had run its course were accordion jokes.[51] Many of these jokes were encouraged by accordionists themselves.[52] Another indication was parody. Former accordion teacher and accordion studio owner Pete Barbutti brought personal observations of accordion culture into his comic routines. As Barbutti rose to popularity on late-night television and on the Las Vegas club circuit, his alter ego, the Accordion Professor, rose to notoriety. In one routine, the Professor, who also owns a studio, sells a series of increasingly expensive accordions, one priced at "fifteen hundred hogs," to a father who is made to believe that his son will display talent on the accordion if he has a better instrument. The gag is that the Accordion Professor can only play one song. The routine ends with the son opening a rival accordion studio down the street as soon as he learns to play a song. But, like the Professor, he can only play that one song.[53] On airing such material, radio and television stations could expect a round of outraged telephone calls from the AAA and its network of accordion defenders—a devastating indication of the accordion movement's increasing irrelevance.[54]

The accordion, for all intents and purposes, drifted away on a sea of wearisome stereotypes. However, the perceptions of the accordion as tired, clichéd, dated, and kitschy and images of accordionists as mediocre hacks purveying substandard repertoire become highly significant later (discussed in chapter 6). This later "revival" of the accordion depended in part on the willingness of some of its advocates to confront and take ownership of the accordion's image.

Although the accordion was particularly vulnerable to the influence of rock 'n' roll in the 1950s, it did not fall out of favor in all regions of the country. As I will explore in the next chapter, it remained a significant force in the midwestern and East Coast ethnic communities that had nurtured its rise to prominence.

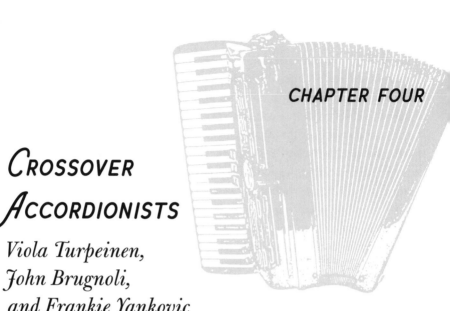

CHAPTER FOUR

CROSSOVER ACCORDIONISTS

Viola Turpeinen,
John Brugnoli,
and Frankie Yankovic

ACCORDIONIST VIOLA TURPEINEN began her career entertaining Finnish-American farmers and mineworkers in Michigan's Upper Peninsula in the 1920s. Furthering her art through studies with Italian accordion teachers, she moved to New York City, where she won a larger audience in the city's Finnish halls as well as in theaters and ballrooms throughout Manhattan. Although Turpeinen recorded for Victor and performed on radio broadcasts, it was her live performances and her regular appearances in her hometown of Iron River that earned her a unique Finnish-American title: Hanuriprinsessa (accordion princess).[1]

In the 1940s, John Brugnoli, an accordionist from Borgotaro, spent five nights a week in his Manhattan cabaret near Times Square playing lively arrangements of tuneful waltzes, polkas, and pasodobles, entertaining *compaesani* as well as non-Italian audiences who were ready to pay for "good accordion music." He also played, and arranged, pop standards and Irish-American favorites for accordion. When Brugnoli's business venture succumbed to rising Manhattan rents, he and his fellow Italian accordionists continued playing at casinos, restaurants, and social functions and making commercial recordings for ethnic labels.

In 1946, riding a "national polka craze,"[2] Columbia Records eagerly signed Frankie Yankovic and His Yanks, whose leader was a young Slovenian accordionist, tavern owner, and factory worker from Ohio. Within two years, Yankovic had composed two hits that each sold over a million copies: "Just Because"

(1947–48) and "Blue Skirt Waltz" (1948–49).[3] Such results were unexpected by both Yankovic and Columbia, who had been concentrating their efforts on regional polka audiences in heavily German-American and Polish-American centers such as Buffalo, Cleveland, and Milwaukee. Explaining why his music succeeded in the nation's entertainment capitals and with the media generally, Yankovic commented: "I'm a blue collar guy and so was my father. I'm just an average guy who is lucky enough to understand what a lot of average guys in the country like to hear."[4]

The experiences of Brugnoli, Turpeinen, and Yankovic, along with a handful of other accordion soloists, bandleaders, and recording artists, suggest a complex picture of accordion culture in America at midcentury. As musicians, each of these three individuals shared a common trajectory. Two of them graduated from button boxes to the piano accordion. All aspired to a national reputation. All made recordings with the explicit intent of disseminating them beyond their local ethnic audiences. All learned and developed skills for entertaining diverse listeners, earning the status of royalty—particularly Turpeinen the accordion princess and Yankovic the polka king. Their stories reveal, however, that American piano accordionists worked under a variety of conditions and influences, maintaining different degrees of autonomy over their work, different business strategies, and diverse attitudes about their work. These artists, along with the recording industry, did help to shape accordion culture. Their efforts entwined them in a variety of social and political relationships with their respective "regional" audiences and beyond that help to define the parameters of accordion playing. To understand these parameters, and to get beyond the sentimental, kitschy notion of ethnic music for accordion that emerged in America at midcentury, we need to explore the identities of these musicians and the ways they themselves adapted their own repertoire and style to the demands and structures imposed by their audiences and the music industry. What were the circumstances and conditions under which these accordionists worked? What were their creative processes? How did they market and sell the music they produced and how did they identify themselves? Through such inquiries, we can reveal the ways American piano accordionists negotiated their musical and cultural worlds in a changing context increasingly defined by the workings of the commercial music industry. As this chapter will show, these accordionists were deliberate actors in a specific historical moment and represent much more than a vague, nostalgic, and shadowy impression of a distant past.

A significant theme in my previous discussions of Welk, King, and Contino, one frequently found in American popular music studies, is that of ethnic and regionally based performers catering to their audience's assimilation to the media-disseminated strains of American popular music in order to become successful in their careers. Unlike these performers, who were highly eclectic, the three accordionists discussed in this chapter all remained rooted in folk music practices and repertoires that have been canonized by folklorists as well-springs of authentic tradition.

It has long been accepted as an established truth that the midwestern United States, its dairylands and its large cities, are laden with accordions and with rich, vibrant ethnic musical traditions in which free-reed instruments play a key role. Folklorists James Leary and Richard March have riveted our attention on accordion-centered midwestern phenomena as diverse as Finnish-American dance bands in Michigan's Iron Range, German-American "Dutchman" bands, Slovenian polka styles, and the success of a variety of local accordion clubs, accordion makers, and small record labels in sustaining interest in the instrument. Leary sees the accordion as an instrument "wielded by and for people who have made their living through physical labor," a kind of musical working-class emblem unifying the diverse styles and idioms of the Midwest.[5]

Viewed broadly, since the beginning of the nineteenth century, several profoundly important cultural processes have gone on in the Midwest that have set the stage for the accordion playing a privileged role in the region's music: mass immigration from Europe, primarily by people of peasant origin who had already encountered the accordion in their respective old-country ethnic musical styles and repertoires (see chapter 1); proliferation of dance halls and lodges as places for socializing and music making; and (re)discovery of the accordion by bandleaders, musicians, fans, and amateur players who saw the instrument's potential to serve as a cultural bulwark against encroaching modernity and culture loss. In the heavily German-American communities of southern Minnesota and Wisconsin, polka bands satisfied the local tastes for social music making among blue collar workers. These bands' typical instrumentation—brass, percussion, and accordion—evolved into the popular "Dutchman" style, or what scholars have come to recognize as the "American polka sound."[6] Iconic Dutchman accordionists such as "Whoopee" John Wilfahrt, Syl Liebl, Harold Loeffelmacher, and Jerry Schneider made the sound of the accordion (as well as the concertina) a trademark of polka bands of the 1930s and 1940s. Such bands invoke their "Germanness" by displaying accordions on their album covers alongside beer steins.[7] Another German cultural contribution, the beer hall, provided many opportunities for polka bands to play, beyond church picnics, house parties, and other social functions demanding music. From the 1920s to the 1950s, many

Dutchman bands in the 1950s aspired to—and achieved—commercial success, helping to give accordions wider exposure.

As Wisconsin's largest ethnic group, German Americans may have contributed most to the transformation of the accordion into an iconic polka band instrument. But Germans were not the only ones to put the accordion on the musical map of the Midwest. Other European immigrant groups who embraced and popularized the piano accordion in their music were the Poles, South Slavs, Swiss, and Scandinavians. The use of the accordion was intimately linked to the working-class, old-country culture of these immigrants. Bohemians, Finns, and Slovenes who migrated to the region to work in lumber camps and mines seemed to share a common penchant for filling their leisure time with music making and dancing in social halls.[8] As James Leary points out in his study of accordion-based dance traditions in the Upper Peninsula, a wide range of beliefs, attitudes, and values circulated around the instrument, not all of them positive. In the old country, Swedes and Finns had confronted Lutheran fundamentalist positions against dancing and drinking. This had sometimes included screeds against the accordion, an instrument that served as driving force behind "scandalous" new couples dances such as the waltz and the polka. Yet, at the same time, the instrument developed a significant role in "establishing a common, creolized, regional and enduring working class culture that was substantially formed between the 1890s and the 1930s."[9]

The nature of and impetus for the use of the accordion in midwestern communities, which involved the changes in musical practices, is a complicated issue. Button boxes, or diatonic accordions, were highly prized by all the major central European groups who immigrated to Wisconsin. Its colorful, reedy sound and its "honking" bass notes were highly prized in the various polka styles.[10] This instrument was particularly important among Slovenians, and dozens of Wisconsin Slovenian bands, such as Richie Yurkewitch's, featured it in their standard repertoire.[11] In Chicago, the Slovenian community witnessed a "button box revival" and several active button box clubs that thrived throughout the 1970s. The button box was also highly prized in Wisconsin's localized but significant Swiss music tradition. Summertime celebrations of dairying and cheese making that began in the late 1800s began to feature "Swiss" and "Alpine" festivals, most of them idealized versions of traditional culture that were cleverly marketed to tourists. Twin button accordionists were often featured in Wisconsin's "Cheese Days" and at house parties among cheese makers.[12]

Although button boxes were highly valued in the region, the piano accordion gained a special status. As ethnic groups came into contact with American popular music, they expanded their musical tastes and sensibilities. They gravitated toward an instrument that appeared to reflect both modern and traditional sensibilities. They admired the "new" sound of the piano accordion. They heard the piano accordion not only played virtuosically by American stars such as Dick Contino but also played by ethnic piano accordionists who were beginning to enjoy wider exposure throughout the region—most famously, the Goose Island Ramblers' Bruce Bollerud.[13] As accordionists like Bollerud navigated through an increasingly eclectic, cosmopolitan repertoire—from bluegrass covers to jazz—audiences came to view the piano accordion as a gateway to other internationally popular styles of music beyond their own. One hallmark of this transition was that ethnic bands were beginning to adopt the conventions of society dance bands: a mix of brass, reeds, and percussion in which the piano accordion was featured as a solo instrument. Audiences saw piano accordions—and skilled accordion players—in bands such as Lombardo's and Welk's, as well the various Polish and Scandinavian bands, as their distinctive texture became a fixture in both mainstream and ethnic bands.[14]

One unique feature of midwestern accordion culture was the unusually high prevalence of accordion schools, retailers, and accordion-centered businesses, compared to the rest of the country. As noted earlier, Chicago was a leading center for accordion production, manufacture, and instruction in the 1930s, 1940s, and 1950s. By no means did Chicago rival New York in the quality and quantity of instruments produced, but it was the nation's band instrument capital, producing the majority of America's low- and mid-priced instruments for students. Milwaukee was as well known for its accordions as for its beer breweries. In the late 1950s, *Accordion World* touted Milwaukee as the "best accordion city in the country, enrolling 8,000 students in accordion schools."[15] Accordionists in that city were served by two accordion manufacturer-retailers: George Karpek and Emil Baldoni.[16]

The piano accordion, an instrument developed and produced in the United States, seemed to have particular appeal to ethnic populations as a musical tool for upward mobility and progress. As noted in chapter 2, The diatonic accordion is limited in the tones it can produce: diatonic scales on the treble side and two or three basic (major) chords on the bass side. Playing music with chromatic scales, runs, or blues progressions is nearly impossible for all but the most proficient players of the button box. On the other hand, the piano accordion's bass side offers a wider range of chord buttons (major, minor, dominant seventh, and diminished seventh) as well as single tones, for the jazz player, or for polka musicians who wish to incorporate chromatic scales, runs, and other melodic flourishes into their playing. Indeed, a generation of ethnic musicians emerging in the 1930s developed roles for the more "modern" sounding piano accordions. Two musicians who contributed most to the rise of the piano accordion in the Midwest were Viola Turpeinen and Frankie Yankovic.

VIOLA TURPEINEN

She may not have been the only Scandinavian accordionist to become a celebrity, but she had the most appeal beyond that community. She was certainly among the best known female accordionists and capitalized on her image to launch a successful performing career.

Turpeinen was born in 1909 in the town of Champion in Michigan's Iron Range, an area rich in natural resources that sustained a large Finnish-American population.[17] In the era prior to World War I, this was a hardworking community of loggers, iron and copper miners, and farmers supporting a number of dance halls where Scandinavian bands performed. Raised on Finnish popular music, Viola learned the two-row button accordion from her mother. Her repertoire included not only traditional Finnish polkas, waltzes, and schottisches but also a pan-Scandinavian array of Swedish, Danish, Estonian, and Norwegian tunes.

When the Turpeinen family moved to Iron River, Viola's musical horizons broadened significantly. Across the street from the family's house was an Italian social hall (Bruno Hall). Hearing the music of the piano accordion, Turpeinen sought lessons with the Italian teachers whom she recognized as master players of the instrument. She began her studies with a succession of Italian teachers and mentors, leading to a respectable reputation both within and outside the Finnish community. She played dances at Bruno Hall and the local Finnish Workers' Hall. At sixteen, she attracted favorable attention from Finnish émigré violinist and impresario John Rosendahl (nee Juho Hugo Hemming). Rosendahl was a flamboyant personality who held a variety of jobs in show business, such as painting signs and showing movies, before becoming a full-time professional entertainer. Rosendahl toured the Finnish communities in Michigan, Minnesota, and Wisconsin with two other Finnish accordionists. When he first heard Viola Turpeinen play, he recognized not only her talent but her potential appeal as a blond, blue-eyed Finnish beauty who could captivate American and Scandinavian audiences. Such was the image Turpeinen conveyed in many of her publicity photos and album covers.

In 1927, when Turpeinen turned eighteen, Rosendahl invited her to tour with him as a duo (first seeking permission from her parents). They embarked on

Viola Turpeinen. (Photo courtesy of James Leary)

a crosscountry tour of Finnish-American communities, beginning in Duluth, Minnesota, and Superior, Wisconsin, where many Scandinavian Americans sought work in the factories surrounding Lake Superior.[18] A 78 rpm recording of a standard Finnish-American number from that year, "Viulu Polka," demonstrates Turpeinen's competence as a dance musician. Her left hand plays rhythmic accompaniment throughout the piece, providing a rock-solid tempo. She doubles melodic passages with Rosendahl in what appears to be a dynamic display of virtuosity for both, a kind of friendly race. It is spirited playing, just what her audience must have admired. A fan who recalled seeing Turpeinen play at a dance in Brule, Michigan, has said: "the crowds were huge . . . more than when (Frank) Yankovic played. You could always dance to what Viola played.

She was precise, good timing, rhythm, good fingers. The way she handled that accordion! I made up my mind to play like that."[19] Indeed, it is astonishing that Turpeinen, who was first and foremost a dance musician, could have been seen as bigger draw than Cleveland polka king Frankie Yankovic (discussed in the next section). But perhaps part of Turpeinen's appeal lay in the fact that she was not a singer, like Yankovic. Her fans could admire her without having to understand her music linguistically and appreciate her as an outstanding instrumentalist. Therefore Turpeinen had more potential to inspire enthusiasm for the accordion than most of her contemporaries in the ethnic music field. She was likely to have been, as one scholar has pointed out, as popular with non-Finns as she with Finnish Americans.[20]

Aiming for wider exposure beyond Lake Superior's Twin Cities region, the duo moved to Chicago, which provided a home base for further touring of the Upper Midwest. They thrived on the working-class Finnish dance hall circuit in Ohio, Massachusetts, New York (Manhattan and Brooklyn), and New Jersey. They drew crowds with not only music but also ethnic comic sketches. In 1928, they reached New York City. With a population of over ten thousand Finns in Brooklyn's "Finntown," New York City offered the largest possible audience for Turpeinen, as well as the opportunity to record four sides with Columbia.[21] In addition to traditional Finnish dance tunes, the duo recorded a schottische composed by Swedish-American composer-accordionist Edwin (Eddie) Jahrl, (discussed later). One notable piece in Turpeinen's repertoire was "Finnish Woods," a familiar Scandinavian folk tune arranged by Swedish accordionist Carl Jularbo. It has become a well-known accordion "standard" and has been published in many collections, such as *Music, Scandinavian Style*, AMPCO's folio of Scandinavian popular songs, from the 1940s. Another six records made for Victor included "Variety Polka" by Guido Deiro, a revered figure among Scandinavian accordionists; however, the piece is listed as "Violan Polka," as if Turpeinen herself had composed it.[22]

The duo returned to the Midwest in 1928, where they toured Finnish communities in Minnesota, Michigan, and Ohio. They made their way back to New York in 1929, playing the Finnish Workers' Hall in Manhattan, the Kalevela Hall in Brooklyn, and in New Jersey. Their audience consisted of working-class Finns and Norwegians who worked in the shipping industry. Rosendahl's diary indicates that on April 4, 1929, the duo sold over eight hundred tickets at the Finnish Workers' Hall. Their typical audience ranged from two hundred to four hundred.[23] That year, Rosendahl and Turpeinen together with a new third musician (Andrew Kosola) who made the group a trio, moved to Harlem.

There the group faced considerable challenges. Rosendahl, a heavy drinker, died tragically in an alcohol-related accident in 1933. Without their promoter, the group had to scramble to get bookings at the height of the Great Depression. Fortunately, they could draw on many talented musicians to fill Rosendahl's place. One of these was a female second accordionist from Michigan, Sylvia Pölsö, known as the "Greta Garbo of the Accordion." Joining the group on drums and cornet was composer-arranger William Syrjala, who married Turpeinen in a ceremony that was, with many accordion luminaries in attendance, the highlight of the accordion world's social calendar in 1933.[24]

From the 1930s until 1958, Turpeinen made appearances in Finnish-American communities from coast to coast. Although confined to a particular ethnic group, these barnstorming tours mirror the success of her predecessors Guido Deiro and Pietro Frosini on the vaudeville circuit fifty years earlier. Although Finnish Lutherans eschewed dancing, social halls and social dances were regular and well-tolerated features of community life. Accordionists were often the focus of such events. Like other working-class Scandinavian immigrants, the Finns "relied heavily on accordionists to create a lingua franca amid the house parties and hall dances that highlighted their scant hours of leisure."[25] At these Saturday night dances, accordionists would play the familiar repertoires of polkas, schottisches, waltzes, and serenades, with children and families present. The social organizations also sponsored appearances by visiting celebrity musicians, a slot that in Hubbardstown, Massachusetts, was filled each July by Viola Turpeinen. She would appear reliably each year on a tour of Finnish and Scandinavian communities in the Upper Midwest and Massachusetts. At one such performance, at a Finnish hall in Michigan, a performance by Turpeinen and her ensemble was followed by a slide lecture featuring rustic scenes of Finland and narration in Finnish.[26] Such events suggest that Turpeinen's musical performances were deeply entwined with notions of traditional and communal identity among Finnish Americans.

As some of her audiences have described her appearances, Turpeinen had an almost magical effect on her audience. She was regarded as a symbol of Finnish ethnic identity and "THE dance musician of her community," admired not only as a musician but as a friend of the community.[27] A few community members still recall Viola stopping by for a home-cooked Finnish meal or a sauna, an important form of Scandinavian hospitality. Greene writes: "her fans nearly deified her—some Finnish Americans felt she gave them a new sense of themselves."[28]

As Turpeinen built her reputation in the Finnish community, she also became prominent in the mainstream accordion world. She was associated with Pietro

Deiro's music school in Manhattan, as well as with the Excelsior Accordion Company, from whom she purchased a $1000 instrument.[29] She later appeared in advertisements as an Excelsior artist. She was a protégé of the great Deiro himself and was also linked with Frank Gaviani, Arvid Franzen, and a host of other Scandinavian and Italian accordion virtuosi in New York. Publicity photographs of Turpeinen's trio, probably from the 1930s, shows what looks like an elegantly dressed mini–society band. Both women, Turpeinen (seated) and Pölsö (standing), clad in 1920s-style short skirts, smile alluringly at the camera.

Beyond their success in numerous live performances, Turpeinen's ensemble continued reaching wider audiences by continuing to record for Victor and Columbia, whose ethnic musical recording activity continued full steam through the Depression. Turpeinen cut eighty-nine sides from the late 1920s through the 1930s. (Most of these were issued by Columbia.) After 1946, when the major labels curtailed their ethnic recordings, and few Finnish-American artists were recording regularly, Turpeinen moved from RCA Victor to Standard Records, where she recorded about a dozen sides a year. There she joined another leading Scandinavian accordion luminary, Walter Eriksson, the noted Swedish-Finnish composer-arranger of Scandinavian music. Most of her Standard recordings were Finnish pieces; some were solos and others duets with Sylvia Pölsö on second accordion.

Recordings of Finnish and Norwegian popular songs made between 1949 and 1951 suggest that Turpeinen responded to the changing tastes of the Scandinavian community. Several of these recordings reflect the influences of big band jazz and mainstream American polka music (discussed later). In 1951, Turpeinen made her last recording. The Finnish Workers Hall closed in 1951–52; the building was converted into an African-American church—evidence of the Finnish-American community's dissolution and the eroding market for Turpeinen's music.[30] Turpeinen's and Syrjala's subsequent move to Florida was undoubtedly a tactical decision to follow their Finnish audiences as they aged and retired from their shipyard jobs. After Turpeinen's death from breast cancer in 1958, Syrjala and several other musicians (including accordionist Jorma Vuorinen) continued to appear as the "Viola Turpeinen Orchestra" well into the 1980s.[31]

Although Turpeinen reached beyond Finnish traditional dance music with her repertoire of light classical favorites and popular Scandinavian tunes, becoming a "crossover" performer did not mean making significant changes in her repertoire or instrumentation, as Yankovic would do with traditional Slovenian music. Although she never became a "staff accordionist" on a radio station,

Turpeinen made one appearance that was highly successful in reaching Finnish *and* American audiences—her appearance on *Major Bowes' Amateur Hour* in April 1936, transcribed below:

> **MB:** Next we have Viola Turpentine.
>
> **VT:** No, Major, it's Turpeinen.
>
> **MB:** Sorry, an accordion player specializing in Finnish music. Were you born in Finland?
>
> **VT:** No, I'm from Michigan.
>
> **MB:** Why do you specialize in Finnish music?
>
> **VT:** My grandparents are Finnish, but I play Danish, Swedish, Norwegian, and Estonian music.
>
> **BM:** What's your work? What do you do?
>
> **VT:** (Pause) I have to do everything. You see, I'm married.
>
> (Laughter and applause.)
>
> **BB:** And what Finnish music would you like to play?
>
> **VT:** I'd like to play a Finnish schottische, and then my own polka, named after the place where my grandparents were born: "Kivijarven Polka."[32]

If this brief clip is any indication of her style, Turpeinen presented herself with lighthearted charm. She cleverly did not share her ambitions to become a professional female performer, which might have been off-putting to many listeners in the 1930s, but sidestepped the issue in a disarmingly amusing way. She did not play up her sexuality or flaunt her fashionable style, as some female musicians of her era did, although one Victor advertisement portrayed her as an "accordion-wielding, short-skirted bobbed-hair flapper."[33] Her success was never predicated on image. Turpeinen's gift to the accordion world was her virtuosity and her hard work sustaining two musical careers: one with a busy schedule of concerts, recordings, and radio appearances in New York and the other as a touring musician concertizing for her midwestern "base."

Indeed, Turpeinen was not the only successful Scandinavian accordionist of her time. Edwin (Eddie) Jahrl and Eric Olzen, both Swedish Americans, opened popular accordion schools in Brooklyn. Olzen published sheet music in popular styles bearing English titles—"In the Hay Loft," "Sunbeam Polka"—and became well regarded among local Scandinavians for his Saturday morning radio show on WBBC in New York; he also recorded widely. Jahrl launched his own record labels, Scandinavia and the free-reed–centric Cordion, which offered pieces by Olzen and other accordionists. He was especially popular in the 1940s, as he appeared often on WBBC and WBYN.[34] These two performers sold thousands of records, filled dance halls, and generally appealed to Scandinavian and American audiences. Walter Eriksson was an industrious and resourceful conductor, arranger and admired musical figure among Scandinavians and accordionists of many backgrounds, but not a barnstorming virtuoso. What made Turpeinen's career unique was that while based in New York during the Depression, she succeeded in marketing her accordion performance style and a relatively static repertoire of Finnish polka to *all* Americans.

JOHN BRUGNOLI

Like Turpeinen, the Italian-American accordionist John Brugnoli capitalized on his community's fondness for ethnic music and dance, and the rising popularity of the accordion. While Turpeinen relied on barnstorming crosscountry tours to build her reputation, John Brugnoli and his colleagues chose to develop their audience locally by investing in the nightclubs that aimed to be the heart and soul of Manhattan's northern Italian community.

In 1936 Brugnoli, an immigrant from the town of Borgotaro in Italy's Emilia region, opened the Val-Taro Restaurant and Bar at 869 Second Avenue, between Forty-Sixth and Forty-Seventh streets.[35] This club, located in the heart of a tightly knit northern Italian community in Manhattan's Turtle Bay neighborhood, was to feature dancing to live accordion music and a small orchestra four nights a week. Surely Brugnoli must have been anxious with anticipation. The club brought to fruition years of hard work, saving, and self-sacrifice and the traditional lengthy wait for a liquor license in New York City. Finally, when the required document arrived, the restaurant opened its doors for the first time on Christmas Eve. The new establishment was jammed—"an instant success."[36]

This account echoes, to some extent, the experiences of Frankie Yankovic, who also owned a tavern. But Brugnoli's were less dramatic in that he, unlike Yankovic, spent his entire career in an ethnic musical enclave. Yet Brugnoli was highly significant in that he was responsible for the development of the only accordion repertoire and style created in New York City: "Valtaro musette" (also called by its practitioners simply "Valtaro"), a song repertoire and style of Italian accordion music with roots in nineteenth-century Europe. Created in Manhattan's Italian nightclubs in the 1930s and 1940s by Brugnoli and a tightly knit group of musicians and composers with roots in northern Italian culture, Valtaro found a small but cherished place in accordion culture, as well as the memory culture of Italians and Italian Americans today.[37]

I first encountered Valtaro music when in search of repertoire to play at my accordion band's "community service" gigs in upstate New York, where

I lived at the time. We performed at nursing homes operated by Catholic charities. Our audience seemed to respond well to Italian songs. When we performed a northern Italian standard tune, "Tutti Mi Chiamano Bionda,"[38] an energetic contingent of people often sang along in Italian. A year later, at a concert sponsored by the AAA in New York City, a pair of accordionists announced a piece in "Valtaro style." I again heard the same tune, "Tutti Mi Chiamano," but performed in a dynamic, highly ornamented style. In their duet performance, the lead player performed the melody "straight" (but in much livelier fashion than our band did); the second player added florid ornamentation: trills, fills, and arpeggios (broken chords); and all improvised seemingly effortlessly. Their performance made our band's version sound austere by comparison: if our performance was a whitewashed Protestant church, the "Valtaro" version was a magnificent Gothic cathedral. My inquiries about what "Valtaro" style was led me to accordionist Dominic Karcic in New York City and ultimately to his teacher, eighty-eight-year-old accordionist Peter Spagnoli, a contemporary of John Brugnoli and his one-time business partner. (Spagnoli especially was eager to discuss this repertoire, which he had not performed in public for some decades, and his observations form the basis of the following discussion.)[39]

The accordionists who invented a new playing style and repertoire they called Valtaro provide important insights into the accordion's crosscultural appeal in America. Brugnoli's lively reinterpretations of northern Italian (among other Italian) songs reveal a genius for the use of the accordion as a means of bringing people together through sonic spectacle and participatory dancing. They often encouraged audience-participation sing-alongs of Italian songs, while including their own arrangements of Irish, French, Spanish, and American tunes. Brugnoli and his fellow exponents of the Valtaro repertoire understood that the Italian songs they performed in these purely instrumental performances, absent the lyrics and the language/dialect barrier, would appeal to American audiences. He would draw his Irish, Irish-American, Polish, and Anglo audiences in closer under the universal ethnic "sign" of the accordion. By encouraging them to dance to the rhythms of the polka, mazurka, and fox-trot, the musicians gave others (of different ethnic origins and nationalities) a way to participate more fully in the American multicultural scene of the 1940s and 1950s than they ever had in the days of vaudeville and ribald ethnic comedy.

From his northern Italian (Valtarese) upbringing and early interactions with French, German, and other American musicians, Brugnoli learned to use music as both a powerful means of individual and collective ethnic expression and a reliable source of income. He followed the lead of fellow Italian Americans such as Guido Deiro, an immigrant from Turin who was the first to play piano accordion in America and the only accordionist to become a vaudeville headline act, and Guido's brother Pietro Deiro, who had made the first-ever recordings of accordion music. Like the Deiro brothers, who were from Turin, Brugnoli had both formal musical training and informal exposure to the rich musical influences of the north. As a young man, Brugnoli played the accordion at town dance halls (*ballo lisci*), which featured the popular waltzes, polkas, and mazurkas that had circulated to Italy from the Alps; like Guido Deiro, he had achieved the status of a minor celebrity in Europe. When migrating to France, Brugnoli could not help but absorb the charming French-Auvergnian musette music he heard (and played) on the streets of Paris. In addition to his informal training, Brugnoli incorporated jazz and the new forms of popular dance music that were circulating in the hotels and nightclubs of midtown Manhattan. Indeed, the story of the accordionists from northern Italy demonstrates different stages or levels of cultural interaction; their choices set them apart from the old-world immigrants who journeyed to New York and other American cities. They were immigrants not only from Italy but from Europe; they had to come to grips with changing American tastes (i.e., the jazz craze of the 1920s and 1930s), which they did by becoming students of American music in New York, as Yankovic had done in Cleveland.[40]

The relationship the Italians developed with the accordion has an important bearing on another issue relevant to this book: the accordion as a distinctively Italian contribution to the world of music. The accordion's unique role in Italian American culture and its capacity to engage issues of class and ethnicity was the subject of a recent symposium on the accordion as an "Italian-American icon."[41] The accordion for a time formed part of the vibrant, lively culture of urban and suburban first- and second-generation immigrants who saw playing the accordion as a key part of maintaining their old-world cultural connections. As Italian immigrants worked their way up the economic ladder in the first decades of the twentieth century, playing the accordion could become a particularly risky practice, particularly among the second and third generations of immigrants who wanted to conform to the suburban cultural order. James Periconi, who learned the accordion as a child growing up in the Bronx during the 1950s but abandoned it in his teens, noted in a memoir: "the accordion and my skill with the instrument have been . . . a stigma for me, not unlike my frizzy hair, emblematic of a certain rejection by straight-hair American culture, a denial of my *Italianità* ("Italianness")."[42]

How was it that in the climate of postwar America, Italian Americans made use of the accordion to symbolize their ethnic identity to themselves and others? During the post–World War II era, immigrants from northern and central Italy recontextualized a broad repertoire of Alpine, pan-Italian, and European folk songs, as well as film music and jazz standards, by arranging it for accordion ensembles and performing it in handful of Manhattan nightclubs. This newly created subgenre of accordion music—an original Italian-American musical repertoire and style created in New York City and performed at Italian-American cabarets—reveals how a remarkably talented and diverse set of Italian- and American-born artists gave a distinct voice to these familiar and widely circulated popular songs and marketed their creations as "authentic northern Italian music." They accomplished this in the context of a vibrant and changing entertainment industry.

In the 1930s, Manhattan's entertainment district began to spread east and below Times Square to the forties blocks. This neighborhood, known as Turtle Bay, also had the distinction of being a popular destination for immigrants from northern and central Italy—Genoa, Parma, Tuscany, and Emilia—as did the seven blocks of Manhattan's West Side in the twenties (Chelsea). These "northern Italian" neighborhoods consisted of only a few city blocks: essentially Sixty-First, Sixty-Second, and Sixty-Third streets between First and Second avenues, with some northern Italian immigrants on First Avenue between Sixty-First and Sixty-Third streets.[43]

The idea for an "Italian cabaret" that would be open to the public began in the 1930s with John (Gianod "Scud'lein") Brugnoli.

Born in 1901 in Borgotaro in the Parma region, Brugnoli inherited his nickname from his grandfather, who loved wine and drank it from a soup bowl (*scud'lein*).[44] The region had long sustained a vibrant *ballo liscio* (dance hall) tradition in which local and regional bands circulated through a network of public dances in local towns and villages, and John's brother and father played at these events.[45] His older brother Luigi was known on the dance hall circuit as an outstanding accordionist and eventually migrated to Paris, where he is said to have pioneered the use of the piano accordion. Under Luigi's tutelage, John established himself in Paris as a virtuoso piano accordionist and bandleader, playing and conducting bands in public dance halls throughout Borgotaro. Aiming higher as a professional musician, he emigrated first to France and then, following a short stint in the clubs of Paris, to the United States in 1928. Earning his livelihood playing accordion in Italian cabarets such as the Francino, Brugnoli realized that his ambition was to open one of

John Brugnoli.

his own that would feature the popular musette repertoire as well as music of his own region. But he needed a business partner. He heard that fellow accordionist Pietro (later Pete) DelGrosso, whom he had met in Borgotaro, had emigrated and was well established as a musician in New York City. They did eventually meet at a West Side nightclub called Bel Tabarin where DelGrosso was performing. They agreed to go into business together, and friends provided capital to support their vision. The opening of their club, the Val-Taro, became a significant moment in the memory of New York's northern Italians: "The Val-Taro became a mecca for people who loved good dance music, good times, and above all, the accordion. It was a place where notable accordionists . . . all worked . . . over the years."[46]

The Val-Taro's success was also an incentive for other entrepreneurs to establish similar types of cabarets featuring northern Italian accordion music.

Many eventually flourished in the New York midtown, area but "not one quite equaled the Val-Taro."[47] After selling his share of the business in 1939, Brugnoli left the Val-Taro and entered into another partnership with his longtime friend and landlord, Emilio Spagnoli. The new cabaret was known as the Terrace (at Second Avenue and Fifty-Ninth Street).

Spagnoli's son Pete, tutored by Brugnoli in exchange for room and board, was emerging as an accomplished accordionist, and in time he joined the roster of notable, Italian accordionists who were regularly featured at the Val-Taro and the Terrace.[48] These notables included Mindie Cere, Addie Cere, Emilio Chiesa, Hugo Nati, and Aldo Bruschi.[49] The Terrace's two house musicians—pianist Norma McFeeters, an Afro-Caribbean woman from Dominica, and Jewish drummer Willy Wohlman—joined with these accordionists in arranging and performing Valtaro music. Spagnoli later claimed that McFeeters and Wohlman learned to play Valtaro repertoire "as if it were in their DNA."[50] To Spagnoli and other musicians, the presence of musicians and listeners from many backgrounds seemed to validate the broader appeal and significance of their work, as well as the viability of the clubs themselves. The opportunity to play four or five weeks gave Brugnoli, DelGrosso, and eventually Spagnoli

The Terrace nightclub in Manhattan, 1940s.

the opportunity to polish Valtaro as a distinctive repertoire and unique style, continuing to build on its foundation of familiar, traditional northern Italian and European popular songs by adding jazz, popular tunes, and Irish favorites like "Danny Boy."[51]

It is evident through their prolific work as arrangers and composers that Valtaro musicians, like the Slovenian polka musicians discussed in this chapter, intended for their music to circulate beyond their community. Peter DelGrosso's work made up the first and third volumes of *Let's Waltz and Polka*, the ethnic dance folios published by Deffner. While performing four or five nights a week and teaching accordion at Elsie Bennett's music studio in Brooklyn (and eventually his own), Spagnoli managed to arrange most of the songs that are considered part of the Valtaro repertoire. As I found when interviewing Peter Spagnoli recently, what Valtaro musicians consider their core repertoire consists of over one thousand Valtaro songs, most of which Spagnoli arranged himself.[52]

An analysis of the Valtaro repertoire can help to demonstrate the wide spectrum of songs and musical influences it has absorbed from French, central European, Italian, and American popular culture. In their discourse about the origins of the music, the players tend to privilege native folk influences while glossing over its hybrid commercial, high-cultural, and crosscultural musical influences. Some songs in the repertoire, such as "Mazzolin del fior," hail from the Italian film industry. Medleys like one that conjoins snippets of Robert Schumann's "Carnival of Venice," the traditional Italian song "Vieni sul mar" (popularized by Tito Schipa and Enrico Caruso), and the ballad of "Il Sirio" (Val-Taro Musette Orchestra, 1953) may seem like haphazard pastiche. But such productions can be seen as strategic as well. I would argue that Spagnoli and DelGrosso engaged in the process of "folklorization," an important thread in this book.[53] Folklorization of Italian culture appropriates local music for the pleasure of its listeners but at the same time creates spaces in which the community (northern Italians) can assert their own claims to be true custodians of a national cultural patrimony (the accordion). The proponents of this music succeed in producing a collective identity based on their mastery of their local folksongs, in order to enhance the visibility and legitimacy of their community and to foster integration into American culture. With his accordion and his arsenal of one thousand songs, Spagnoli was armed for any occasion. He aimed to satisfy not only listeners from his own region but all audiences: northern Italian, southern Italian, American, Irish, and German, and others. He learned that the greater his flexibility, the greater the demand for his services (as accordion teacher and bandleader), and the greater his financial success.

It is impossible to overrate the significance of regional repertoire and of the way these songs were associated (at least in the minds of northern Italian-Americans) with the idea of the accordion. Dance sets played in Valtaro clubs invariably included waltzes, tangos, mazurkas, and polkas, which have been part of not only the German (Dutchman) but also the Italian regional repertoire since the eighteenth century.[54] The songs musicians know as "Italian polkas" were usually performed by musicians (including accordionists) during *maggio delle ragazze* ("young girls' May Days") at dances in village squares and in prominent families' palazzi. Linked historically to the Emilian *ballo liscio* tradition, they also became part of New York City's nightclub and cabaret scene.

While many songs in the repertoire are valued as expressions of identity or even documents of historical experience, Valtaro accordionists typically create with little concern for "purity" and "authenticity." In Valtaro, as in other instrumental performances of polka, there is no vocalist and lyrics; the songs themselves are simply raw material to be carved and chiseled by the accordionist. As Spagnoli has said, the skill of the accordionist provided a point of connection with the musical traditions and with his audience, who would frequently sing along. Folk songs and traditional ballads provided an important sense of cultural continuity, but the draw for the audience was the accordion, and for patrons of the Val-Taro nightclub, the name was synonymous with "good accordion music." No doubt proud of and attuned to the potential to capitalize on the "cult of the virtuoso" phenomenon in the accordion world, Valtaro players sought to develop their own local following in Manhattan. They aimed to do this through the resignification of the music through a unique instrumental performance style and sound.

Seen on paper, most songs from the Valtaro repertoire appear indistinguishable from other Italian and central European dance tunes. They share the same rhythms, harmonic progressions, and in many cases melodies. In spite of generalized, nonregional, and central European characteristics of much of this repertoire, the players aimed to construct a distinct style. By employing an instrument with a sense of an artistically rich past (the Italian accordion) and simple, unadorned folk and popular songs, Valtaro musicians forged what might otherwise be heard as simple or "generic" material into a unique style. One way to understand this process would be to compare two performances of the polka "Tic Tic Ta." I first encountered this tune as a Polish polka in my accordion band's repertoire. When I compared the "Valtaro" version of "Tic Tic Ta" (performed on Mario Tacca's album *Nostalgia*) with the pounding and hard-driving renditions performed by my band, I detected a more lighthearted and easygoing quality, with distinct operatic influences present in the Italian polka. The instrumentation of a polka band most familiar to practitioners of the Slovenian style features a piano and/or a diatonic accordion, guitar, bass, and drum set and is similar to that used by Valtaro bands.[55] The accordion often plays lead (melody), using a single reed or a pair of reeds, high and middle, tuned at the same pitch, which enables the accordion to "cut" through the band texture.[56] For this purpose, many "Dutchman" accordionists choose instruments with so-called dry tuning or polka tuning.[57] This piercing single-reed sound enables the instrument to be heard over the brass instruments, particularly the oom-pah-ing tuba. Most Italian-made piano accordions, however, unless the player specifically requests that they be "dry tuned," are equipped with a "musette" switch, a pair of reeds that are tuned higher and lower than the desired pitch. This, the musette sound or "wet" sound, is the one desired by Valtaro accordionists.[58] The ever-present vibrato of Valtaro—the singing accordion—evokes the resonant operatic voices of bel canto tradition and the historical significance of the Italian opera casting its shadow over this popular folk tradition.[59] The importance of singing and the ever-present vocal soloists and choruses at Valtaro events may explain why players value the "wet" musette sound and strive for a lighter sound (easier to blend with the voices) than their eastern European colleagues in the polka field.

As Valtaro is seen as an "accordion-centered" tradition, a performance of "Tic Tic Ta" at a 2006 "Reunion" of Valtaro musicians in Walkill, New York, showcased not only the vocal soloist, Mary Mancini, but also two accordionists presenting the song as a minicomposition-improvisation for accordion duet. The lead accordionist, Dominic Karcic, played the "Tic Tic Ta" melody in fairly straightforward fashion, with a harmony in thirds unfolding in the right hand (keyboard). The second part, improvised by Ray Oreggia, embellished the melody with triplet runs and arpeggios, creating a rich and varied texture. The tempo of the Valtaro version of "Tic Tic Ta" was slower and more elastic than my band's driving Polish polka version. As presented by the pair of accordionists, the tempo was much more relaxed, with plenty of rubato, which was much appreciated by the dancers, who exploited the slow ends of phrases to add turns, dips, and other embellishments as they moved across the dance floor.

Although many players believe that Valtaro music is "innate" or absorbed in the womb,[60] Karcic has taken on the mission of teaching workshops at accordion conventions to newcomers. Karcic is concerned with perfecting the "duet style" of accordion playing, developed by Brugnoli, in which the players take turns performing the lyrical melodic line and playing rhythmic chords, adding arpeggios, dynamic shifts (through the bellows), and ornaments.[61] Indeed, this style also reflects many other styles of music, such as classical, jazz, and the scores of lighthearted popular songs (Italian and American) that Valtaro musicians played at their audience's requests. Karcic also has offered a lengthy discussion of the French musette tradition, a parallel repertoire and style developed by Italian accordionists in Paris, and its boundary-crossing influences on Valtaro musicians. The transnationalism of the accordion—and its repertoires—may help to explain why Karcic, who is of Croatian descent, can present himself as a leading Valtaro tradition bearer without being perceived as an outsider.[62] Indeed, the Valtaro phenomenon displays the significance of the accordion as part of a much broader cultural icon, beyond "Italian-ness," within the shifting landscape of "refolklorized" musical culture.

A pivotal moment in the decline of the Valtaro tradition among Italians was the decline of old-country identity, which had been ongoing since the 1920s, as Italian Americans (and other southern European immigrants) left Little Italys for the suburbs. Whether or not one chooses to view this migratory pattern as a harbinger of a permanent decline of the accordion's significance as an icon for Italian Americans, evidence exists of major shifts in the group's entertainment choices and musical tastes.[63] The Val-Taro, the Terrace, and all the Italian cabarets closed down between 1961 and 1974. In addition, there was a general decline in live music at social functions and clubs, replaced by less costly deejays and the rise of the discotheque, largely catering to a younger crowd.[64] Brugnoli and DelGrosso were savvy businessmen who were aware of these trends and their erosive effects on their income. After their nightclubs had to close, they ensured that their music would continue reaching a paying audience. They continued to perform, compose and arrange Valtaro music. They played it at club dates, church functions, casinos, and summer resorts; they taught it to their accordion students.[65] The demand for ethnic recordings in the languages spoken by immigrant Americans allowed more stable future for this music took shape in the recording studio. In 1961 the Colonial record label, which published "sing-along" albums for the Italian-American market, gave Brugnoli the opportunity to release a series of albums called "Sing-Along in Italian."[66] These consisted primarily of songs from the Valtaro repertoire and featured Brugnoli's work along with that of the Norwegian-American accordionist Walter Ericksson. In addition, the Fiesta label released a series of Valtaro LP records for accordion solo and ensemble, which reduced this originally forceful music to a pretty background sound.[67] The sing-along albums seem to capture the spirit and energy of the Valtaro style through the ardent singing and the virtuosic yet spontaneous stylings of the accordionists. The albums, not yet available on CD, remain in the possession of collectors.

Although Valtaro musicians could hardly have predicted it, one possible route to greater visibility for this music has been the Italian "ethnic feast" phenomenon. These summer festivals have become a significant part of the revival culture of Italian Americans as well as profitable ventures for the entrepreneurs who sponsor them. These festas, presented by city tourism boards in collaboration with local Italian-American organizations, are in the realm of "Italian family FUN."[68] Although the musical entertainment at such event usually focuses on a headline act that has been proven to draw large audiences outside the Italian-American community, a band playing traditional Italian music with an accordionist is often part of the mix: Valtaro accordionist Mario Tacca and vocalist Maria Mancini appeared at Milwaukee's "ethnic feast" in the summer of 2008. San Jose's festa promises "ample accordion entertainment," along with a grape-stomping contest and folkloric dance companies performing the tarantella.[69] Italian festas in the San Francisco Bay Area and the wine country region are an income-generating mainstay for accordionists. In the context of an event that promotes Italian "heritage tourism" and the exotic and familiar appeal of participant-friendly Italian "traditions," audience reception of these events, and their music, and how live festive performances figure in the perception of the accordion is a topic worthy of further consideration. Certainly the foregoing evidence suggests that the accordion has assumed a unique place in the memory culture of all Italians and Italian Americans.

FRANKIE YANKOVIC

Of the three accordionists discussed in this chapter, Frankie Yankovic was the most admired and famous nationally. He not only was crowned "Polka King" by Milwaukee audiences but also brought the music to Hollywood royalty as well as to the living rooms of working-class fans of the polka. Yankovic's astute reflections on the surge of polka music in America of the post–World War II era, recorded in Robert Dolgan's definitive biography and an informative, late-life interview with historian Victor Greene, provide a valuable context for understanding the postwar rise and fall of the accordion.[70]

Yankovic was born in 1915 in the logging community of Davis, West Virginia, home to many recent Slovenian immigrants (as well as Italians, a connection that would prove crucial in Yankovic's professional career). When local authorities discovered his father's bootlegging activities, the family moved to Cleveland's Collinwood area, where they had family and could feel at home in the most "Slovenian of all American neighborhoods."[71] Most of the immigrants worked in the railroad yards or at the Fisher Body factory.

Frankie Yankovic, 1940s.

The Slovenian-American cultural milieu of Yankovic's boyhood was steeped in music. The fraternal lodges had oldtime brass bands playing at social events—and parades, which fascinated young Frankie. Indeed, most cities, including Cleveland, had a variety of ethnic communities, each featuring its own bands, band events, and wedding band circuit. The Yankovic household was especially rich in culture. Yankovic's parents ran a boarding-house for Slovenian bachelors, and their home had become a social hub for the community. One of their tenants, a talented accordionist by the name of Max Zelodec, made a strong impression on young Frankie. At nine years of age, Frankie began lessons with Zelodec on a three-row Hohner diatonic accordion (possibly in exchange for a portion of rent, as the family was likely too financially strapped to afford lessons). In 1931 at age fifteen, against the objections of his father, Frank switched to the piano accordion. Why the resistance from his father? At the height of the Depression, purchasing a $500 instrument may have seemed like an unwise idea. And in this insular family and community, the piano accordion must have also signified "American" ways and the potential loss of their beloved Slovenian tradition. Frankie's father could have also seen the piano accordion as a symbol of Frankie's pending professional musical career, a choice to which he was opposed—no doubt wishing for his son the job security of the factory and the trade union. But perhaps the high-class image of the piano accordion to an immigrant family persuaded the father to accept his son's choice. Or was it the Slovenian waltz Frankie prepared for his father on the piano accordion? Yankovic recalls his father expressing tentative confidence in him with the cryptic statement "If you're going to play it, play it well."[72] Most likely the parents knew, from hearing performers like Pietro Deiro and other radio virtuosi, that if their Frankie was going to be a famous musician, he certainly wasn't going to play a button box.

Yankovic formed his first band as a teenager: a trio of accordion, banjo, and drums, a combination that was characteristic of the acoustic Slovenian polka style then popular in Cleveland. Slovenian-style polka (SSP) is a musical style and repertoire that developed from the Slovenian-language popular song tradition as well as German, Austrian, and Istrian traditions. Developed into a modern popular style by Slovenian immigrants in Ohio, it is also known as "Cleveland style" polka. The instrumentation is lighter than the previously discussed "Dutchman" bands and parallel polka styles that developed in the Midwest, featuring piano and accordion (button box or piano accordion), with banjo, bass guitar, and a drum kit providing rhythm. The repertoire consists of traditional Slovenian-language songs arranged in upbeat, duple-meter tempos, the classic polka style.[73]

While the acoustic texture of SSP remains consistent, some of its practitioners were bringing change and variation to the style during the time Yankovic was coming of age as a musician. William Lausche incorporated the elements of early jazz and swing, a flavor that is apparent on some of the early Yankovic recordings. Johnny Pecon and Lou Trebar extended the style as well, using blue notes, "jazzy" modulations, and altered chords. Collaborating with some of these musicians and observing their innovative and experimental approach to traditional music must have been extremely helpful to Yankovic. It was also significant that at this early point in his career, he worked with Italian-American arranger-composer Joe Trolli, composer of the polka "Tic Tic Ta," a song that has become as familiar in the accordion repertoire as "Lady of Spain." Trolli's collaborations encouraged Yankovic to modify his many ethnic Slovenian pieces to appeal to the wider audience he was seeking.

Radio and recordings advanced Yankovic's career during the 1930s, just as they had for other accordionists discussed in this book. The Slovenian Sunday program on WJAY offered Yankovic his first radio audience in 1932. He became a regular feature on Slovenian programs throughout the 1930s: for example, WGAR's popular Slovenian show hosted by Martin "Heinie" Antoncic. Yankovic's group was in high demand all over Ohio, Pennsylvania, and Michigan, at clubs, weddings, and other social events. At that point, Yankovic approached Victor and Columbia for contracts. Rejected, he turned to Antoncic and a Czech promoter, Fred Wolf, for help in making his own recordings. Both were happy to oblige, and in 1938, "Yankovic and His Yanks" put out his first records under a label whose name would not prove apt for another decade: Yankee Records. Yankovic's early recordings, with groups he called the "Slovenian Folk Orchestra" and the "Joliet Jolly Jugoslavs" demonstrate that at this stage in his career he never sought to reach audiences beyond the local ethnic community, which rewarded his efforts by promptly buying up his first run of six thousand records (distributed by a fellow Slovenian on the Joliet label). By 1941, the Yanks' band members had married and started families and the constant touring was taking its toll. Yankovic shrewdly opened his own bar in Cleveland, which quickly became a gathering place for local polka musicians such as accordionist Johnny Pecon, who would contribute to Yankovic's rise to national fame.

When America entered World War II in 1943, Yankovic enlisted, believing at first that his polka career would be put on hold for the duration of his military service. Yet in several respects his military service speeded his path to becoming the Polka King, while helping him rediscover his love for the instrument. Fighting a bout of frostbite after the Battle of the Bulge, Yankovic rehabilitated himself through "accordion physical therapy" in a military hospital, defeating a severe gangrene infection moments before he was to undergo amputation of all of his fingers.[74] During the war, Yankovic found an enthusiastic audience for the polka. The war, with millions of men absent from home and community, had created a surging demand for ethnic music, and Yankovic had returned home on leave several times, ready to fill that demand. While enlisted, he continued cutting records, fifty in all, for the new Continental Records Company, which was actively promoting ethnic music.

In the postwar era, as historians note, the polka's popularity surged. The jitterbug craze was winding down, and some performers evidently promoted their wholesome image of polka music in contradistinction to the jitterbug's unsavory youth culture image.

Indeed, while the polka world was dominated by the brassy, boisterous sound of "Dutchman" bands, SSP was finding its niche as an internationally popular polka style. In 1946, Yankovic badgered Columbia into reconsidering its earlier rejection of him and signed a contract. Yankovic suggested that his band record "Just Because," but Columbia wanted nothing to do with the song because the Sheldon Brothers had recorded it years before without success. Yankovic threw a temper tantrum, kicking over chairs and throwing sheet music around the room, but the record executives would not budge. He then offered that if he were allowed to record the song, he would buy the first ten thousand records himself, "because I know I can sell them."[75] He recorded the song in a Slovenian-style arrangement with banjo, accordion and drums. It sold over a million copies. His next big seller, "Blue Skirt Waltz" (1949), was adapted from a Bohemian (Czech) folk melody with Mitchell Parish's English lyrics. "Blue Skirt" seems to have been a best seller for about six months, turning out to be Columbia's second most popular record in 1949 after Gene Autry's "Rudolph the Red-Nosed Reindeer."

Indeed, having signed Yankovic and putting up with his temper tantrums, Columbia must have known that he could deliver on their expectations: to break the barrier between polka music and popular music and to create a "national polka star." In 1948, the major record labels promoted a national polka contest in Milwaukee. With over eight thousand spectators voting, Yankovic and His Yanks won by an eight-to-one margin. They also won the next two years, after which the competition ended. Frankie Yankovic and His Yanks even won a "Battle of the Bands" against Duke Ellington in Milwaukee and hosted polka variety shows airing in Cleveland, Chicago, and Buffalo during the early 1960s. The "heyday" period of his career lasted twenty years, with his move to RCA in 1968 before recording a succession of albums on smaller labels such as Cleveland International. In 1986, the Academy of Recording Arts and Sciences awarded Yankovic's album *70 Years of Hits* the first Grammy in the polka category. Weird Al Yankovic (no relation) immortalized the occasion with a medley of songs that were nominated for the Grammy that year, performed as polka-style duets by the accordion-playing Yankovics (no relation). In 1986, Frankie Yankovic was the first artist selected for induction in the Polka Hall of Fame (of the American Slovenian Polka Foundation), an organization devoted to promoting Slovenian-style polka.

Yankovic's rise to stardom did not hinge on astonishing virtuosity—he himself admitted he was not as "good" a player as Myron Floren—but in his ability to deliver SSP in the way he knew his audience loved to hear it, but with new stylistic twists.[76] Perhaps Columbia's earlier rejection of him was instructive for him. He made up his mind never to limit himself to the Slovenian or Yugoslavian audience but to play for the public in general, particularly, as he stated, for the working-class audience. Indeed, Yankovic himself had worked at a variety of blue collar jobs: as patternmaker in a foundry and at the Fisher plant in Collinwood. On jumpstarting his postwar playing career, this loyal son of Slovenia attempted to find interethnic common denominators, and he had a great deal of support in his efforts. While he was stationed in Europe, his sergeant (Sidney Mills) offered him a significant family connection—the famous Mills Publishing House was owned by Mills's uncle. The younger Mills persuaded Yankovic that he could reach a much wider audience by associating with his uncle's firm. Yankovic did so quickly, helping to become a popular American accordionist, not just an ethnic accordionist and bandleader. His music helped to symbolize not just immigrant working-class culture in its old-country purity but also a progressive, modernizing strain that would have appealed to Slovenes and other European working-class immigrants, like Yankovic's father, who had experienced the shift from rural to urban culture.

After scoring his first two major hits, "Blue Skirt" and "Just Because," Yankovic brought the Yanks to Hollywood in the early 1950s, where they recorded with Doris Day and made several short films for Universal showcasing their stage act. He had his own television show, *The Yankovic Hour* in Cleveland, which later had to be renamed *Polka Varieties* and feature a variety of polka bands and styles, owing to his constant absence from the show (he toured most days of the year). He also broadcast a television show in Chicago and Buffalo, *The Frankie Yankovic Show: America's Polka King.* Continuing with Columbia through the 1950s and 1960s, he recorded some of the polka genre's most iconic songs: "Beer Barrel Polka," "Who Stole the Kishka?" "Too Fat Polka," and "In Heaven There Is No Beer." He recorded over two hundred songs, and they sold in the millions.[77]

He and his colleagues were hardly sectarian in their choices of repertoire. Here is how Yankovic, Pecon, and Trolli, worked together to "Americanize" Slovenian music: "We would take old Slovenian folk tunes that had been around hundreds of years, put new piano and accordion arrangements to them, and add American titles."[78] This composing trio exploited Trolli's Italian background in composing the polka "Tic Tic Ta," and from the German repertoire they obtained "Rosalinda Waltz." Mills Publishing Company published the first of these ethnic crossover pieces by Yankovic in 1947.

In order to become a prominent polka artist in a genre dominated by the boisterous, brassy "Dutchman" style, Yankovic had to build a fuller band sound. In 1946, he abandoned his acoustic sound and added a Solovox electric organ, along with a second accordionist—Johnny Pecon. Smodic notes that it was a "first" in Slovenian music for two accordionists to play in the same band."[79] (That configuration had been common in other accordion-based ethnic styles, such as Valtaro.)

It was an important moment in Yankovic's career when Milwaukee had a major polka festival in 1948, sponsored by the major record companies, at which Yankovic was crowned "Polka King." The occasion prompted the press not only to heap praise on Yankovic—who was between two chart-topping hits— but also to observe that the general polka fad might be supplanting previous teenage dance fads with a more wholesome revival of a tradition that appealed across cultures and generations.[80] "Teenagers are jumping from jitterbugging to polka dancing," one Milwaukee reporter observed. "This latest trend of the younger set was inescapable at the Auditorium when . . . students of the 'jump and toss' school of dance gathered to crown the Polka King."[81] If the reporter was correct in his observation that dancing schools were "swamped by requests from high school kids who want polka lessons," it stands to reason that accordion schools in Milwaukee (and other midwestern cities) experienced a surge in enrollees. It is safer to assume that the decline of the accordion discussed in chapter 3 must have proceeded more slowly in places like Milwaukee, with its strong core audience of Slovenian, Polish, and Slavic ethnics. Perhaps this is why *Cleveland Plain Dealer* columnist Dick Feagler recalled in his tribute to Frankie Yankovic that when he was a boy the accordion was not the scorned instrument it had become later, in the 1960s. He recalled that half the boys in his neighborhood, including himself, took accordion lessons. Feagler indicated he preferred the polka to the anger and fury of contemporary rock music.[82] Indeed, there is plenty of evidence to suggest that Yankovic played an important role in contributing to the wider popularity of polka music and elevating a formerly maligned lower-class dance.

In 1962, perhaps aware of changing teenaged musical tastes and the limits of polka's popularity with younger audiences, Yankovic hired the talented thirteen-year-old Chicago accordionist Joey Miskulin to perform regularly with the band. It proved a wise decision for Yankovic, who continued to exude a strong presence as a vocalist while conceding the spotlight to his younger colleague. In a performance of the song "Hoop De Do Polka," Yankovic all but congratulates himself for his choice of Miskulin: "there's a young accordionist stretching out a mile . . . we'll all smile, that's the style."[83] (After Yankovic's death, Miskulin went on to enjoy a successful career as an accordionist, founding a country and western band, Riders in the Sky, based in Nashville.)

How did Yankovic's popularity and his musical choices shape accordion culture in and beyond the "polka belt"? There is scanty but fascinating evidence to suggest that Yankovic may have inadvertently contributed to the decline of the button box among his own people while contributing to the popularity of the piano accordion. He never promoted the accordion, taught the accordion formally, or developed accordion pedagogy, nor did he make appearances at accordion conventions. The accordion world responded by ignoring him. Perhaps Yankovic, who refused to style himself as a virtuoso, was never able to earn the esteem of the "accordion old guard." Nor was he intent on becoming the Slovenian Lawrence Welk, and he was evidently not interested in Dixieland or sweet-style "society" jazz band arrangements. However, of all the ethnic musicians discussed in this volume, Yankovic was unique in his ability to transform ethnic music into unique arrangements and performances that would appeal to *all* Americans.

The musical activities of Turpeinen, Brugnoli, and Yankovic express a wide range of aspirations surrounding the accordion. Turpeinen and Yankovic wished to make national careers. Brugnoli aspired to remain settled in Manhattan, at the center of an Italian community. All three careers suggest, succinctly, the cultural tensions and possibilities underlying the accordion: the accordionist as a bearer of both modernity and local cultural traditions. Neither Turpeinen, Brugnoli, nor Yankovic appear to have located themselves at either extreme, but available evidence suggests that they all felt the tension on some level. It is clear that in all three cases, the accordion was the touchstone both of culture's authentic roots and its destination. The piano accordion was the key to perceiving one's distinct cultural identity, to energizing one's motivation as tradition bearer, and to preservation and rejuvenation.

CHAPTER FIVE

NEW MAIN SQUEEZE

*Repositioning the Accordion
in the Music Industry*

ANYONE WHO READ MAGAZINES and newspapers or heard popular music on the radio and television in the 1990s might have noted a new wave of fascination with the accordion. *Keyboard* was among the first observers of the phenomenon, reporting that "against all odds, despite the image problems and all the high-tech hoopla, the accordion is back."[1] There had been dramatic surges earlier, in the 1930s and 1940s, peaking in 1955 when accordion sales reached their height. The midcentury accordion craze was precipitated by causes different from those of the 1990s, fueled primarily by postwar prosperity and the educational and cultural aspirations of returning GIs; lingering associations with victory, patriotism, and success; and an early backlash against rock 'n' roll. It centered mainly on the accordion industrial complex, reaffirming its hegemonic values and musical aesthetics. Although the accordion continued to be the primary featured instrument in polka and a number of American ethnic musical styles, an unbridgeable divide remained between the accordion industrial complex and the proponents of the accordion-based ethnic styles discussed in chapter 5. The accordion revival of the 1980s and 1990s, if it can be called that, was more complex and more abstract, consisting of several interrelated social and cultural developments: the increasing presence of the instrument in popular and world music styles, a desire for acoustic sounds, and the proliferation of accordions and accordionists on television and the Internet.

In the 1990s and continuing today, more overtly self-conscious uses of the piano accordion have appeared, such as Those Darn Accordions, John Linnell of the alternative rock band They Might Be Giants, and Weird Al Yankovic, grimacing like a deranged rock 'n' roll idol on the cover of *Keyboard* in 1987.[2] Weird Al (no relation to Frankie Yankovic the Polka King) and his flat, inexpressive style of accordion playing subverted this listener's expectations of exaggerated virtuosity ("accordions can rock, too!") or deliberately bad playing ("see how schlocky!"). What is Weird Al doing to/with the accordion? The answer to this question offers much insight into this chapter's discussion, raising key moral and aesthetic issues. The accordion is present not as an object of parody but as the subject—an accomplice to Weird Al's explicit attacks on the popular music industry's banality and endless repetitions of mediocre musical formulae (note the song title "It's Just Billy Joel to Me"). That such charges were once leveled against accordionists is an ironic twist that would have been, for many accordionists in the 1980s, hard to miss. From the perspective of accordionists, Weird Al's rise to fame constitutes both a liability and an asset.

That the accordion's new presence in popular culture was documented by the media and on websites makes it unique in the music world. After *Keyboard* heralded the return of the accordion in 1987 (preceded by an earlier "squeezebox update" in various Gannett papers) came a wave of articles in the mainstream press and a broadcast on National Public Radio stations that covered the accordion revival (see table 5.1).

Table 5.1 lists only some of the many articles that appeared on websites, local radio broadcasts, television spots, and alternative weeklies such as the *New Times Los Angeles*.[3] Also noteworthy are the scores of profiles of accordion performers, coverage of AAA conventions and accordion festivals, and hundreds of news spots about Accordion Awareness Month (June; discussed in chapter 6). All these items give evidence of the accordion's wider exposure in the 1990s and 2000s in the mass media. While press coverage of the accordion movement seemed to decline in the first decade of the new century, the accordion players and industry players continued to document the "revival" and evidence of a critical mass of accordionists. Long after the ripple of media coverage died down, collectors and enthusiasts continued to track accordion sightings in the industry. The blog letspolka.com tracked accordionists and accordion players in the industry. The Dutch blogger Jeroen Nijhof's attempt to collect and document bands in every style and genre that make use of accordionists and accordion sounds is a remarkable and unique accomplishment and labor of love, one that has enriched this book. Some observers marked the accordion's steadily escalating presence in rock music from as early as 1967. In an article for *Music Trades*, Faithe Deffner, the vice president of Deffner Affiliates (the accordion manufacturing company and

Table 5.1: Accordion Articles

Date	Title	Publication
1980 (?)	Squeeze Box Update	Gannett Newspaper Syndicate's Sunday Magazine (reprinted in *Accord* 1 (4–5) (1979–1980), 26–29
1996 (?)	Un-hip, Now Hip: Accordions Coming Baaack [*sic*]	Undated clipping from *Kansas City Star* (and other Knight-Ridder newspapers), WOA
September 2, 1996	Some Attention and Respect for the Humble Accordion	*New York Times*
November 8, 1997	National Accordion Day	*All Things Considered,* National Public Radio broadcast
December 16, 1988	The Big Squeeze	*Wall Street Journal*
August 1990	Guido's Revenge	*GQ* "Man at His Best" feature
October 31, 1990	Re-evaluating the Accordion	*Baltimore Sun*
April 8, 1995	Accordions Return from Obscurity	*Baltimore Sun*
January 3, 1998	Fresh Squeezed: The Accordion Is Cool Again	*Boston Globe*
Aug. 27, 1999	Squeeze Boxes with Attitude Come Screaming into the '90s	*San Francisco Chronicle*
August 24, 2001	Yes! Accordions! The Squeeze Box Is Making a Comeback in the East Bay	*San Francisco Chronicle*
July 13, 2003	Is the Accordion Making a Hipster Comeback?	National Public Radio
September 19, 2005	Accordion Cool: Once Ridiculed Squeezebox Finding New Audiences	*Albany (NY) Times-Union*
June 9, 2006	Ready, Set, Accordion!	*USA Today*
October 23, 2006	Can Accordions Be Cool?	*USA Today*

makers of the Titano and Pancordion instruments), predicted that despite the industry's failure to promote the accordion to the general public over the previous few decades, the instrument would gain a wider following, claiming that the "do-all instrument has arrived."[4] As if to fulfill Deffner's prophecy twenty years later, Maddalena Belfiore, a New Jersey accordion teacher and officer in the International Confederation of Accordionists, told a *New York Times* interviewer in 1988: "The young people are beginning to talk accordion again. . . . Since the Talking Heads started pushing the accordion, they see the time has come to switch." (The Talking Heads' influence will be discussed later.) Deffner also noted the accordion's ubiquity in television commercials and film scores. "In numerous radio and television advertisements, the accordion has become a prominent voice enhancing the sales of a wide variety of products and services. Accordions seem to be fanning the bellows of all media," Deffner has said.[5] Indeed, accordion music has been used to create a wide range of effects in television commercials: from a Volkswagen ad featuring romantic accordion music in the background, to Northwest Airlines' "Now's the time to 'squeeze' in fall travel" campaign featuring a humorous photo of Those Darn Accordions, San Francisco's accordion band.[6] In 1997, an independent list maker documented over a dozen "accordion sightings" in television, radio, and direct-mail advertising for a wide variety of consumer products and services, most of them conveying the idea of luxury, sophistication, and European culture, but some, like Three Musketeers candy, catering to a more populist image of their product (see table 5.2).[7]

What insights can be drawn from these observations? Weighing in at a moment when the accordion's status was ambiguous, observers of the accordion revival offered a new perspective on a musical scene that was changing rapidly in the 1990s: hopefulness, an excitement about the future, a fascination with the exotic musical styles emerging on the scene, embrace of the unconventional, and resistance against dominant trends and tastes in the mainstream popular music industry. These themes, I would argue, define the careers of the accordion artists and projects featured in this chapter: Carl Finch and Brave Combo; Guy Klucevsek and Polkas from the Fringe; and John Linnell and They Might Be Giants. In addition, I link each of these artists to three main routes by which the accordion registered in the 1980s, 1990s, and today. Carl Finch's success is tied to the world music phenomenon and the resurgence of interest in traditional ethnic styles. Even before *Billboard* created the World Music category in the 1990s, there was a veritable explosion of this category of music in the 1980s. In a book by an ethnomusicologist, this issue is subject to

Table 5.2: Advertisements Featuring the Accordion, 1990s

Medium	Product advertised	Comments
Television	Folger's French Roast Coffee	Accordion music, aired 1996–1997
Television	Home Box Office Network	Accordion and yodeling
Television	Hollywood Fashion Magazine	Accordion playing for Paris styles
Television	Kraft Parmesan Cheese	"Cheesy" accordion music played by Guy Klucevsek
Television	Mitsubishi	Cars seen, accordions heard
Television	Plymouth	1997 coupe, accordions heard
Television	Soft Scrub household cleanser	Accordion heard
Television	Sprint	Accordion heard—"Germany" segment
Television	Thomasville Furniture	Accordion
Television	Three Musketeers candy bar	Accordion heard
Direct mail	AT&T	Enclosure featured drawing of accordion, mentioned accordion band

close scrutiny. But some of these styles, particularly polka, had been alive and thriving since the 1950s, although primarily known to regional audiences and ethnic-radio listeners. But for many new aficionados in New York, Chicago, and San Francisco, this music was local no more. This section will examine the work of Carl Finch of Brave Combo as a case study in crosscultural polka.

The accordion's visibility in the world music scene attracted the interest of artists in the rock scene—first, in the alternative bands, followed by greater visibility thanks to the program *MTV Unplugged*, which featured a variety of artists playing acoustic instruments, including Sheryl Crow singing her poignant ballad "Are You Strong Enough to Be My Man?" while accompanying herself on the piano accordion.[8] Bruce Springsteen, John Mellencamp, and other mainstream rock 'n' roll artists featured accordions in their bands—some because they preferred the sound of the accordion to the electronically generated sounds of the Hammond B-3 or the synthesizer and others because they played the instrument as kids. In this chapter, I will discuss John Linnell's unconventional route to the accordion, why he chose to feature an accordion in his rock band, and how this choice was pivotal to his transition from the world of alternative rock to mainstream rock.

A third route by which the accordion reappeared is the contemporary and avant-garde musical scene. Although fewer people know the works of Guy Klucevsek, his projects are, of those discussed in this chapter, the most ambitious in their scope and their potential to expand the possibilities of the accordion in the contemporary music world.

All of these uses of the instrument provide a counterpoint to my discussion of "crossover" accordionists in chapter 4. That chapter introduced accordionists who attempted to reach broader audiences while retaining what they considered to be their core musical ethos, that is, Slovenian, Finnish, and Italian-American traditional music. While the crossover artists seem to have capitalized on postwar nostalgia and 1950s constructions of ethnicity, the artists discussed in this chapter are responding to subtler forces of musical hybridization and globalization that infiltrated the Western musical scene in the 1980s and 1990s.

In the 1950s, Flaco Jimenez, who learned the three-row diatonic button accordion from his father, Santiago Jimenez, Sr., was among San Antonio's most admired figures in conjunto, an accordion-based genre of instrumental music and song associated with working-class cantinas in the Texas Mexican borderlands. As a teenaged fan of Elvis Presley, Jimenez was aware that "there was something out there I didn't know."[9] His first chance to explore the vocabulary and syntax of rock and jazz came when his fellow Texan Doug Sahm recruited him to play alongside Bob Dylan, Dr. John, and himself. Shortly thereafter, Jimenez met Ry Cooder, a musician who had spent his career uncovering and reinterpreting "lost" musical cultures, and tutored Cooder in the diatonic button box. Jimenez has since performed with the Rolling Stones and Dwight Yoakum, earning five Grammys. Jimenez is proud of his rise from humble roots to international stardom, but more important, he has realized his dream to "share cultures" and bring conjunto music beyond its regional boundaries. "Let's make a big fiesta!" he told an interviewer with characteristic spontaneity. "Let's make jamming things between our cultures."[10]

Stanley "Buckwheat" Dural, born in Lafayette, Louisiana, was the son of a farmer who played traditional Creole button box. But it was the organ, not the accordion, that captivated young Buckwheat. Zydeco music, a local music of the bayou region that evolved from Cajun, Afro-Caribbean, and Afro-American traditions, was seen as too "country" in Lafayette.[11] Local youth gravitated toward the popular music they heard on the radio. Dural's talent and ambition led him to become a successful keyboardist in local funk and R & B bands. But a 1978 gig with Clifton Chenier and the growing popularity of zydeco beyond the bayou region persuaded Buckwheat eventually to take up the accordion and form the Buckwheat Zydeco band, which made its debut in 1979. When he "returned" to the accordion, he did not choose his father's button box but the mightier piano accordion, which would allow him to play jazz and blues riffs. The band signed to Island Records, becoming the first zydeco act on a major label. In 1988, Eric Clapton invited Buckwheat Zydeco to open his tour, and he has since played in major music festivals, as well as the 1996 Summer Olympics in Atlanta.

In 1979, after forming a "polka rock band," Carl Finch, a musician from Denton, Texas, traded his guitar for an accordion. Listening to recordings of polkas in dozens of world music styles and instrumental configurations and teaching himself to play piano accordion, he recorded his first album, *Music for Squares*, in 1979. Unlike Frankie Yankovic and other polka artists who had focused on regional audiences in "polka centers," Finch, who grew up in Texarkana, Texas, positioned his music for audiences in Denton's alternative music scene. His band has received two Grammy awards in the polka category: for the albums *Polkasonic* (1999) and *Let's Kiss!* (2005).[12] Accounting for his success, he comments: "I found that everyone was open to polka if it was played by more conventional rock instruments in a more rock way, rather than traditional polka instruments."

Although they represent different influences and experiences, the careers of Buckwheat Zydeco, Flaco Jimenez, and Carl Finch help to reveal the conditions of the world music scene in the 1970s and 1980s. They worked under a variety of conditions, maintaining different ties and affinities, and their attitudes about their work as culture bearers are diverse. These accordionists, as well as the bands they founded, helped to shape perceptions of the accordion among popular music audiences. Their endeavors entwined them in a variety of social relationships that constructed the boundaries and possibilities of the accordion in mainstream popular music. To understand these boundaries, and to get beyond the media hype about the accordion in the 1990s, we need to explore the identities of some of these musicians and the ways they themselves adapted their own practices to the demands and structures imposed by the industry. What were the conditions under which they worked? What were their creative processes? How were their contributions perceived by others? Through such inquiries we can reveal some ways accordionists have found places in and around the increasingly global world music scene. As the following discussion shows, they were deliberate actors in a specific historical time rather than vague and shadowy remnants from the 1950s age of champagne music.

All three of these influential world music accordion artists' rise to success was conditional on changing tastes and sensibilities in the 1980s: the rise in popularity of world music, world beat, Afropop, klezmer, and Celtic. Offshoots of these genres included techno-tribal, trance, ambient, and new age. *Downbeat* coined the term "world music" in 1990. By 1991, the market share of world music was equal to that of classical music and jazz. In the same year the Grammy Awards created a "world music" category. An astonishing range of accordionists in different world music styles achieved public visibility, from the Gipsy Kings (Philippe Eidel and Antonio Rivas)—a group that produced *Billboard*'s best-selling world music album in 1995[13]—and Paul Simon's "Graceland" (Jonhjon Mkhalali and David Hidalgo).

The recording industry has made several attempts to capitalize on the "universal" appeal of the accordion by issuing compilations of accordion-based musical traditions around the world. The *Accordions That Shook the World* series of LPs, produced on the London-based label Ace, was distributed in the United States by Rounder in the late 1980s. The 1995 Ellipsis Arts three-CD compilation *Planet Squeezebox* juxtaposes performances of accordion-driven musical traditions from around the world with the work of contemporary accordion artists like Guy Klucevsek and Art Van Damme. This project demonstrates the producers' perceptions of the raw emotions expressed by the accordion and its (non-Western) practitioners. "Somewhere an immigrant may have stepped off the deck of a ship, holding his only link to home and heritage, the accordion," writes producer Michael Shapiro in the liner notes. It's a clever sell. These CDs promise (and deliver) authenticity and depth of feeling, as well as historical accuracy (the notes give a brief paragraph on each of the traditional music styles featured on the album). The very title *Planet Squeezebox* and the producers' mission to tell the story of how the accordion became a "respected member in the family of musical instruments" presents the instrument on an elevated, almost cosmic plane.

Space doesn't permit a discussion of all the projects, musicians, and artists who have made use of the accordion in their explorations of world music genres or the range of perspectives they reflect, from alienated insider to curious outsider. The political and legal implications of the interventions made by Western artists in world music traditions have been explored in greater depth by Tim Taylor, Simon Frith, Louise Meintjes, and other scholars.[14] In this section, I want to focus on just one musician and band, Carl Finch and Brave Combo. Finch has pursued a radically different musical path that helps to delineate a new range of musical practices available through the accordion, and he speaks in an articulate and heartfelt way about learning to become an accordionist and to master the polka. Finch has attempted to explore the instrument's function in various styles of music—the accordion as instrument of musical fusion—while preserving traditional ethnic styles of accordion playing.

Formed in 1978 in Denton, Texas, Brave Combo—Carl Finch, (accordion and guitar), Jeffrey Barnes (guitar, reeds, and woodwinds), Danny O'Brien (brass instruments), Little Jack Melody (bass guitar), and Arjuna Contreras (drums) is one of the most adventuresome polka bands of the last thirty years, and Finch is one of America's most visible and groundbreaking accordion players. Thanks to Barnes, a multi-instrumentalist, the band's instrumentation, unconventional for polka, juxtaposes the traditional textures of the accordion, brass instruments, and guitar with pennywhistle, harmonica, and flugelhorn. Their catalog of over twenty recordings features Latin American dance genres (cumbia, conjunto, merengue, and cha-cha), zydeco, blues, opera and the classics, and pop tunes. Sporting wild costumes and hats, the quintet has appeared at venues as wide-ranging as punk rock clubs, folk festivals, and Lincoln Center's Midsummer Night's Swing dance festival in New York City.

Brave Combo brought about unique visibility for the accordion on both large and small screens. Their music can be heard (and seen) in films such as *Fools Rush In*, *Envy*, *The Personals*, and David Byrne's *True Stories*, which features Brave Combo, along with conjunto artist Esteban Jordan, playing a memorable part in constructing a kaleidoscope of folksy Texan curiosities, which include accordions playing an important part in a local town's "Celebration of Specialness." Brave Combo even appeared (animated) on *The Simpsons* as Springfield's Oktoberfest band. They have contributed music for the ABC series *Ugly Betty* and Fox Television's *Bakersfield P.D.* They have also scored music for the ESPN and the Big Ten Network.

It might be fair to say that Brave Combo plays a significant role in the contemporary accordion world not because they are on the front lines advocating for the instrument or any particular musical genres with which they are associated but because of their willingness to present themselves as a new kind of polka band. This strategy may have helped them find new admirers for the accordion among contemporary audiences as well as the genre's traditional fans. Carl Finch's experimentations with the accordion, as well, were intended to extend the repertoire and practices of mainstream polka performance. "I was turned on by polka in the 1970s, because it represented a whole new world of music," he has said. "Nothing related to it anywhere. I wanted to mess around with the idea of polka, a style of music that was the butt of jokes and rarely taken seriously in the mainstream. I wanted to examine why there was such a prejudice against this music. I thought putting together a rock band to play polkas might be an interesting experiment."[15] Their departures from traditional polka are worth noting. Their first four albums, recorded on the self-owned Red Dot label, feature "old school" polkas (i.e., "Julida Polka" and "Clarinet Polka," student staples found in many of the older accordion method books such as Willard Palmer's) as well as the polka combined with other ethnic styles and genres from tango, conjunto, cha-cha, bluegrass, klezmer, and a wide variety of Balkan dance forms.[16] A typical strategy for Brave Combo is to reinterpret highly familiar popular songs in unusual ways. For example, the Italian popular song "Return to Sorrento" (another staple from the student accordion repertoire), originally written as a waltz in moderate tempo, is presented in a fast-paced, heavily syncopated soca rhythm.[17] Also noteworthy about the quintet is not just their repertoire and instrumentation but also the many artists who appear with them on recordings and in live performance, from Tiny Tim to Tex-Mex/conjunto artists David Hidalgo and Mingo Saldivar to the children's folk duo Cathy Fink and Marcy Marxer.

Finch, whose home town of Texarkana, Texas, is distant from the midwestern and Texan centers of polka, said that he was attracted to polka music for many years. "I started buying records in 1978 or 1979, when distributors were dumping their polka vinyl," he recalled. He was delighted to discover a small record store in Denton that had been "inundated." "East Coast, Midwest, Slovenian, and Polish style—I didn't realize how much variety there was. So I started force-feeding myself polka for the next three years." He began to play everything he heard, trading his Fender guitar for a green 42-bass Weltmeister piano accordion. What Finch tried to avoid in his independent study program was anything evoking "mainstream" polka of the kind popularized by Lawrence Welk and Myron Floren. "I always wanted to see, hear, and feel differently from what the media dictated. I felt that this was cool music, and it could work in lots of different ways," says Finch. He wanted to bring to polka a sound that it had "never had before."

Finch invested several years in perfecting his technique and reworking the band aesthetic to incorporate free-reed textures. He found himself on an ongoing quest for an approach to playing accordion that would express his personal vision for the band as well as capturing the flavor of polka and other traditional styles of music. He was intrigued by sounds and techniques that were idiomatic to the accordion, particularly the bellows shake and the "clacking" noises produced when keys are depressed on the accordion. As he watched players and attempted to emulate their technique, the Tex-Mex accordion players impressed him the most. Again, as he had done with polka, Finch capitalized on the marginal status of Tex-Mex music vis-à-vis the dominant Anglo musical tastes. "Some of the small distributors out of San Antonio were dumping their conjunto, Tejano, and norteno catalogs," he recalls. He also tuned into Tejano stations on AM radio. He reveled in the sounds and textures of conjunto accordion players such as Flaco and Santiago Jimenez, Mingo Saldivar, and Steve Jordan, all rooted in San Antonio's thriving conjunto scene. "There's really nothing like the accordion. You can do so much with the bellows—you can go from a whisper from a sharp attack with very little movement." The bellows technique on these instruments is quite distinct, as bellows changes produce different tones. This results in what some hear as a more dynamic, percussive, and choppier sound in performance. In addition, his experiments with Tex-Mex music were conducted at much higher volumes. "One thing about the accordion is how loud it is. You should never play accordion with anybody but loud musicians. There has to be a kind of punch." Of course, loudness is an iconic feature of punk rock music, whose audience Finch hoped to attract. Finch's observation that the accordion was "cool" in the punk crowd is worth further consideration, as both punk rock and a return to "folk sounds and styles" can be seen as responses to the crass materialism of the 1980s. "The folks who really supported us were into the anti-mainstream thing. When we played punk clubs, we were met with total acceptance. In 1979, the accordion was the symbol of defiance against the system. Anyone or anything considered geeky or nerdy was cool."[18]

Finch's discussion of Brave Combo's work and his development as an accordionist and practitioner of polka music indicate that his personal artistic vision was as important to him as cultural authenticity. By treating "polka" and "Tex-Mex" as raw material for his personal musical vision, Finch continues the practice of musical hybridization, a feature of the world music scene in the 1980s and 1990s. In so doing, Finch helped to shape the world music scene of the 1990s. Like his contemporaries Paul Simon, Ry Cooder, and Peter Gabriel, Finch migrated from rock 'n' roll to ethnic musical styles in an effort to reinvigorate his music and reach wider audiences. He perceives his project as a personal mission rather than an attempt to recreate an authentic style that would be recognizable to "insiders" of a particular cultural tradition. He is in complete control of the music he arranges and presents; he is at liberty to cull and combine different styles, repertoires, and sonic tidbits. Though the founding fathers of polka music whom Finch idealizes have a palpable presence in his music, it is more performer driven and idiosyncratic than anything I can think of in the polka world. His five intrepid band members have journeyed to the Lost Atlantis of polka and come back with some cool stuff, ethnographic goodies, and impressive moves in live performance—ideal for the antiestablishment, affluent, and cosmopolitan world music audience of the 1990s.

It is true that instances of Western musicians who were drawing on world music styles schooling themselves in ethnic musical styles—their own and other peoples—were common in the world music scene in the 1990s. Artists who were at the forefront of these practices included Johnny Clegg and Savuka, Sheila Chandra, Angelique Kidjo, the African-Belgian vocal group Zap Mama, and a wide range of North American klezmer, bluegrass, and Celtic acts.[19] What is special about Brave Combo is the way the quintet stage-manages the presentation of polka music by relying on marketing strategies in the popular music field, in which performers want to be rock stars, responding to the fact that polka music, after all, is not something to be "appropriated" or rescued; it is a living tradition, and (as Finch is aware) its primary exponents are idolized as "rock stars" by their own regional audiences.

Another unusual feature of Finch's career, one that may make him appear out of place in a book about the accordion, is his refusal to position himself as an exemplary player. Although he has played the accordion for twenty-nine years, Finch still speaks about his accordion pursuits as a kind of apprenticeship; throughout the course of our interview he reminded me that the accordion was his third instrument and he is not a highly skilled player, and he kept referring to other players whom he revered. One of Finch's collaborators, whom Finch reveres as an accordion virtuoso, is Guy Klucevsek.

GUY KLUCEVSEK

Like Finch, he has devoted his career to a variety of boundary-crossing musical experiments in and beyond the contemporary music world. However, Guy Klucevsek also presents himself as a new kind of accordionist who aims to change popular perceptions about the instrument and to completely transform, or perhaps deconstruct, its core musical repertoire, the polka.

Although this chapter has been concerned with the complex ways the accordion has been used musically and culturally in a context that blurs global and local styles, Klucevsek presents an even more complicated case study. Unlike Finch, Klucevsek describes himself as an accordionist from an early age; he chose the instrument and a program of classical accordion study to pursue from childhood. In the 1990s, while an active member of New York City's "downtown" experimental music scene, he began exploring diverse paths through the various styles and subgenres of polka I have mentioned so far. Klucevsek is a different kind of accordion virtuoso and composer, reaching out to audiences beyond the "uptown" world of avant-garde composers in New York City in which he has traveled. Nor does his music fit cleanly into polka or anything in the "world music" category I discuss here. His music has been powerfully driven by his fascination with the accordion and awareness of its marginal role in American music culture. He never felt "marginalized" as an accordionist, but his current discourse on his music shows affinity with the agendas of accordion advocates throughout the ages. The 1990s accordion revival clearly owes much to Klucevsek's music and ideas.

Klucevsek was born in 1942 in New York City. The impact of accordion culture came early; his choice of instrument was made largely as a result of hearing Dick Contino on Horace Heidt's *Original Youth Opportunity Program*, Ted Mack's *Amateur Hour*, and watching the *Lawrence Welk Show*. Guy learned popular standards from his first teacher, Joe Macko, who sold his father a 12-bass accordion when canvassing door-to-door. After his parents divorced in the early 1950s, Klucevsek was sent to live with his aunt and uncle in the Pennsylvania coal mining town of Springdale. There he studied accordion with Walter Grabowski, who owned and operated a studio. He received a solid education in music theory and musical appreciation as well as accordion technique. "From the beginning, my training with Grabowski was both highbrow and lowbrow," Klucevsek recalled. "I was learning transcriptions of opera overtures, piano and violin concerti, and solo piano pieces; but I was also playing novelty pieces like 'Dizzy Fingers,' 'Flight of the Bumble Bee,' and 'Carnival of Venice,' and polkas and waltzes by Frank Yankovic, the hero of my Slovenian-American community."[20] Apart from Yankovic, all this was standard fare for most accordion studios. But Grabowski was also determined that his talented student should explore the wide range of twentieth-century American and European composers whose had composed works commissioned by the AAA. "In the early 1960s, Grabowski introduced me to pieces by Paul Creston, Nicolas Flagello, Alexander Tcherepnin, Elie Siegmeister, and Henry Cowell. These pieces were written expressly for the accordion and they instantly felt and sounded natural on my instrument. And I was young enough to be open to the new vocabulary which these composers used."[21] Indeed, that these highly difficult, dense pieces felt "natural" for Klucevsek is a testament to his virtuosity, about which he remains modest.

Within his community of Slovenian coal miners, Klucevsek capitalized on the accordion's strong cultural roots. He formed a band called the Fascinations, made up of accordion, tenor sax, guitar, and drums, which played club dates and dances. Their repertoire consisted of instrumental versions of 1960s pop songs, jazz standards, and Slovenian-American polkas and waltzes. "I was transcribing tunes from the radio and records and began writing my own polkas, which became my introduction to the world of composition."[22]

In 1967, Grabowski introduced Klucevsek to the free-bass accordion, another remarkable feature of his accordion studio training. Few American accordion studios taught the free-bass, because the left-hand system of single notes and its four-octave range were seen as too demanding for the average student. As noted in chapter 3, the free-bass could be controversial with studio owners whose financial liquidity depended on regular sales of traditional Stradella piano accordions. But Klucevsek soon realized that the free-bass accordion had opened up a whole new world of music for him. "I was able to play Bach and Scarlatti pieces directly from the keyboard manuscripts, with no transcription involved. And modern composers were using the left-hand button board of the free bass as an equal melodic partner to the right-hand keyboard."[23] Klucevsek joined the teaching staff at Stanley Darrow's Acme Accordion School in Westmont, New Jersey. Darrow further expanded Klucevsek's horizons with literature for accordion by avant-garde Scandinavian composers Per Norgaard, Arne Nordheim, Ole Schmidt, Torbjorn Lundquist, and the recordings of Mogens Ellegaard, a chromatic accordion composer-performer whose works have been extremely influential on American classical accordionists. "It was from studying these scores and hearing these recordings that I learned about extended techniques for the accordion, which I incorporated into my composing and performing vocabulary," Klucevsek said.[24]

Klucevsek's postsecondary education consisted of studies at the University of Pittsburgh and California Institute of the Arts. Because the accordion was not seen as a classical instrument at either of these institutions, he majored in music theory and composition. Early on in his studies, he became heavily involved in electronic music making. "Working with electronic music for three years stressed to me the importance of timbre as a primary musical element and developed in me a love of drones," he said. In the early 1970s, Klucevsek decided to explore new ways of organizing music while contributing to the extended range of techniques and sounds of the accordion. "I began writing solo accordion pieces in which subtle harmonic shifts took place over long periods of time and in which tones would slowly crossfade between the left- and right-hand keyboards. Often times I used analog or digital delays to cover the changes of bellows, providing a continuum."[25]

In 1977, Klucevsek began collaborating with members of the Philadelphia-based contemporary music ensemble Relache. The group specialized in what Klucevsek calls "performer choice" pieces, compositions for classically trained performers that entail a significant amount of open-ended improvising based on a set of procedures prescribed by the composer. Relache collaborated with many younger American composers like Malcolm Goldstein, Daniel Goode, Thomas Albert and Mary Jane Leach, and Pauline Oliveros. Klucevsek composed in this style as well, composing *The Flying Pipe Organ of Xian* (1985) for Relache. This was an important period for Klucevsek in which he discovered new compositional processes involving the accordion.

In 1984, hearing John Zorn perform at a new music festival, Klucevsek offered his services as an accordionist and was invited to join Zorn's band Cobra. In it, Klucevsek found exactly what he was seeking: more elaborate and challenging procedures for free improvisation. His collaborators in Cobra included some of the most admired experimenters of New York's "downtown" new music scene: Bill Frisell, Elliott Sharp, Arto Lindsay, and Anthony Coleman. During Cobra's tour, Zorn agreed to write a solo accordion piece for Klucevsek, *Road Runner* (1986). This became the first of over fifty accordion pieces commissioned by Klucevsek for American composers.

In the 1980s, Klucevsek began to reassess his own musical style, which he describes as fitting squarely in the "minimalist mold," on encountering the Tex-Mex polkas of Flaco Jimenez and the Cajun two-steps of Nathan Abshire. He realized, with regret, that he had sorely neglected his own ethnic musical heritage. "Serious composition study at the college level put an extended halt to my life as the polka musician: getting the accordion (and myself) taken seriously in that environment meant avoiding music that reinforced accordion stereotypes," he recalled.[26] This "avoidance of polka" ended as Klucevsek realized that polka, like the avant-garde circles in which he traveled, had its own "fringe" elements, "culturally isolated communities in which the form had developed outside of the mainstream."

In the mid-1980s, he composed his first polka in twenty years, "The Grass, It Is Blue," for a modern dance score. "My thought was, if I can write a polka without giving up my avant-garde credentials, why don't I ask other composers to try to do the same?" he recalls. "The idea was to bring together two parts of my schizophrenic musical background: growing up in a Slovenian-American community, where I played polkas and waltzes for picnics, weddings, and club dates, while at the same time studying classical accordion."[27] Klucevsek then came up with the idea of commissioning different composers to write polkas, a project he called Polkas from the Fringe. As he invited composers of avant-garde, pop, and jazz music to participate, Klucevsek's only specifications for the project were to write a two- or three-minute piece in duple meter that could be played either solo or with the group he assembled for the project, Ain't Nothin' but a Polka Band. The quartet produced two recordings: *Polka Dots and Laser Beams* and *?Who Stole the Polka?,* both released in 1992, and toured the United States and Europe.

In these projects, Klucevsek has managed to create a repertoire that stretches the boundaries of the polka, an upbeat genre of music distinguished by simple melodies in a major key and upbeat duple meters suitable for lively social dancing. *Polka Dots* features polkas in a minor key, polkas played at breakneck thrash-metal speed, and one polka consisting entirely of sustained chords played in free rhythm (that is, with no meter apparent).

Ain't Nothin' but a Polka Band, the band for Guy Klucevsek's "Polka from the Fringe" project. Left to right: Bill Ruyle, drums, percussion; John King, electric guitar, electric violin; Guy Klucevsek, accordion, vocals; David Garland, vocals; Dave Hofstra, bass. (Photo by Michael Macioce)

The 1990s were productive years for Klucevsek. In 1992, he arranged material for another dance project, Passage North, creating a working band with accordion known as the Bantam Orchestra. "Accordion Misdemeanors," a folk-inspired suite, was written as a series of short pieces for the audiobook version of Annie Proulx's novel *Accordion Crimes*.[28] The plot evolves by following an accordion on its travels across America, as it finds itself passed from one immigrant community to another, and Klucevsek's compositions reflect the influences of these styles.

In 1995, Klucevsek performed on the *Planet Squeezebox* CD compilation—one of the few nonethnic, non–world music artists to do so. In 1996 he formed a new group, Accordion Tribe, consisting of himself and five other accordionists who represented different national and folk traditions. Its offshoot, Four Accordions of the Apocalypse (founded in 1998) featured Amy Denio, Pauline Oliveros, Alan Bern, and Klucevsek. Throughout his years as a performer, since the 1980s, Klucevsek has noted a sea change in attitudes toward the accordion. "The most amazing thing about being an accordionist for forty years has been to experience the dramatic shifts in public opinion about the instrument. I began playing in 1952, when the accordion was the most popular instrument in America. By the late fifties, however, the guitar had replaced the accordion in popularity. During the sixties and seventies the accordion was decidedly and totally out of fashion. Not only were fewer people playing it, but the future of the instrument seemed relegated to camp and nostalgia."[29] In 1988, the producers of the long-running children's program *Mister Rogers' Neighborhood* invited Klucevsek to perform on the show. He was asked to play serious repertoire in order to show children that the accordion could be used as a classical instrument. "For me, it was like coming full circle," he recalled. "I had a chance to play accordion on television and just maybe there would be one child out there watching for whom the accordion would spark an interest, and perhaps even a life, in music."[30]

In our interview, it was difficult to pin down Klucevsek's agenda as an accordionist and composer. Part of this may have been an effort to avoid labels or tying himself down to the mainstream accordion world. Klucevsek understandably wants to be considered a composer instead of an "accordionist" or "bandleader." To call Klucevsek an accordion composer would be to put him in a small, isolated niche (an accordion ghetto?). He wants new kinds of polkas and new music for the accordion (and other instruments), where aesthetics drives him as much as music that he feels showcases the power and range of his instrument. Aesthetics and politics appear to be inseparable, but gut instinct and personal choice trump these agendas. He notes, "I've continued playing the accordion through all these attitude adjustments. People often ask me why. I used to explain that I made the choice when I was a five-year-old, but that always made it sound like, had I been a sensible adult instead, I would have known better. Would I have made the decision knowing the negative image that came with the instrument? I don't know. I'm just thankful that I made the choice at an age when we act first and foremost on our instincts."[31]

As an accordionist, the politics of exclusion and inclusion positioned Klucevsek (at least initially) on the margins of the mainstream Euro-American musical world into which he sought entry. He knew that identifying himself as a composer was the best means available to him to define himself, and his weekend polka gigs were for money, not for career advancement or creative self-fulfillment. Yet it turned out to be the accordion and the polka that made new modes of consciousness possible for Klucevsek. He used the accordion to create new sounds and the polka to construct new musical forms. Further, although Klucevsek defines himself apart from the world music scene, he nonetheless participates in reinforcing some of its basic assumptions (the appeal of ethnic styles, including the polka) by choosing to make music that he believes the mainstream music world has ignored. He has not only returned, as he puts it, "full circle" to his own community's music but also helped to cultivate notions about the value of this music by encouraging other composers to write their own polkas. And, like Finch, he has succeeded in putting these "appropriations," and the accordion, to positive use. Nonetheless, the task of putting the accordion on the map of mainstream popular music was not a project for Finch or Klucevsek but a new generation of artists and bands that capitalized on the appeal of the accordion for younger listeners in the 1980s and 1990s.

"MACHINE OF JOY"

As American and British pop artists began exploring alternative sources of music in the 1960s and 1970s, the door cracked open for the accordion, which had been all but banished from the concert stage and the studio. No "accordion rock stars" were to make it through that crack, but some accordion advocates certainly had their hopes. More typically, the accordion was featured as a side instrument: examples include the Grateful Dead (Bruce Hornsby on keyboards and accordion), Hot Tuna (Pete Sears on keyboards and accordion), Bruce Springsteen (the E Street and the Sessions Bands, whose keyboardist-accordionist members included Danny Federici, Roy Bittan, and Charlie Giordano), and John Mellencamp's band (John Cascella on keyboards and accordion). Keyboard and guitar players who occasionally doubled on accordion include Billy Joel, Nils Lofgren, Sheryl Crow, and Pearl Jam's Eddie Vedder, who played accordion as a child. The Beatles famously made use of the accordion in "Rocky Raccoon" and of free-reed textures in many other songs, and Beatles enthusiasts are proud of the fact that John Lennon once played piano accordion. Other contemporary experimental artists who have made use of the accordion are David Byrne, Peter Gabriel, Tom Waits, alternative artists and rock bands such as REM, Cyndi Lauper, the Smithereens and U-2, singer-songwriters Suzzy Roche and Christine Lavin, and a wide range of jazz artists and vocalists such as Leslie Uggams, James Carter, Rebecca Pidgeon, Cynthia McCorkindale, and John Miller.

As anyone who lived through the 1980s can attest, the dominant musical textures of the new wave, punk, and techno era were electronic, not acoustic. So what did the accordion, a mechanical instrument, have to offer the musical world? Several observers have commented cogently on the tendency of listeners to ascribe value of different musical sounds that they might not have been able to hear, imposing gut-level, romantic ideas and feelings to these sounds. The accordion came to be seen as a "natural" and emotional choice in response to the overload of electronic and computer-generated sounds and the repetitive rhythms of punk and techno.

William Schimmel, an accordionist who worked in the popular song industry for a time, has said: "the accordion started to come back in the late 1970s, early 1980s. We just got overloaded with all the drum machines, and the bleeping and beeping. The accordion, you can hold it in your arms, it weeps, it sobs, it breathes."[32] Lest this statement reflect too much of Schimmel's bias as a player of the instrument, one can compare the 1996 article "I Have Seen the Future and It Is Squiggly" by art rock composer and producer David Byrne in which he offered an analysis of developments in the music world that point to the possibility of a slot for an the accordion in the avant-garde musical world.[33] Beneath Byrne's pseudo-ethnographic, satirical description of "Northern European" culture is what appears to be a critique of techno music. While the article is overreaching in its satirical intent, Byrne appears to be arguing for the use of mechanical instruments as a response to the current vogue for electronic music. While electronic instruments are limited in their emotional range, Byrne's "mechanically-produced" sounds, or acoustic instruments, can "laugh, sigh, and swoon"—because they are "machines of joy."[34]

Could the accordion be seen as a "machine of joy"—at least to ears that had been oversaturated with what Byrne refers to as "blips and beeps and mechanically produced sounds" for an entire decade? Although he does not mention free-reed instruments, Byrne's essay offers some interesting insights into the accordion's appeal in the contemporary music scene of the 1970s, 1980s, and 1990s. I parse these appeals as follows: the attraction of "natural" sounds, produced by physical movement, breath, or air; the preponderance of "smooth," lush textures, in contrast to the herky-jerky-ness of rhythms and beats in techno music; and the attraction to musical structures and effects not possible through the use of the computer. On the accordion, the player can heighten the percussive sounds that fingers and keys make when coming into contact (techniques noted by accordionist Carl Finch earlier in this chapter).

As a "corrective" or antidote to music produced by artificial means, the accordion might be seen as a kind of emotional, "irrational" choice. There is apparently a willful attraction to rhythms and styles that have no obvious connection to mainstream techno music, house, funk, and rock 'n' roll—or Western music in general (as will be discussed later). Indeed, Byrne followed through on his argument. He has used the accordion (and a wide range of unusual acoustic instruments) in his music since his earliest student art-rock experiments at the Rhode Island School of Design. Although he may not have "pushed" the accordion in the manner described by Maddalena Belfiore and her fellow accordion advocates, Byrne's collaborations with accordionists over the years, in his various CD and film projects, have earned him a lifelong honorary membership in the Texas Accordion Association, and provided many American accordionists with a special connection to "new wave" culture.

Especially noted by observers of accordion culture in the 1970s and 1980s were the mainstream bands that departed from the core instrumentation of the rock band—guitar, bass, and drums—to include free-reed textures. Arguably, Springsteen began the trend by featuring keyboardist-accordionist Danny Federici in his first studio album, *Greetings from Asbury Park* (1973). For Springsteen's second album, *The Wild, The Innocent, and the E Street Shuffle*, Federici recorded "Sandy," using the accordion to evoke the carnivalesque, transient pleasures of the Jersey shore. In this ballad about falling in love with a waitress Federici spins out lyrical accordion solos and accompaniment. Doubling on melody, the accordion softens and embellishes Springsteen's raspy voice, tempering the bitterness with sweetness. The result is a lyrical ballad full of pathos and feeling, mechanically produced swells and sighs.

Roy Bittan, also a keyboardist-accordionist, joined the E Street Band for the *Born to Run* recording. Bittan, explaining the accordion's new presence in recording studios in the 1980s, noted a shift away from electronic sounds in popular music. "There is a reaction away from the electronic stuff that everybody has been using. Synthesizer sounds. . . . a particular kind of sound. . . . becomes the latest trend, so you go along with that, although you know that in six months, everybody will get tired of it, and somebody will come out with an instrument that has newer sounds. In the long run, though, it all begins to sound very much the same. As that happens, the accordion starts to sound fresh again."[35]

Although Springsteen has presented his accordion sidemen in many concerts and recordings over the course of his thirty-year career, nowhere has he featured the instrument more prominently than in his "Seeger Sessions Band." This eighteen-piece acoustic band includes horns, violins, banjo, sousaphone, pennywhistle, and the pioneering accordion and keyboard work of New Yorker Charlie Giordano. Giordano may have done more to disseminate the accordion in the mainstream popular music industry than any other musician. A self-taught accordion player and multiinstrumentalist, Giordano's hundreds of recording studio credits include side work with Roseanne Cash, Pat Benatar, James Carter, Cyndi Lauper, Madeleine Peyroux, Dan Zanes, Marshall Crenshaw, and pit orchestra work for Broadway productions such as *Victor, Victoria*.[36] Giordano currently tours and records with Springsteen's E Street Band, playing accordion side by side with Roy Bittan.

Giordano has been widely admired for taking pains to absorb a variety of musical genres—country, blues, jazz, and pop—and adapt them to the principal artist's personal style. Although Giordano's success puts him in a privileged position, he does not set out to promote the accordion or himself as an accordion artist; he sees himself as a sideman, and his job is to make the accordion blend in as a band instrument, not to stand out.

The Seeger Sessions Band features traditional American songs and acoustic, "Pete-Seegerized" reworkings of Springsteen songs ("Atlantic City" and "Blinded by the Light.") According to Giordano, playing accordion allows him to incorporate several different ethnic styles of music into the band: zydeco, blues, and Tex-Mex, which Giordano states is most important to the "Sessions" sound. (Giordano is yet another piano accordionist who cites Flaco Jimenez as an important stylistic influence.)[37] Like Carl Finch, also influenced by Tex-Mex music, Giordano attempts to capture the dynamics and flavor of the diatonic button accordion and recreate them on a piano accordion (for this purpose, he plays a small instrument, the Hohner Student V). "I like the small Hohner because it has the same reeds and very similar sound to the diatonic accordions used for the Tex Mex style. On a smaller accordion, I

Bruce Springsteen's E Street Band onstage in Buffalo, New York, in 2009, featuring accordionists Roy Bittan and Charlie Giordano (right to left). (Photo by Danny Clinch)

find that you can be a little more expressive with single-note runs and solos, and use a little bit more technique."[38] Giordano recommends to his students that when attempting to play pieces in Tex-Mex style they use the musette switch, which evokes the "wetter" sound of the diatonic button boxes. For the syncopated, percussive "zydeco" sound (heard on the Seeger Sessions Band's performance of the spiritual "Mary Don't You Weep"), Giordano prefers a 120-bass Excelsior accordion, which can deliver a "dry" sound through switches like the Bandoneon (two lower reeds). The heavyweight piano accordion can thereby capture the sound and flavor of the Cajun button box. In all the styles he plays, Giordano emphasizes the use of the bellows and its importance in expressing emotional intensity.

Another rock icon, John Mellencamp, has given the accordion prominence in his band. His album *Lonesome Jubilee* (1987) is a set of musical portraits of downtrodden and disenfranchised Americans. It is scored with mandolin, acoustic guitar, and accordions, ostensibly, as some admiring critics have pointed out, to achieve a rustic, "heartland" flavor. Like Springsteen, Mellencamp has emphasized his working-class authenticity and his connections with his audience by gravitating to these acoustic textures. The lyrical, heartfelt accordion solos are played by John Cascella, who took lessons as a child in New Jersey. Cascella, who joined the band as a keyboardist, recalls Mellencamp telling him, "I want you to try something different. I want you to play accordion."[39] Cascella was astonished and a bit embarrassed at the idea of playing accordion in a rock 'n' roll band. But "when we started rehearsing, it was so much fun, because no boundaries had been set around it. I could try anything! Maybe someone could say they didn't like what I was playing, but no one could tell me that it was wrong." For Cascella, and perhaps Mellencamp, his explorations of the accordion signified creative freedom and escape from the limitations of the conventional rock 'n' roll band.

Beyond sound, physicality and the feeling of playing the instrument was a theme surfacing around the accordion in the age of synthesizers. Bittan comments, "when you play a synthesizer, there's a dissociation between player, instrument, and sound. There's something about the mechanical aspect of playing the accordion that I've always loved. That's why I never turned my back on it, even when it wasn't hip to be an accordionist." Indeed, the days when it was "unhip" to play an accordion were over by 1987. A case in point is the career of John Linnell and They Might Be Giants, the band that precipitated the rise of the accordion in the alternative rock movement.

This band began as a duo on the margins of popular culture (John Linnell, accordion and keyboards, and John Flansburgh, guitar) and rose to mainstream prominence in the 1990s. At the core of the band's ethic is a deeply ironic sensibility. Their crisp, sharp-edged tunes and witty commentary focus on topics that are deliberately atypical for rock songs, for example Mesopotamia, electricity, and James K. Polk, the eleventh president of the United States. Their musical style, indebted to punk-rock minimalism, is simple and catchy, delivered in the cheerful and bouncy style of nursery rhymes. Their self-promotion strategy was as innovative as their music. In the mid-1980s the duo created Dial-a-Song, a free answering-machine-based song service (these songs were later compiled and reissued on their CD *20 Years of Dial-a-Song*). They became the first independent band to have a music video in regular rotation on MTV and were signed by a major record company, Elektra, in the 1990s. Numerous articles in major daily newspapers and magazines such as *Rolling Stone* identified the band with "nerd appeal" and "geek chic," a 1990s sensibility and style that were seen as a refreshing alternative to the debauched (and clichéd) image of the conventional rock 'n' roll icon. According to their admiring chroniclers, They Might Be Giants' meteoric rise to fame was quite unexpected from a band that neither adhered to rock 'n' roll conventions nor aspired to mainstream success. One critic cited the band as "emblematic of the hardy, independent spirit of the alternative-rock movement," which they helped to establish.[40]

Though the duo became a full band in the early 1990s and other instruments are featured, the accordion is often the musical and visual focus of the band's live performances. Before incorporating the accordion, Linnell had never played one, nor did he bring conventional preconceptions to the instrument. Growing up in Boston, he knew no one who played or owned an accordion and had no exposure to the instrument "other than Lawrence Welk . . . until I was in my 20s." On a whim, he borrowed a friend's accordion for a street performance. "I discovered that it was the solution to every keyboard player's dilemma, which is that you can't move around onstage," he said. "Plus, it's much more direct for controlling the kinds of things that an organ player uses a volume pedal for. You have this enormous amount of direct dynamic control. It's like breathing."[41] Linnell was also intrigued by the accordion's potential to transcend its cultural baggage. "There's a style thing that's very appealing about the accordion," he said. "On the one hand, it's associated with schlock–adult popular music from the 1950s. But it also cuts through a lot of other cultures—European musics and various American subcultures."[42] Linnell has no intention to improve the image of the instrument or the repertoire with which it is traditionally associated. Unlike Finch, fighting the accordion's associations with Lawrence Welk, Linnell simply views the accordion's historical legacy as raw material for experimentation. "There's something to be gotten out of things like that," he said. "There's something worth mining, even with a cultural devil like Lawrence Welk. I'd say I probably owe as much to that as to any real European tradition."[43]

Linnell says that he spent a year getting acclimated to the accordion. "I've never completely gotten the chord and bass buttons down. I don't really use them in a live show, since we have our bass lines on tape."[44] He does not present himself as a virtuoso practitioner; he is more interested in using the instrument to develop the band's unique voice. They build their music around familiar pop music foundations, drawing on the accordion to provide elements of strangeness and wonder. "Number Three" starts with a pounding country beat and "old-timey" harmonies and moves through random saxophone fills in different tempos, unrelated to the main pulse. "Boat of Car" evokes Zappa and early psychedelic rock, with some Johnny Cash–like vocal fills intruding at odd moments. Other songs have straightforward pop and rock-song armatures but blossom into a profusion of postpunk, underground musical directions. In these songs, the accordion is a constant trope, providing full-bodied, swelling chords on "The Day," rhythmic ostinati on "She's An Angel," timbral variety on "32 Footsteps" and "Rabid Child," and a sweetly sentimental texture on "Hideaway Folk Family."

While other keyboards are played in "Folk Family," they do not sound as distinctive or stand out from the band texture in the way the accordion does. On the final chorus, a Casio synthesizer with backward-sounding tonal distortions is blended into the accordion, and the two instruments become a single sound. Linnell was delighted to discover the range of sonic effects he could get with the accordion, with a little help from electronic technology. For "When It Rains It Snows," Linnell used a sound mixer to lower the accordion bass notes one octave to create a growling, gravelly effect. On another occasion he recorded the accordion through a fuzz box. "That was a really fantastic sound, like a harmonica going into a cheap mike and being blasted through a Fender amp."[45] Linnell also made use of the nonpitched gasping sounds produced when the player pushes the bellows without pressing down keys (note of caution: moving the bellows without delivering air by pressing the keys can result in breakage). Yet it was the accordion's acoustic quality that appealed most to Linnell, so he exercised some restraint in his technological experiments. "If you electronically alter it too much, it moves very quickly into a synthesizer sound that doesn't even suggest accordion. That's why we've kept the accordion almost completely untreated on most of the recordings."[46] Since They Might Be Giants first achieved mainstream popularity, many other alternative bands have emerged with accordion: Gogol Bordello (Yuri Lemshev), Oingo Boingo (Doug Lacy; disbanded in 1995), The Bad Things ("Jimmy the Pickpocket"), and Flogging Molly (Matt Henly), a band that mixes traditional Irish and hard-core punk sources. Julian Hintz (aka Julz A), a touring performance artist from New York City, performs what he calls "Squeeze Rock Hip Hop." He records multiple accordion tracks with a drum machine running in the background, while rapping on the themes of difference and the difficulty of fitting in. Hintz believes he's the only artist to combine rap with the accordion. "It's definitely not your usual mixture of sounds, instrument, and voice. And most people don't believe it when I tell them. And sometimes even after they see it they don't believe it."[47]

Clearly, the accordion was proliferating quickly in ways accordionists of the previous generation could have hardly predicted. There is quite a bit of divergence in contemporary discussions of how to characterize this moment. I have been alluding to world music and musical styles identified as "global," "postmodern," and "global postmodern" by scholars, and I have sketched out some possible motivations for using the accordion to create new sound textures and musical styles. But what might these terms mean for our discussion of accordion culture in the 1980s and 1990s?

I consider the notion of "revival," prevalent in the ripple of media coverage about the accordion's return, partisan and problematic. Most of those using the term were invested financially and emotionally in the idea of revival. One could easily argue the opposite: the accordion continued to be the object of ridicule throughout the 1980s and 1990s. As evidence, one might point to the proliferation of accordion jokes through the Internet, Weird Al's performances, or the stereotypical images of the accordion that persisted in newspaper articles with titles like "Nothing Hurts Quite Like the Sharp Sting of a Polka."[48] Indeed, while Faithe Deffner observed that the media was "fanning the bellows" for the accordion, some were fanning the bellows of contempt. Guy Klucevsek likes to tell the story of how he was hired to play "Italian" or "ethnic"-sounding music on television commercials in the 1980s. "When they need something that sounded really square, they would use an accordion," he recalls. "I once did a commercial for Polly-O mozzarella cheese. They used me to do the music for their competitor's cheese, which was hard and dry and tasted bad."[49]

At the same time, among most of my informants the term "revival" surfaces as a universal theme in discussions about the accordion in the 1980s and 1990s. No other instrument has had such a dramatic fall from grace and return to popularity. In the drive toward more "authentic" acoustic sounds in the popular music industry of the 1980s and 1990s, few other instruments could symbolize the natural, nontechnological aspects of music making that a wide range of artists—from David Byrne to Bruce Springsteen to Paul Simon—wished to emphasize. Few other instruments seemed as "universal" as the accordion, integrated into so many folk and traditional world music styles that became recognized by the music industry in the 1980s and 1990s. Therefore, I embrace the idea of revival, but in a limited way. The accordion's appeal may have been seen as universal, but it was limited to western European and American artists and audiences. Nor was it equally powerful in all media markets. The musics for accordion discussed in this chapter are made by influential arbiters in the music industry who have had the power to play around with the accordion's meanings and references (or, in the case of They Might Be Giants and audiences too young to assign 1950s cultural baggage to the accordion, its complete nonreferentiality) in a way they find profitable. Record companies, producers, and high-profile artists like Paul Simon and Ry Cooder with large amounts of cultural capital are at liberty to play with "other" cultural identities, sounds, and instruments and concoct the kinds of pastiches that are characterized by postmodern music.

In this period, musicians, producers, and the press identified the accordion as "ethnic" and "hybridized"—in a positive way, as I observed of *Planet Squeezebox* and other accordion compilations. Some, like Carl Finch, saw the accordion as inspiration to explore new sounds and cultural projects. Others, particularly audiences in their twenties and thirties, may have seen the accordion as a more "authentic" sound and an alternative to techno music—as a National Public Radio reporter observed in 2003.[50] Few of these musicians were concerned with the cultural context of the music they undertook to master on the accordion. They were more interested in its potential to aid in their personal and musical growth and help them voice their dissatisfaction with the musical conventions of rock 'n' roll—most notably, the classic rock band formation anchored by a guitar as lead instrument. To add an accordion to the configuration of the "traditional" rock band and to challenge guitar hegemony is to confront certain expectations and assumptions underlying rock, from its electronic, volume-driven technology to its "masculine" image. The accordionists introduced in this chapter talk about playing the accordion in terms of style and affect, not just as an aesthetic exercise or a meaningless play of sounds. Cooder, Jimenez, Simon, Buckwheat Zydeco aimed to produce musical products that crossed boundaries. Simon claimed: "I work outside the mainstream."[51] The accordion is the musical signifier of the "other," demanding entry into the mainstream. Springsteen's and Mellencamp's efforts to include the accordion in different band configurations played to their working-class audiences, while sending the message that they were attempting something groundbreaking and important in their music.

While there is some value to the idea of revival, I would like to propose a broader perspective. We are dealing with an accordion "movement" with many phases and motivations, and I would be wary of characterizing it monolithically. I would summarize the revival this way: *different accordion sounds, genres, and styles coming together in new ways, all over the United States.* Viewing the accordion movement from the perspective of its users in different communities and locations, the motivations of its makers and audiences do not always line up. For example, Finch has claimed that his project was to create a different kind of polka music and expand the polka's appeal to rock 'n' roll audiences; in our interviews, he did not aspire to draw a following for his music among the German and Czech communities in rural Texas or the Slovenian communities of the Rust Belt. When I interviewed Finch for this book, our conversation focused on his high-profile appearances and recordings and how his band sees itself vis-à-vis the "world music scene." Yet according to the *Slavic and East European Journal,* Finch also has a growing fan base within the Czech-Texan community, particularly the younger generation. About Brave Combo, a Czech-American fan of Czech traditional music observed: "they're a cross between Czech dancing and American, they sort of mix the two together, they're hippie style, long hair, but they play fast-paced Czech music, and kids love it. I would say that 15 or 20 percent of younger people come strictly because of Brave Combo—but at least they bring in the Czech music to the younger kids and they're accepting it."[52] That a non-Czech, nontraditionalist polka band could contribute to cultural expressions seen as profoundly authentic is a phenomenon that could have only happened in the diverse, fragmented, and postmodern world of the 1980s and 1990s.

CONCLUSION

The musicians I've discussed in this chapter continue to find new sounds and new contexts for the accordion to project new musical selves, selves that find commonalities across different genres, from conjunto to rock. At the same time, they are also continuing some of the policies and practices of Western pop music and even the basic premises of accordion culture. Musicians who took up the accordion in the 1980s were implying that the metanarratives of rock and techno-music were dead or moribund, and rock 'n' roll musicians at midlife were discovering the potential of the accordion to invigorate their bands and provide emotional depth to their songs. As someone who lived through the Reagan era, I would characterize the many enthusiastic sightings of accordion-playing geeks, nerds, and squares as an implicit challenge to the consumeristic, materialistic, and conservative ethos of the period.

Just as dominant groups in the music industry made radical positions available through accordion sounds, it is important to acknowledge their debts to the "subordinate" groups that kept the accordion in circulation during the "dark ages" prior to its revival and continue to do so in the twenty-first century. It is also important that a discussion of the contemporary accordion include not only ethnic tradition bearers but also the diverse contingent of professional, lay, and aspiring accordionists it takes to shape a movement. That contingent is the subject of the next chapter.

CHAPTER SIX

OUT OF THE CLOSET

*Reimagining the Accordion
in American Popular Culture*

SOME OBSERVERS OF THE ACCORDION WORLD, and at least one prominent composer-accordionist (Pauline Oliveros) expressed optimism about the accordion in the 1980s and 1990s, a time when Americans began to unravel some of their assumptions about the accordion and the people who played it:

> The accordion is shedding its square image—this generation doesn't know who Lawrence Welk is. It's a new era.[1]

> The accordion has come out of the closet. In fact, it has practically broken down the door, and strange things are happening.[2]

> The accordion is a symbol of the outsider.[3]

Ten years into a new century, it is time to evaluate these observations and measure the inroads the accordion has made into the musical lives of Americans. I've described how, in the 1960s and 1970s, many Americans suddenly felt uncomfortable with the accordion and wished to shed its wholesome, mainstream, and white ethnic cultural baggage. As America moved into the era of disco, electronic music, and rap music, the dramatic changes in the musical environment sparked an interest in the accordion's acoustic sounds and physical dynamics and the idea of cultural difference it represented. These longings are not simply the products of nostalgia, the lure of the exotic and the ethnic, or a kind of "false consciousness." Frank Busso, the first observer of the three just quoted, may be right that "it's a new era," and we are right to consider that this transformation has real impact not only in the world of the AAA, over which he presides as president, but on a larger cultural stage. The challenge is to figure out what these changes might mean in the context of the twenty-first century.

In the previous chapter I discussed the accordion revival in terms of the mainstream music industry and the activities of prominent musicians and producers. But it takes more than institutions and money to make a movement; it takes a mass constituency that participates and benefits from the movement in tangible ways. In this chapter I discuss the cultural work the accordion has accomplished at the beginning of the twenty-first century. To understand some of these developments, I once again invoke the term "social capital." At the dawn of the new century, the social capital built by enthusiasts had completely deteriorated, and the accordion community had ebbed. One notices its effects in the scarcity of surviving accordion studios, schools, and bands and accordion-related businesses. The most serious consequences are reminiscent of the old parlor game "What's missing from this picture?" The accordion's weakened social capital is manifest in the activities that have vanished—community accordion bands, get-togethers with friends and neighbors, accordion performances, and shared pursuits surrounding the accordion. The hundreds of accordions that have been donated to the World of Accordions museum are visible evidence that thousands of people, and perhaps more, interrupted or neglected their studies of the accordion and destroyed the evidence of such pursuits. Naming this problem—"the decline of the accordion," "the death of the accordion," and the accordion as the butt of parody and satire—was an important first step toward confronting it, just as the climate of the 1980s allowed more Americans to hear and appreciate world music and to articulate what they found lacking in the mainstream musical offerings of the 1970s and 1980s.

Disentangling trends in a musical instrument's popularity from broader cultural and economic currents is a tough challenge. In a world irrevocably changed, a world in which people and markets are global, leisure time diminished, and entertainment electronic, how can there be a renewed interest in music making, or any one particular musical instrument? Like most social phenomena, this one has two faces—one institutional and national and one local. To use a metaphor of the market, we need to consider both the supply of opportunities for engagement with the accordion and the demand for those opportunities.

Just as their predecessors did in the golden age of the accordion, advocates felt a need to create new music for the accordion, new events and activities, and—in the Bay Area (San Francisco and Cotati, California)—new policy and civic actions to facilitate renewed personal and civic engagement with music. As

I shall explain in more detail, accordion players and advocates in many spheres of American life sought innovative ways to respond to the eroding appeal of the instrument they inherited from the previous generation. One strategy is self-deprecating humor: for example, the Closet Accordion Players of America (capa.org), an Internet group, was founded in 1991. While playing it tongue in cheek, the members of this group fortified their resolve to play the accordion and connect with other accordionists in what seems like a deliberate collective action. If I poke fun at myself, I make it harder for you to poke fun at me, and I make it harder for you to impose your idea of the accordion on me. Humor and irony are not sufficient to restore the accordion community on their own, but they are essential.

The challenge for accordionists is to restore not only the image of the instrument and its visibility in mainstream music and media but also a sense of community around it. I recognize the impossibility of there being a single "accordion community." Throughout my years attending accordion festivals and accordion conventions, I have noted increasingly intensive interchange among accordionists and accordion enthusiasts across different genres of music (polka, Tejano/conjunto, and zydeco) and across different subcategories of the accordion family: players of diatonic button box, concertina, and melodeon attending conventions that had once catered exclusively to piano accordionists. Accordion enthusiasts are optimistic that Americans can once again engage with the accordion, but in a different way from previous generations. The objective of many conventions now is to make their audiences aware of the diversity of playing styles and traditions and their cultural significance, and second, to spark interest in their fellow citizens in discovering the accordion and finding their own way of connecting with it that fits into their own interests, backgrounds, and playing abilities.

Figuring out in detail how people renewed their interest in the accordion and its varied repertoires is not a task for a single scholar or book. My intention in this chapter is more modest: to identify key facets of accordion culture and its challenges in the twenty-first century, by sketching two sites that illustrate the paths by which the American accordion is returning to popularity: the San Francisco Bay Area and the Houston metropolitan area. In San Francisco, the work of innovative performance artists and promoters was pivotal in setting the tone for the national accordion revival of the 1990s. Their immediate success, and the influence of the San Francisco accordion band Those Darn Accordions, provided momentum for the highly successful and popular Cotati Accordion Festival, which was widely copied in cities and towns across the nation. In contrast to San Francisco's experimental scene, Houston accordion advocates pursued their interest in the accordion through more traditional channels, accordion schools, clubs, and a major academic accordion program. Yet Houstonian accordion advocates and promoters are becoming aware of the potential of the city's ethnic populations to provide both musical inspiration and a significant customer base. I will discuss the way advocates in both cities have rebuilt the accordion's social capital through accordion schools, festivals, retailing, even the sphere of politics and government.

THOSE DARN ACCORDIONS AND THE ACCORDIONISTA RAIDS

On a balmy May evening in 1990, ten accordionists gathered outside an elegant restaurant in San Francisco's popular and heavily touristed North Beach neighborhood. With piano accordions strapped to their chests, fingers poised on keyboards, they awaited a signal from their leader, Tom Torriglia. "C'mon, we have to move quickly, before the maitre d' has time to throw us out." They marched in, storm-trooper style, encircling the tables of diners and blocking the waiters' access to the kitchen. Food service halted. Then the band let loose with "Roll out the Barrel," each accordionist extending his or her bellows to the fullest to produce maximum volume. "Thank you, ladies and gentlemen!" announced Torriglia. "Come join us this evening for a performance by Those Darn Accordions!" After announcing the particulars of the event, the accordionists filed out, ambling down Columbus Avenue in search of their next target with a television cameraman in tow.

The seemingly spontaneous performance was organized by members of the all-accordion rock band Those Darn Accordions. When the band first formed, in 1989, it was a thirteen-piece "novelty band" that intended to give a single appearance at a nightclub in San Francisco. Then Linda (Lou) Seakins, an early band member, generated interest in the idea that gave rise to a widespread interest in the band's activities in and beyond San Francisco. Her preoccupations were not artistic—her music concerned features that transcend barriers between the accordion and rock and highlight the crosscultural identity of the accordion. Seakins and the band produced a highly stylized music and mode of performance that has been widely imitated by other accordionists.

When she was in her twenties, Seakins had moved from her native Los Angeles to Austin, Texas, and found work as a waitress at the Broken Spoke, a legendary dance hall where country and western stars like George Strait, Ernest Tubb, and Asleep at the Wheel made regular appearances. Seakins was

In a publicity stunt orchestrated by their manager to promote an upcoming concert, Those Darn Accordions barges in on unsuspecting diners in the North Beach neighborhood of San Francisco. (Source: Getty Images)

well aware of the riches of country and western music, as well as the diverse musical scene she inhabited in Texas: rockabilly, alternative music, and various styles of polka. She was especially attracted to the lively sound and feel of the accordion in bands she heard at the Spoke, and she decided to master the instrument herself. During her years of practice, she struggled particularly with the right-hand manual because she is left-handed. In her spare hours—she worked part-time as a geologist—she also carefully studied Lawrence Welk's programs, still in syndication on public television. She admired his technical skill and his success in introducing the accordion to television viewers. But she realized that his smooth, tepid sound had been unpopular among her generation. She had grown up on rock, and Welk's music was too "cornball." But her experiences in the Austin music scene suggested that ethnic polka music could be just as fast and furious and uninhibited as rock.

Five years later, moving to the San Francisco Bay Area in 1989, Seakins found a way to make her case publicly. She had joined a country and western band called Thee Hellhounds (*sic*), which played an eclectic repertoire that ranged from Beatles songs to polka to the theme song from the 1950s television show *Perry Mason*. She decided to call up everyone she knew who played the accordion to play together at a nightclub concert. Another band member, Tom Torriglia, a music journalist who ran his own public relations business, determined that he could garner a great deal of media coverage with "accordionista raids." The restaurant owners apparently appreciated the publicity and began paying the group for return appearances. "Then Apple computers called and asked us to barge in on their early morning seminars," said Torriglia.

The band, now calling itself Those Darn Accordions, swelled to eighteen members, including an electric guitarist and drummer. All of the members had day jobs and little time to practice. Former band members I interviewed recall being poorly rehearsed and underprepared. Most of the band members appeared ill at ease onstage. "Everyone had to have sheet music on stands and the music would keep falling off. It was just not a band," recalls Paul Rogers, a current member. Early video footage supports this appraisal. Whether the band was performing rock covers in earnest or as parody depends on the perspective of the viewer/listener. In a performance of Rod Stewart's "Do Ya Think I'm Sexy?," seventy-four-year-old cable car mechanic and band member Clyde Forsman "sings" lead—or rather, chants the words in an inexpressive monotone, reading from note cards. The band plays the guitar and keyboard lines as Stewart wrote them, but they sound (and look) cluttered onstage. Entrance cues are often missed, and there is a lack of cohesion in the arrangement. No monitors are present onstage, and it often appears that the band members cannot hear each other or perhaps are not listening. Performances of Jimi Hendrix songs and other rock covers proceed in the same fashion, although the band sounds slightly more polished on their recordings. Yet the band is clearly enjoying its performance, egging on Forsman as he casts sultry looks at the audience.

The band continued to find engagements—not only in the San Francisco Bay Area, where Torriglia's publicity efforts had paid off in nightclub gigs—but at music festivals. They appeared at South by Southwest (Austin) and Summerfest (Milwaukee). But the band members were responsible for their own travel expenses, and the financial burden caused nearly half of the members to drop out. Although they did not release their first album until 1992, they made use of the Internet to garner numerous television and radio appearances in the 1990s. They have been the subject of profiles in the *New York Times*, the *San Francisco Examiner*, the *San Francisco Chronicle*, and *Stereo Review*. Most authors of these profiles and reviews seem to be "in on the joke," never taking the band to task for their sloppy musicianship and theatricalized performances. Yet this slew of admiring coverage of this band contributed to a national wave of "accordion revival" stories: "Band Wants to Tune Up Accordion's Status" (*Chicago Tribune*, November 24, 1989), "Raiders of the Night on a Mellifluous Mission (the *New York Times*, January 23, 1990) and "Those Darn Accordions Redeem a Ridiculed Instrument" (*San Francisco Chronicle*, February 3, 2005). These headlines echo some of the quasi-moralistic and spiritual themes sounded around the accordion in the 1990s and 2000: enhanced status, or even redemption, and the idea of the accordion as a "mission."

When Tom Torriglia felt that the accordionista raids had saturated the media, he explored a novel strategy for legitimizing the accordion and heightening its visibility—making the accordion the "official instrument of San Francisco."

SAN FRANCISCO'S OFFICIAL INSTRUMENT

A native of the Bay Area, Torriglia had played accordion on and off since his childhood. He had taken lessons at the Pezzolo Brothers' accordion school in San Francisco's Mission district and performed with his father at weddings and parties. Unlike other teenaged accordionists in the age of rock 'n' roll, he never experienced humiliation, and he looked for opportunities to show off his skill at school pep rallies and talent shows. He wanted others to share in his sense of pride and self-worth as an accordionist. Aware of the city's unique history as an accordion center, he proposed that San Francisco adopt the accordion as its official instrument. According to his research, the city had yet to bestow this distinction on any instrument.

A San Francisco city supervisor agreed to schedule the proposal on the city's official calendar, but she insisted that Torriglia first present a position paper making the case for his proposal. Torriglia then delivered a compelling twenty-page report that presented the history of the accordion in San Francisco since Guerrini opened the first factory there in the early 1900s. Torriglia's account of the process that followed is vivid, offering a unique snapshot of accordion culture and civic life in San Francisco:

> I called a press conference. I called all the old fucks from the accordion clubs and musician's union: "Come on down, we're having a rally in support of the accordion becoming the official instrument. We're going to play Italian songs and polkas. It'll be fun." I called every freakin' accordion player in the Bay Area—like forty or fifty of them. I sent out press releases. I had every medium there, radio, television, newspapers. *Time* called. Then CNN picked it up, and that was it.
>
> The city officials are ready to vote, but they have to have public comment. All these people show up: saying "I hate the accordion!" in front of the Board of Super-

visors. They bring up Lawrence Welk. Then the younger people: "the accordion is cool." People just went on and on. The board decided that it wasn't worthy of their time to vote on an issue like this. They moved it to some mock court, where people can give testimony, but it's nonbinding. I said, I don't want a mock court! I want legislation! Then I'm on the radio, talking about the accordion as the official instrument. I said I needed an attorney. The phones lit up. I got a lawyer to represent the "good" side of the accordion. The "bad" side had an attorney. There was a judge and an audience, and a whole contingent of them with kazoos. It was farcical. I got a ton of press. I didn't understand that, but just went with it.

The supervisors finally voted. One supervisor, Angela Alioto, was the daughter of the mayor, who plays the violin. Of course, she wanted the violin to be the official instrument! How, as an Italian, could you not vote for the accordion?[4] I presented all the evidence—the piano accordion was invented in San Francisco, and what more do you need to make the accordion the official instrument?[5]

The mayor didn't want to sign it. But after ninety days, it becomes law by default. But that is not the same as signing an endorsement. The spin I put on it was that the issue was too hot, too political, for the mayor. He ended up looking like a buffoon. And it did become law![6]

Indeed, Torriglia's campaign had ramifications beyond the next day's headlines. The forty musicians Torriglia recruited for the rally remained in contact, and they revived the San Francisco Accordion Club, which had been dormant for several decades. The same year, in cooperation with the management of the Anchorage Center Mall at Fisherman's Wharf, Torriglia launched San Francisco's Accordion Festival, featuring, in unique San Francisco style, a coed pageant in which women competed with men in drag for the title of "Ms. Accordion." The event later moved to the Cannery, where it continued for the next eight years, through 2006.

These events of the 1990s inspired Torriglia to continue seeking national media coverage for the accordion. As a former radio reporter, he knew that many disc jockeys relied on the events listed in the annual publication *Chase's Calendar of Events* to fill space between music and news items. He sent the publisher his suggestion for a new entry for the month of June: National Accordion Awareness Month. Then, early in the morning of June 1, 1990, Torriglia recalls, "my phone starts ringing like crazy. '*It's WJL in Upgrove, Indiana! How are you today? Hey, it's National Accordion Awareness Month! Could you play us a song?*' It's four A.M. on the West Coast! I had to play 'Beer Barrel Polka' in my sleep or get their name and call back." Torriglia continues to receive an annual barrage of inquiries from caffeinated deejays regarding the *Chase* entry, so he is armed for the calls with tidbits about celebrities who play the accordion ("Did you know Lucy Liu plays the accordion? Who wouldn't pick that up?!") and information on upcoming engagements for his current band, Bella Ciao, which specializes in "1950s Italiano song." On June 9, National Public Radio member stations aired an Accordion Awareness spot featuring Astor Piazzolla's music and Norwegian folk dances for accordion.[7] In addition, Torriglia is certain to mention appearances and recordings by local accordionists in the radio station's area of coverage, in order to attract attention to the diversity and scope of accordion culture beyond San Francisco.

As these stories illustrate, Torriglia and Those Darn Accordions were an important part of the process of renovating the accordion's image in the Bay Area—and beyond. The band learned—and demonstrated to others—which aspects of accordion culture captivated the imaginations of contemporary audiences and the media. Their ideas—and their music—spread rapidly in the climate of the 1990s and beyond. Functioning both as publicity and parody of San Francisco culture and the city's circus-like political spectacles, the "official instrument" campaign was effective in bringing public attention to the accordion's significance in San Francisco history. Torriglia has since begun investigating the possibility of having the city place markers at the sites of former accordion factory buildings on Columbus Avenue. However, innovation and change in accordion culture was not the work of any one band, citizens' group, or politician. It is the work of an entire community of musicians, listeners, and fans outside the official public spotlight.

Perhaps more significant to accordion culture than the accordion's status as "official instrument" of the city is its unofficial status as a key instrument in alternative rock bands in the Bay Area and the Pacific Northwest. As of 2009, at least a dozen bands in the Bay Area featured the accordion; each of them (judging from the colorful descriptions on their websites) appears to occupy a musical niche of their own invention.

After leaving Those Darn Accordions in the 1990s, Lou Seakins and her husband, a bass player, founded Polka Casserole, a band that incorporates many kinds of polka sounds: the Cleveland Slovenian style, the Chicago Polish style, and a style Seakins identifies as "San Franciscan": with tinges of jazz, country and western, rock, French musette, and Hollywood film music. Polka Casserole's international perspective on the polka and other types of ethnic music is shared by other bands with their own niches and with accordions at the forefront: Polkacide ("punk polka"), the Mad Maggies ("Celtic ska"), and Five Cent Coffee (a jug band specializing in the blues).

Maggie Martin of the Bay Area Celtic-ska-fusion band
Mad Maggies. (Photo by John Clayton)

Like Seakins, Maggie Martin is a seasoned musician with eclectic tastes who
has, in a self-conscious and tongue-in-cheek way, promoted the accordion (her
bio on Polkacide's website describes her as an "accordion rights activist).

A trained opera singer and former student of composition at Sonoma State
University, she studied classical Western and Indian vocal music and sang with
a Cajun band. Like other accordionists I have spoken with in this community,
Martin's attraction to the instrument occurred late in life, because she was not
exposed to it as a child. But in the Bay Area she had some unique opportunities

to deepen her appreciation for the instrument and to be part of a community of alternative musicians. "It was love at first sight, really. I went to the first Cotati Accordion Festival and shortly after that, I went to San Francisco and competed in the Ms. Accordion Pageant."[8] After joining Polkacide, the polka-punk band, Martin wished to found her own band with a more diversified repertoire: eastern European, Celtic, Balkan, and Tex-Mex.

Solo accordionists are a visible part of San Francisco's vibrant performance art scene. They have the opportunity not only to showcase their artistry at local alternative clubs and music venues but to perform for tourists as well. According to Tom Torriglia, the wineries in nearby Napa Valley hire accordionists (and sometimes small combos) to entice tourists and add European "flavor" to the wine-tasting experience. Also significant to the professional accordionist's income is the club date and corporate party (an early mainstay of Those Darn Accordions). Seakins promotes herself as a solo "artiste" who "can provide the perfect atmosphere for French, Italian, German and Eastern European-themed events."[9] Other solo artists making use of the accordion include Amber Lee Baker, Fannie Mae Farrell, Esmerelda Strange, who identifies herself as a "one-woman vaudeville accordion band," and Oakland-based Tara Linda, a Hohner-endorsed button accordionist, who describes her repertoire as "jazzy blues, Latin torch, and 'Tortilla Western.'"[10]

The West Coast's thriving cabaret and neo-vaudeville scene in the Bay Area, Seattle, and Portland has given accordionists opportunities to perform and compose for theater venues. Without necessarily being aware of the accordion's historical roots in vaudeville, accordionists like Heidi "Doodles La Rue" Wohlwend (of Five Cent Coffee), Eric Stern (leader of the Portland-based band Vagabond Opera), Suzanne ("Kitten on the Keys") Ramsey, and Maggie Martin (who once had a theater troupe in Petaluma) have approached the instrument with a highly theatrical sensibility. "Kitten on the Keys" uses the accordion in her burlesque act featuring off-color humor and original songs.

Fronting his band with the accordion, Stern, who describes Vagabond Opera as a "Balkan Arabic klezmer-based, original absurdist cabaret ensemble" uses the instrument to underscore his dark, rich baritone voice. He moves with his instrument when he plays, making it a central visual element in his performance.

All these performers appear regularly in the nightclubs and venues in the Bay Area and the Pacific Northwest (Vagabond Opera is based in Portland). My brief interviews with many of these musicians seem to indicate that all of them respect each other's musical niches, which do not compete with one another. Many describe themselves as part of an "accordion community."

Portland-based "Bohemian cabaret" act Vagabond Opera with Eric Stern, accordionist, bandleader, and operatic tenor (center). (Photo by Brian McLernon)

Another factor in the growth in accordion-based bands, at least for those who aspire to national and international notoriety, may be the success of Those Darn Accordions, which reconfigured itself after most of its original members, including Clyde Forsman, departed in the early 1990s. (Forsman made occasional appearances as a guest star–elder statesman until he was unable to travel.) When founding member Paul Rogers, an aspiring rock 'n' roll musician and keyboardist, assumed leadership in 1992, he whittled the band down to four accordionists, including himself, making it more feasible for the band to tour. Forsman's retirement made it possible for Rogers to move the band in a new direction, away from novelty antics. "We need to go in a new direction now," he told me. "If we're living and dying by having Clyde sing two or three songs, then I'm in the wrong band." Aiming for a tighter, more "professional" sound, he banned the use of sheet music in performance. The three female accordionists who perform with Rogers on lead are polished singers and dancers as well as practiced and precise accordion players. The "new" stage choreography and musical arrangements of this band reflect their meticulous attention to detail and their success in creating a professional image for their full-time touring band. Instead of playing in unison, as the former band did, the current one plays arrangements in which harmonies and solo parts are assigned to each musician and worked out in advance. Although they adhere to the band's traditional mix of rock covers, polkas, and original compositions in a humorous vein, their performance style is tight, direct, and focused on pleasing the audience rather than wallowing in self-indulgent kitsch. Having put aside broad comedic strokes, TDA aspires to demonstrate that accordions can really "rock."[11] It is a clever strategy that has allowed the band to outgrow its novelty-band roots and be seen as a "serious rock band."

Through the accordion festivals in cities like Los Angeles, and New York City, and San Antonio, American accordion advocates have attempted to turn around the accordion's image, connect with the wider public, and acknowledge ethnic communities that have traditionally included the accordion in their music. For accordion bands, festivals create an important stop on their circuit, a reliable meeting place for accordion fans, and a place to market their music. As my previous discussions of accordion bands and solo artistes has shown, accordion festivals sometimes also serve as a place to inspire new players or, in the case of Mad Maggies, launch the careers of new bands. Taken as a whole, the wave of accordion festivals that began in the 1990s has become an impressive feature of popular accordion culture, creating thousands of opportunities for people to hear, play, and purchase accordions and creating the impetus for new bands. Of all these gatherings, Cotati's is most significant.

THE FESTIVAL IN COTATI

While by no means the largest or most popular of the free-reed festivals, the Cotati Accordion Festival in a small Sonoma County town marks a dramatic moment in the story of the accordion's changing image. Like trade shows and competitions, this festival is a grand exercise in what folklorist Simon J. Bronner might identify as "impression management" for the accordion.[12] Because it raises cultural issues with respect to how the accordion is presented and the engagement of citizens in that project, the accordion festival offers some insights into both the ways the accordion has been presented to popular audiences and the development of alternative musical practices surrounding the accordion vis-à-vis performance art and contemporary music. Complementing the story of accordion culture, this section examines the accordion festival as a festival, a genre of performance and civic-cultural display, providing a context for understanding public representations of the accordion.

The Cotati Accordion Festival was founded in 1990 by a group of Cotati civic leaders on the completion of a bandstand in La Plaza Park in the center of the city. Clifton Buckman-Kauffman, owner of Prairie Sun Recording in Cotati and a festival founder, noted: "We were looking for something musical to draw a crowd, some kind of multicultural event, without attracting too many unruly kids and a lot of potential problems."[13] The idea for an accordion festival came from Jim Boggio, an accordionist who performed a variety of ethnic music genres (Cajun, zydeco, polka, and jazz standards) at local wineries, hotels, and restaurants. He had recorded a solo album, *Accordion to the Blues*, with Prairie Sun, and Buckman-Kauffman was impressed by the possibilities of the instrument. "We realized that there seemed to be an incredibly untapped demand for accordion entertainment, especially among older folks who recall the golden days of the accordion," he said.[14] Boggio believed that an accordion festival could also be useful in his personal mission to overcome the accordion's Lawrence Welk stigma.[15]

Buckman-Kauffman, a native Cotatian descended from Italian-American chicken ranchers (the area was originally populated by immigrant farmers) had a long track record of civic involvement. Buckman-Kauffman helped to establish the Cotati Festival as a nonprofit organization that would donate proceeds to support performing arts programs in local schools reeling from sharp budget cuts. For the festival's funding, he turned to the local chamber of commerce and the Cultural Arts Council of Sonoma County, and he collected private contributions.

The charter for the nonprofit Cotati Accordion Foundation states: "we believe the CAF [Cotati Accordion Festival] has a very positive effect on the resurgence of the accordion and community spirit and more opportunity and fun for accordion players."[16] That is, the festival helped to enhance a sense of community and build credibility for advocates of accordion teaching in schools, while creating a highly visible place for accordion players. This sentiment, which animates the Cotati Accordion Festival, brings together civic pride, social action, and accordion culture. Through this festival, with its strong participatory component, accordionists really can represent themselves, their feelings about the accordion, their accomplishments, and what they have found significant about their instrument.

Beloved by the general public, tourists, the press, and city officials, and heartily embraced by participants, the festival nonetheless raises problematic issues. It represents a maligned instrument and unfamiliar, exotic genres of music. Recall from the San Francisco mock court proceedings that the accordion still had its haters in the Bay Area. Furthermore, the festival embraces the satirical, the comic, and performances by novice and amateur players, which old-line accordion advocates who view the event as their own find objectionable.[17] Bumper stickers produced for the festival issue the tongue-in-cheek warning "Use an Accordion—Go to Cotati," a slogan the city's mayor quoted in his welcome message in the festival program. In combining categories such as advocacy, public service, and entertainment, the authentic and the carnivalesque, the satirical and the serious, the festival can be misinterpreted on many levels. While it earns kudos for its celebration of accordion culture and the contribution it makes to the community, there are those who do not appreciate its eclecticism.

The Cotati Festival is an annual concert of solo and ensemble musicians whose instrumentation features an accordion (including concertinas, chromatic accordions, diatonic button boxes, Cajun button accordions, and melodeons, but most participants are piano accordionists). It is produced by the Cotati Accordion Festival organization each August for two full days, in cooperation with the city of Cotati, which oversees events taking place in La Plaza Park. Both days open with an accordion parade.

The festival (in its early years) was free and offered to the public as a "community service" in recognition of the "festive ambience" city leaders wished to sustain.[18] In keeping with Boggio's wishes to increase and diffuse awareness about the accordion and specifically its grassroots cultural heritage, the festival has featured diverse ethnic and regional musical cultures such as Tejano/conjunto, zydeco, tango, klezmer, Italian popular song, and various polka styles. In 2008 the festival featured nationally known acts like Alex Meixner, a thirty-year-old Slovenian-style accordionist from Pittsburgh. The festival showcases local groups as well, and many of the previously mentioned accordion artists and solo acts have in some way attributed their success (in some cases their very existence) to Cotati.

To date, the festival has covered most of what we might recognize as the world's exemplary accordion traditions, from every region of the United States and many different nations, without privileging any single ethnic group or tradition. Another significant feature of Cotati is its representation of the West Coast's experimental and avant-garde musical-cabaret scene; for example, Polkacide, the Mad Maggies, Those Darn Accordions, Polka Casserole, Amber Lee, and Vagabond Opera. In recent years, the committee has leaned toward presenting "headline" acts, such as Flaco Jimenez (2005), Dick Contino (2008), and Those Darn Accordions (2009). The festival includes zydeco and polka tents, where the public is invited to participate in these traditional dance styles.

Brian Jack & the Zydeco Ramblers playing in the zydeco tent at the 2008 Cotati Accordion Festival. (Photo by Patti Davi)

Dancing is, of course, encouraged in front of the mainstage, and not necessarily in the traditional styles practiced by the performers.

Players of classical and jazz music, representing the Bay Area's old-line accordion culture, gather to play informally in the Golden State Accordion Club's tent (but not onstage). With the emphasis on eclectic and alternative styles of music, performers of classical, jazz, and "standard" fare are notably absent from Cotati's mainstage. However, Dick Contino has been making regular appearances as a headline act at Cotati. The octogenarian accordion legend, who had disappeared from public live performance for decades following the decline of his career in the 1950s, seems to draw two kinds of admirers: much older listeners from his string of fan clubs from around the country and younger listeners who are familiar with Contino as a rebel figure from his B movies such as *Daddy-O* and who have contributed to the construction of the accordion's hip-outsider image in the 1990s.[19] (Contino is also a familiar figure on the national Italian "festa" circuit, which I discuss elsewhere.)[20]

The retail core of the festival offers accordions and accordion accessories for sale, sheet music, recordings, and crafts and food vendors (no outside food or beverages are allowed). There is a heavy focus on the accordion-related businesses in the region, such as Smythes Accordion Center, whose display table is the focal point of shopping, impromptu music making, and live performance.

At a cost of $25 for a two-day pass, the festival annually attracts about five thousand spectators each weekend. Although its size is modest, the event is scaled to the compact size of La Plaza Park, about the size of a square city block; hence it appears full and lively throughout both days. As the only August accordion festival for many years (until Orange County instituted its own in 2009) this one receives reliable media attention, an annual feature story in the *San Francisco Chronicle,* and blog coverage. Since the 1990s, San Francisco no longer has an accordion festival, so Cotati has garnered notoriety as the West Coast's premiere accordion event.

In its first year, the festival was an instant hit, drawing an audience of five thousand and praise from the Bay Area press, which was observing a new wave of interest in the accordion. Support from musicians followed, as many saw their chance for a national spotlight and were eager to share their knowledge and traditions with accordionists from other traditions. The festival's popularity has encouraged the development of similar programs on the West Coast, such as the Orange County Accordion Festival, the Los Angeles Accordion Festival, and the Monsters of Accordion festival in Vancouver, all taking place in the summer months.

Each performer plays a complete set of forty-five minutes to an hour onstage. Most programs consist of about twenty-five musical groups or musicians on stage. In addition, impromptu strolling performances take place on the lawn and private jam sessions in the vendors' and club tents. The tents (on the periphery of the mainstage but inside the gates), provide an opportunity to engage in conversations with professional and lay performers, who provide information about the accordion and its related musical traditions, answers to questions, and advice on such matters as buying or repairing an accordion.

A strong feature of the festival, which also may constitute its greatest limitation, is its informal quality. Although the festival presents tradition bearers who are regarded as important exponents of their culture, they do not have much of an opportunity to represent or discuss their culture. At the festival, musicians are encouraged to simply play. Some musicians presented in the early part of the day have sounded poorly rehearsed or exhibited technique that some accordion aficionados would see as amateurish or bad. The public is strongly encouraged to participate—to dance, eat, wander the accordion "shopping mall," and even to play. During intermission on the lawn, there is a "Lady of Spain-A-Ring in the People's Key of C," and anyone who has brought an accordion for the occasion is encouraged to participate.

In keeping with the festival organizers' efforts to create ritual traditions specific to Cotati, white doves are released from the stage as a finale to the musical performances. While celebrating the diversity of the accordion and the people who play it, the festival celebrates people's ability to talk with and join with one other, to appreciate and bridge differences in musical tastes and styles. Audience participation is a significant feature of Cotati, as it is of most festivals.

As one might expect from a small festival, Cotati does not include a catalog, signage, educational material, workshops, or children's and family programs. It is not broadcast or televised. It does not create much of a context for the traditions represented. The festival is not quite curated, not quite based on research; unlike the San Antonio International Accordion Festival, which has engaged professional folklorists in research and documentation, it is not based on scholarship; rather, it involves the efforts of producer Scott Goree and his fellow citizens, who happen to care a great deal about the accordion. The festival has generated $70,000 in revenue, which has been used to fund an accordion scholarship and music programs in local schools. The festival has had a strong impact on accordion culture outside California and as a significant meeting place for accordionists on the West Coast, and it has earned a reputation as one of the "must see events of Sonoma County."[21]

The need and desire for public celebration is a significant part of Sonoma County's cultural identity and the image it presents to residents and tourists. As stated on the County's website, "Sonoma County is a collection of great food and wine, entertainment, economic opportunity, temperate weather, and a beautiful location. The result is the truly unique and fulfilling Sonoma County lifestyle."[22] Most of the County's two dozen annual festivals focus on food and wine. Yet Cotati is remembered by some longtime residents as a countercultural haven, a place where coffeehouses and alternative music venues like the Inn at the Beginning once thrived in the 1960s.[23] An illegal bandstand built by rogue music fans in the center of La Plaza Park became the focal point of free concerts of psychedelic rock 'n' roll music. According to the city's website, "council meetings played hosts to two disparate factions: one wanted more music, facilities, sandboxes for the kids, the other demanded user fees, permits, an end to amplified music." In that context, perhaps the Cotati Accordion Festival could be seen as an ideal solution to satisfy both factions. Although amplification is used, most of the bands feature acoustic music; the event is welcoming to families and children (who can play in the sandboxes or run around on the sidelines); in 2008 I observed no overdrunkenness or lewd behavior of the kind commonly associated with psychedelic rock concerts. The event also requires a permit; the organizers charge admission, and bracelets are required for entry to the park on both days of the festival. In 1992, the third year of the festival, the festival committee decided to charge admission. Some musicians and participants objected, fearing a betrayal of the populist spirit behind La Plaza concerts and objecting to the closure of La Plaza Park, a public space. However, attendance barely dipped following the institution of the ticket system. The festival continues to draw two to three thousand attenders each day. In 2008, Cotati's mayor, Janet Orchard, took tickets and checked bracelets at the front entrance, perhaps reminding patrons of the festival's egalitarian spirit while adding the flourish of civic pride.

The Cotati Accordion Festival has encouraged uses of the space in ways consistent with what city planners had in mind. After Boggio's death in 1996, his circle of friends and admirers commissioned a sculptor to render—in lifelike exactness—a statue of him, which was erected in La Plaza Park. This bright, copper-colored bronze memorial to Boggio depicts him with impish grin and stout, bouncy demeanor, his left foot in midair as he plays his piano accordion, surrounded by snacking patrons at the 2008 festival.

Although one art critic may have a point when he describes it as an "oversized wind-up toy, waiting to start up as soon as someone drops a quarter in his back," the statue seems like a lovingly personal tribute to an accordionist who was also a beloved local figure. In contrast to other, more somber memorials to musicians—in Vienna's parks, for example—the spontaneous performances that take place near the statue on festival days seem to argue for a certain vision of the accordion as part of lively, people-oriented musical traditions. This statue (the only public statue of an accordionist) portrays the accordion as the "people's instrument," to be used, enjoyed, and owned by them, much like the festival Boggio founded.

It is now time to consider what makes accordion festivals unique and what makes Cotati unique among them. Accordion festivals are a particular kind of festive celebration, not of the same type as Milwaukee's Italian Festa or San Antonio's celebration of Tejano and conjunto music. Nor do they seem to be commercial festivals of the same type Sonoma County sponsors in order to help real estate sales or promote its wineries. It is not a folk festival—a concert of "revival" folk music. Nor does it resemble the international festivals organized by communities to showcase forms of dance, food, music, games, and dress related to their citizens' daily lives. Accordion festivals have yet to attract much scholarly attention, but I would argue that they are as uniquely worthy of serious analysis as an American phenomenon that reflects a worldview that could only have emerged in the 1990s and 2000s. They are not a "living museum" or "live cultural exhibit," such as those presented by the Smithsonian on the

National Mall. They do have a great deal of music, but it is not just a concert; it has other purposes as well.

Cotati's festival is different from other festivals, and from accordion conventions, because it consistently excludes performers and repertoires (classical and jazz) that would be considered "mainstream" and privileges ethnic music and the accordion's appeal in experimental and avant-garde music. Cotati, a festival, concert, and parade that seem to blend into one another, seems to demonstrate "ludic" qualities that folklorists have described in studies of ritual and festival: it demonstrates a strong degree of the carnivalesque; there are few boundaries separating performers and audiences, and the interactions among the spectators and musicians have a spontaneous and informal quality.[24] There are attempts to challenge old beliefs and stereotypes surrounding the accordion, most notably in the cabaret and burlesque style performances of Amber Lee and Vagabond Opera. Accordions evoke peculiar relationships with the past, as we have seen from the numerous stories in the media celebrating the accordion as "cool again" or "back again." Participants and visitors I interviewed at accordion festivals described themselves as "accordion geeks," "accordion nerds," or some variation of eccentric or outsider, and enjoy seeing themselves on display as such. At the festival, people engage in dialog with mainstream perceptions of the accordion and play a role in shaping the representation of their instrument. In 2008, two women accordionists, regular Cotati festival attendees who were not part of the "official" program, wandered the park, playing for anyone who might listen.

Indeed, the Cotati festival has been extremely successful in providing opportunities for nonprofessional players to share their love for the instrument while creating visibility for it in a wide range of ethnic music and performance styles. While Cotati is a very small city, not easily reached from San Francisco (the trip is about ninety minutes by car or bus), the Cotati Accordion Festival has extraordinary name recognition beyond the Bay Area (about half the listeners I spoke to at the 2008 festival were from outside the Bay Area).

Accordion advocates in San Francisco have used two key strategies to place their instrument at the center of a movement: first, invoking the idea of the "outsider" or the underdog, and second, reassessing the accordion's present status in terms of the past. These strategies are regionally specific. Beyond older cities like San Francisco and New York City, and beyond a certain community of performers who embrace eclectic repertoires and performance styles, these concepts do not travel well. In a newer metropolis like Houston, the idea of the accordion's decline and the need to rehabilitate its image is much more evident.

THE ACCORDION KINGS AND QUEENS FESTIVAL

Unlike San Francisco, whose attractiveness to musicians helped to reinvigo-rate the accordion in recent years, Houston is a manufacturing town, not an artists' haven—that was how it was described to me by informants. Most of the accordionists I encountered, with the exception of conjunto artists, were educated professionals who pursued music in their spare time, not as a call-ing or profession. Accordionists in Houston are not likely to invoke terms like "hip" or "cool," and Oliveros's (a Houston native!) concept of the accordion as an "outsider instrument" would be utterly meaningless for them. Indeed, the instrument has established itself in almost every imaginable musical sphere of this sprawling multicultural city. In Houston, credit for the current resur-gence of the accordion belongs to communities of working-class Americans of Mexican/Latino, Czech, German, Cajun, and French Creole descent where accordionists on the margins aspired to gain recognition in the mainstream, not to represent an alternative subculture, as in San Francisco. In 2007 I vis-ited Houston to witness the accordion's lead role in all these types of music and to trace the origins of the instrument's highbrow classical persona as well.

Every year in June, the Austin-based Texas Folklife Resources sponsors a showcase called Accordion Kings and Queens in Houston. The lineup exposes Houstonians to the wide variety of accordion styles found in Texas and be-yond. In 2007 the event kicked off with the Houston-based Knights of Dixie. A straight-Dixieland band that plays traditional mainstream polkas for danc-ing, the Knights featured veteran septuagenarian piano accordionist Weiner Gruman. It was not a memorable half hour but a reminder of an earlier time, in the 1930s and 1940s, when the accordion often played lead in a white soci-ety jazz band. The Knights filled the Miller Theater's sturdy wooden dance floor with veteran, tanned polka ladies with signature sashes tied around their waists, as well as giggling teens trying out their grandparents' dance for the first time—highlighting the essential connections between the accordion and social dancing in Texas.

The lineup of featured performers included revered Houston button ac-cordion master Step Rideau. Like most prominent zydeco players, Rideau is from rural Louisiana, only about one hundred miles from Houston. As zydeco scholars have noted, Rideau is a key figure in this genre, a regional type of music from Louisiana that is seen as both the embodiment of black Creole culture as well as one of the most marketable world music styles to cross over to a white audience.[25] (I commented earlier on the centrality of the accordion in this music.) Rideau's appeal rests not only on his mastery of the button box but also on his singing and his performance style. Hurling his muscular body around the stage, Rideau alternates dynamic button riffs on the button box with shouted-out lyrics in French Creole and English.

Although the featured performers represent a jumble of various styles, the names of three under-twenty-five frontrunners for Accordion King—Craig Zuniga, Heriberto Rodriguez, and Anthony Ortiz, Jr.—suggest how much of the rich, homegrown Texas-Mexican cultural tradition has nourished the accordion. In the 1900s, Bohemians settling in Central Texas and Germans working in the brewing and mining industries brought Hohner one-row diatonic accordions to south Texas and northern Mexico. With the accordion came the popular European-cosmopolitan musical forms: polkas, schottisches, and mazurkas, which enriched the local Texas-Mexican two-steps and *redovas*. To this, players are now adding salsa, merengue, and cumbia licks and opening new channels for distribution beyond Texas and Mexico. While worldly accordion artists like Flaco Jimenez and David Hidalgo introduced conjunto to global and national audiences, the Accordion Kings provided vivid evidence of its significance to local audiences in Texas.

The winner of this year's Accordion King title, Johnny Ramirez, appeared with a well-known norteño band, La Tropa F. Ramirez performed like a rock icon, and from the moment he extended the bellows his fans were screaming their hearts out. A small boy ran across the front of the stage bearing a hand-painted sign that read "Johnny Ramirez for President!" I later spoke with the newly crowned Accordion King's mother. Sixteen-year-old Johnny is only the latest musical member of a prominent Houston conjunto family; his father, Hermenio, plays norteño music at clubs and wedding gigs. Johnny started teaching himself the accordion at an early age; he has never had a formal teacher (his father plays another instrument); yet he now has students of his own. Johnny's mother is proud of him sustaining the family legacy as well as his Tejano heritage. I noted that Johnny plays a custom-painted red, white, and blue Gabbanelli accordion. This, a novel twist on the "Mexican flag" accordions highly prized by Tejano players, provocatively positions him and his music as an essential part of the larger American musical landscape. It also provides evidence of the vitality of the Italian accordion tradition in Houston's accordion scene (discussed later).

During the performance, I stepped out of the amphitheater, situated high on a hilltop. I looked out at Houston's famous skyline and surveyed the territory I was researching. To the north: Frenchtown, a traditionally black Creole working-class enclave where scholars believe zydeco emerged. To the east:

the Latino neighborhoods, with their cantinas and clubs featuring Tejano and conjunto music. Farther north: "Greater Acadia," the part of southeast Texas that the Cajuns and Creoles consider an extension of their native coastal Louisiana. To the south and southwest: Mexico—but the very ideas of "Tejano" and "conjunto" and the sensibilities of its players make this a fluid border when it comes to music and culture.

THE ACCORDION IN CZECH-TEXAN MUSIC

Much farther away, to the west toward San Antonio, are Texas's Czech and German homelands. The ancestors of the people who live and work there introduced the accordion to Texas, along with polkas and waltzes that the Cajuns, Creoles, and Tejanos would rhythmically retrofit to suit their tastes and dance styles. In the 1860s, Czech immigrants, sailing from the German ports of Bremen and Hamburg to Galveston, settled agrarian central Texas in large numbers. Texas outranks all other states in the total number of Czech Americans, with Wisconsin and Minnesota next in line. [26] All these people share a common religion and moral stance—Catholic and conservative—although they define those values differently than one might expect, as I found in my outing to the St. Mary's Church picnic in Hallettsville the following day.

No fewer than ninety miles separate Houston from the Czech heartlands of Texas. I drove fifty miles west through flat, sun-baked cornfields, and then veered south through the fertile farmland that lured the European immigrants to Texas. A sign welcomed me to Lavaca County. Looking out at the well-kept, spacious farmhouses visible from the highway, I could see how cattle ranching—and all the industries associated with it—drew the European settlers to this part of Texas. There were very few stores—none were open on Sunday—and no strip malls or supermarkets, suggesting a self-sufficient and isolated community. I passed a few Catholic churches. These simple wooden structures, more like stripped-down New England Protestant churches in their absence of Gothic and Romanesque ornament, were paired with much larger, hangar-sized parish halls—some attached to the church itself, others separated from the main building by a large parking lot. The church halls' form fits their function: providing space for couples to dance in large circular formations. Although the Czechs were and still are largely Catholic, they were also inclined to create societies of Free Thinkers, an older movement from Europe, and secular social organizations like the Sokol, dedicated to physical fitness and cultural advancement. [27] These social movements also provided a way of advancing their culture outside the church, as has also been the case in the Scandinavian Lutheran communities of the Upper Peninsula (as mentioned earlier). However, attitudes toward alcohol—and dancing—were much more lax in the Texas heartlands.

Three miles south of the town of Hallettsville, I drove into St. Mary's rambling grassy parking lot, which was packed with hundreds of cars and pickup trucks. I followed the sound of the auctioneer's patter to a large covered pavilion where homemade pickles, home remedies, needlepoint goods, and livestock were up for bidding. In the back of the hall was the largest, loudest air conditioning unit I had ever seen. That was because the unit was actually cooling the outside. A nearby pavilion housed the dance floor, also open to the elements—the heart and soul of the church picnic. I was greeted warmly by a closely knit group of men and women in their fifties, sixties, and seventies, "polka people" who travel the "circuit"—church picnics, dances, and beer and sausage fests in the Southwest).

Close to the dance floor and stage were portable lawn chairs and picnic tables that families had piled high with food and soft drinks and claimed as their personal headquarters for the eight-hour event. They were positioned in view of the stage and the dance floor. The crowd was overwhelmingly white, ranging in age from toddlers to teens to the middle-aged and elderly. Several generations of a family would appear together on the dance floor. In contrast to the more dressed-up polka people in their dance-specific leather-soled shoes, the uniform was shorts, T-shirts, and baseball caps. In this casual crowd, the newly anointed Miss Czech Slovak, just minted and ready to compete with her coethnics on the collegiate pageant circuit, smiled and posed in a modest dress.

In the center of it all were the Czechaholics, the Czech American polka band I'd come to hear. Two Svetlik brothers are the core of the group: Greg, in a "Czech Sex Machine" T-shirt, on bass, and Brian, the band's manager, on drums and diatonic accordion. In front of the band was accordion player Mark Hermes, performing melody on a piano accordion.

Czech-Texan music evolved as a style parallel to the Scandinavian, German, and Slovenian styles discussed in chapter 5. In the early twentieth century, Czech immigrant bands abandoned the traditional brass bands and brought in accordions to create a distinctly "Texan Czech" sound. This lighthearted rural sound contains elements of country and western. The Czechaholics' repertoire blends traditional Czech popular songs and arranged folksongs with original tunes written by the band members themselves. The band also performed Mexican tunes in Spanish and covers of Johnny Cash, who is enormously popular among their audience of ranchers and cattle farmers. The crowd applauded warmly at their rendition of "Folsom Prison Blues." Customers eagerly approached the stage to buy the band's new CD, *Spreadin' the Tradition*. Czech-Texas music is distributed through more limited channels than some of the commercial polka styles discussed in this book. Most of the half dozen or so Czech polka bands in the region produce their own concerts and CDs, enlisting their family members to haul their equipment and arrange their gigs. Lavaca County is isolated from the metropolis of Houston; besides, many of the performers cannot leave their crops and cattle to go on tour. But Czech polka music is well supported by its community. *Polka News*'s event listings show players and bands traveling throughout southwestern Texas: Czech and Then Some, Jimmy Brosch, Chris Rybak, and the Ennis Czech Boys. One of the fundamental themes of my conversations at the dance was that the Czech language was dying out among the second and third generations, the Czech radio shows and dance halls were gone, and most of the young people are marrying non-Czech spouses and leaving the farming life. While members of the Czechaholics enjoy "spreadin' the tradition" on weekends, economic survival is foremost on their minds. But they also said they feel that this music is going to survive: "All people love it." "It's fun." "It's irresistible."

Forty-one-year-old Mark Halata, one of the most famous of all the younger American-born Czech accordionists whose songs were played at the St. Mary's picnic, has made "bringing this music to the outside world" his primary calling. Halata, by his own account, did not grow up in a "Czech bubble." After hearing zydeco master Clifton Chenier at age sixteen, Halata had an epiphany. Other cultures—even black folks—played the accordion! It became his mission to explore as many styles of the accordion as he could. So in Halata's Texas-Czech polka waltz music, as he would tell me later in Houston, "you will find American folk, Cajun, and zydeco." On the way back to the City, I considered swinging by Halata's favorite boyhood hangout, the Moravia Store, but my air conditioner had quit. So I missed out on experiencing one of the only remaining Czech social clubs and dance halls in the region. It is a place where Halata used to spend summers with his Czech grandparents, listening and watching his relatives dance the polka and, later, play some himself on his sister's accordion. I decided to explore Halata's other favorite type of accordion music—zydeco—at Houston's most famous venue: the Big Easy.

HOUSTON ZYDECO ACCORDIONISTS

After a long trip back into Houston from Lavaca County, I alighted at an upscale strip mall near the University of Houston. The inside of the Big Easy was anything but trendy. There was a busy billiards area in the back, and the large bar area was loosely packed with people of a certain age. Some of the men had on the Texas cowboy's night out uniform: ten-gallon hat, tight jeans, and a significant belt buckle. Most of the patrons appeared to be regulars and music fans. The club's walls were jammed with press shots and photos of the famous Cajun and zydeco players who had come through there: Rockin' Dopsie, Wayne Toups, Michael Doucet, and Clifton Chenier, the late "king of zydeco." His son CJ Chenier (in his twenties) is an accomplished Texas zydeco player who mainly tours out of the city and overseas. He is based in Houston. One of the patrons remarked excitedly that any minute Chenier could burst in through the doors with his accordion and start jamming with the band.

On this evening the Zydeco Dots, a famous local group, were on stage. Raymond Chavis was out front with a Hohner piano accordion, playing his original but traditional-sounding tunes in a laid-back style. His sound was quite distinct from the lightning-fast, hip-hop-inspired tunes Step Rideau had played at Accordion Kings the night before. Although the smaller diatonic accordions (like Rideau's Gabbanelli) and the Cajun button box are favored by most zydeco players these days, Chavis plays the piano accordion—as did Clifton Chenier and as CJ Chenier and most Czech-Texan polka players do. Unlike the button box, the piano accordion has black notes and can play flats and sharps—ideally suited for chromatic blues licks and the twelve-bar blues progression, which Chavis showcased in his performance. Chavis played French songs, too, and songs that mix Creole and English.

I introduced zydeco earlier as a commercial phenomenon, but it's important to understand that most Gulf Coast zydeco musicians make their livings primarily from community events: church dances at local parish halls, folk festivals, and private parties and weddings—the same types of events Czech musicians play. The atmosphere of the Big Easy was more akin to that of a social hall than a bar. The Zydeco Dots took an hour-long break during which they mingled with the customers. The club's slogan, "House of Mixology," displayed prominently over the stage, seemed to symbolize not only the drinks patrons were encouraged to buy at the bar (there was no cover for zydeco night) but the mixing of musical styles and the people who were enjoying it.

Beyond its significant Latino and Creole accordion culture, Houston also retains the traditional armature of "old school" piano accordion culture. To understand Houston's club scene and the significance of accordion clubs in general, I invited myself to a meeting of one of Houston's two accordion clubs, the Bay Area Accordion Club, located to the south of Houston near Nassau Bay.

HOUSTON'S "OLD-SCHOOL" ACCORDION CULTURE

The bleak stretch of NASA Road leading to Franca's Restaurant—the site of the Bay Area Accordion Club's monthly meeting—is twenty miles south of Houston and worlds apart from any festive church picnic or dance hall. My GPS device squawked in confusion as I made U-turn after U-turn on the new roads not yet detected by its satellite system, and I missed the restaurant each time. When I arrived, I was greeted by a group of friendly, well-dressed elders who had taken over the restaurant's party room for their monthly meeting. No button boxes were present; only high-end, name-brand piano accordions—including a few new Roland digital models—were displayed.

Houston must have a remarkably heavy concentration of players to sustain three accordion clubs. One explanation for this, besides the city's relentless expansion, is the University of Houston's accordion program, founded by 1950s accordion luminary Willard Palmer. In the 1940s, 1950s, and early 1960s, the university's music department offered a major in accordion. After graduation, a number of Palmer's students remained in Houston, performing the classics with the Palmer-Hughes Accordion Symphony and supplementing their income with jobs at nightclubs, restaurants, parties, and cruise ships departing from Houston. Ambitious students established their own accordion studios in town. Two of them, Shelia Lee and Mark Ropel, continue this tradition. Houston, therefore, may be the unofficial center of today's "accordion industrial complex."

Following the sound of accordions to the party room reserved for the club, I was greeted warmly by club leader Joe Brikha, who invited me to sit with him and his wife, Gailen. I told them about my travels thus far to the Accordion Kings, where a few of them had been in attendance, and the polka picnic. When I told the group about my visits to the Big Easy and the Czech church picnic, many expressed surprise that I had gone to such lengths to hear folk music. One lady asked me if I really liked all that "zydeck" and "conjunct" music. After the meal, every member had a piano accordion and a solo to play. In contrast to the accordion dance band events I had witnessed so far in Houston, these performances looked back to one of the piano accordion's most admired features—its ability to stand on its own as a solo instrument. So all the players that evening had an attentive audience and a stage to themselves, even if they weren't quite ready. As one elderly lady fumbled the bass notes for "Batter Up," Shelia Lee, her teacher, encouraged her by calling out the correct notes. That kind of encouragement, a warmly inviting social atmosphere, and moderately priced Italian food, had drawn in about two dozen accordion players from Galveston (on the Gulf Coast) and Sugar Land, a newer municipality twenty miles southwest of Houston. I noted that most of the members seemed to share a common professional and educational background. Most, including the Brikhas, were college graduates who had moved from elsewhere in the United States in order to pursue a job with a corporation in Houston. Most of the men I met worked as engineers, computer programmers, and scientists. A few worked for NASA. Only a few of their wives played the accordion; like Gailen Brikha, they seemed to prefer listening and socializing at the restaurant. The players seemed to enjoy working on their accordions and learning about its unique technology; many of them either owned or planned on purchasing a Roland accordion and were not deterred by its cost (around $1500).

As the group listened to the evening's slate of six or seven players in the casual atmosphere, members ate the lasagna special and sipped wine. There was a heavy air of accordion pride and a lot of talk about accordions

The players' abilities were mixed, but each player received warm applause and enthusiastic encouragement. A few, like the elderly lady who played with Lee, had only taken a few lessons. Quite a few of the members had played the instrument throughout their childhood and teen years and picked it up later in search of a musical hobby. Mark Ropel, an outstanding player in his early fifties, who had been a child accordion prodigy and a member of the Texas Hotshots with Shelia Lee. Then he had dropped it, because "the accordion wasn't any help attracting girls." Evidently, Ropel and the other talented players were rediscovering their passion for the instrument as adults. Lee presided over the proceedings, leading songs for the jam session and doling out encouragement for the beginning players. While most of the others played just a few short Italian and French "continental" pieces, Lee played dozens of songs—her repertoire covers jazz standards, polka, and 1970s pop tunes—the familiar accordion repertoire in the era before rock 'n' roll. But no one at the event seemed to consider it dated or corny. Lee also handed out business cards for her accordion studio in Houston.

Like a few of the club's other members, Lee first got started when her parents fell for a door-to-door accordion sales pitch. "'In just six weeks, I will prove to you that your child is musically talented, and if not, you can just walk away,'" she recalls the salesmen saying. Her mother said, "Fine, we can't afford a piano." Eventually, her two sisters took up the instrument, and "we had a trio." As a student of Willard Palmer at the University of Houston, Lee focused on the classics, as did all accordion majors, and performed with the Palmer-Hughes

Symphony. Lee became aware of the accordion's decline in the 1970s when Chuck Berris invited the Symphony to perform on the *Gong Show* (1978). "We knew we were going to get gonged," said Lee, "so we decided to play the most vulgar thing we could think of: 'The Beer Barrel Polka.'" Sure enough, they were immediately gonged. But their moment of ridicule led to a remarkable triumph: Johnny Carson invited them on the *Tonight Show* the next night.

The Bay Area Accordion Club meeting ended with an accordion jam session led by Lee—more standard accordion band fare—"Green Grass of Home" and "When the Saints Come Marching In." At the end, I watched everyone gather on stage together for an impromptu accordion band finale in which everyone played lead melody. Lee aspires to enroll dozens of children in her accordion school. But her adult students who have chosen to return to the instrument after neglecting it for years and decades are a more reliable revenue stream. "People in late life are looking for something to accomplish in their lives," said Lee. "If they've always wanted to play music, the piano looks intimidating, but the accordion's inviting." In addition, most of her adult students are working professionals or comfortable retirees who are not deterred by a $500 price tag for an entry-level accordion. Lee wants to make sure that they have opportunities to perform in public. In 2007, she organized thirty-seven piano accordionists to appear onstage at the Accordion Kings and Queens Festival. She was adamant that in a festival full of button accordionists, the piano accordion must be featured. For the 2010 festival, she increased this number to one hundred.

While festivals, nightclubs, and community events have been key in showcasing accordion performance, retail stores both provide opportunities for musicians from different backgrounds to interact and make the instrument accessible to the general public. In music stores, musicians provide feedback on the product that reaches the factory, sometimes generating change and innovation. As noted earlier, feedback from accordionists has been crucial to shaping both the sound and appearance of the modern accordion. In an age when most retail accordion businesses have either disappeared or resorted to the Internet, Gabbanelli Accordions plays a unique role in contributing to the vigor of Houston's accordion culture.

THE GABBANELLI STORY

The location of Gabbanelli Accordions is an ideal metaphor for the kinds of interactions that take place in Houston's accordion culture.[28] Situated in the middle-class Jewish neighborhood of Meyerland, the shop occupies a former

Chinese restaurant. The current owner, Mike Gabbanelli, is the scion of an Italian family that has been making accordions in Castelfidardo for over a century. One of the handful of accordion retail businesses in the nation that survived the new century, Gabbanelli Accordions was founded in 1961 when Mike's father, Gianfranco (John) Gabbanelli (d. 2003), arrived in Houston from Italy. He had been making accordions with his father since the age of twelve and hoped to start a thriving business serving the diverse clientele of Houston. Aware that the accordion was then in decline, John wanted to see if he could boost his family's business and the accordion industry in general. Like other accordion craftsmen who aspired to come to the United States, the elder Gabbanelli found a sponsor, "Reno" (Mike does not recall his first name), who made and repaired his own line of accordions. Two years later, John Gabbanelli started his own business at home in his garage, where he sold, tuned, and repaired accordions; his wife Louise managed the business. (Mike bought the business from her when John died in 2003.)

While the university's accordion program had provided John Gabbanelli with piano accordion customers, he recognized the importance of the diatonic button accordion in Houston's conjunto and zydeco cultures. Against his family's advice, Gabbanelli began ordering one-, two-, and three-row diatonic button boxes from the factory. The company did not make accordions for the Cajun/zydeco market, which Gabbanelli felt would be profitable in Houston, so he began building simple one-row diatonic button boxes for Cajun artists. (The Cajun fiddle legend Marc Savoy was one of his clients.) "My father sold a lot of parts to other builders and showed them how to make these instruments properly," Gabbanelli told me.

Throughout its forty-year history, Gabbanelli's shop has shaped accordion culture in two ways: brand loyalty and design. As noted earlier, early German, Czech, and Mexican accordionists in Texas played German-made accordions—Hohner and Weltmeister. Yet the current crop of musicians I saw in Houston—including Mark Halata, Step Rideau, and Johnny Ramirez, the winner of the Accordion Kings contest—all played Gabbanellis. The shop is plastered with publicity photos of Ramon Ayala, a norteno legend, and dozens of norteno groups all playing or showing off their Gabbanellis. One possible explanation lies in the evolution of Gabbanelli's designs. Most Hohner accordions are plain in appearance, and their players describe them as workhorses, designed to sound good, not to look pretty. Gabbanelli's current offerings include accordions sheathed in candy pink, robin's-egg blue, and silver and gold metallic celluloid skins.

When I visited the store, Gabbanelli was introducing a line of cyan accordions that appeared to change color from blue to green depending how the light hit them. During my visit to Houston, I had spotted several versions of Gabbanelli's "Mexican flag" three-row diatonic accordion, finished with red, yellow, and white stripes on the grilles. As other scholars have pointed out, these newer designs contribute to the reinvigoration of this music and the ethnic identity it represents.[29] These expensive new accordions assert for their working-class audiences a pathway up the ladder of cultural prestige. Not all Gabbanelli fans are Latino, and not all are button box artists. Houston-based Czech polka accordionist Mark Halata owns a violet Gabbanelli piano accordion featuring a red, black, and white bellows. He explained that one of his projects is making the accordion a "sexier" instrument, and the Gabbanelli fits that image. "Gabbanelli accordions are so gorgeous," he told me. There are no other accordions that have their look."

CONCLUSION

As my discussions of music scenes in Texas and California show, cultural and geographical differences complicate the picture of accordion culture, which continues to expand and absorb different tastes and demands. In Houston, the Accordion Kings and Queens festival has become a place where the accordion can be showcased unofficially as the "state instrument of Texas," owing to its significance in local and ethnic dance traditions such as norteno and conjunto, zydeco, Czech-Texan, and country and western music.[30] In San Francisco, the accordion's newfound status as the city's official instrument is tied to its evolutionary origins in the city's factories, as well as its more informal status as an emblem of avant-garde and experimental performance. Festivals like those in San Antonio, Houston, and Cotati attempt to cater to all of these perceptions of the accordion. Festivals can also accommodate the desire for a fully participatory experience—whether as part of a seated audience or on the dance floor—and a unique sense of community. Festivals have a democratizing influence that is especially reassuring to new players. As one participant noted of her experience at the Las Vegas International Accordion Festival, "every accordion enthusiast should plan to visit these festivals at least once in their life. Age, nationality, or ability to play an accordion have no bearing on the attractions these festivals bestow on attendees. They are guaranteed to be a highlight of your life."[31]

The expansion and diversification of accordion culture has perhaps come full circle with the blog letspolka.com, a resource for accordion artists, performances, festivals, and conventions, and the recent availability of information on older styles of playing and the accordion in its earliest phases of development. The Classical Free Reed, Inc., "a nonprofit educational and cultural organization dedicated to the advancement of the free-reed instruments in classical music," offers historical and musicological information and scholarly articles about the accordion that are not available elsewhere (the *Free-Reed Journal* went out of print in 2002). Their website is managed by Henry Doktorski, a classical accordionist and composer who has played the Deiro brothers' accordions and aims to record their complete repertoire on CD. Doktorski's work would be particularly helpful to younger accordionists who may not be familiar with the instrument's evolutionary history or may not have reflected on the accordion's position in the world of "serious" art music. One conclusion we might draw from the dozens of headlines invoking metaphors of "return," "comeback," and "revenge" is that accordion culture is undergoing its own postmodern moment, reflecting on its own place and the act of mirroring or reflecting the past. The trend toward increasing variety continues, with festivals, studios, and teachers representing an ever greater range of musical styles and backgrounds.

Accordion instruction, that traditional stronghold of musical conservatism, has been diversifying over the years as well. Accordion teachers like Shelia Lee (Houston) and Charlie Giordano and Walter Kuehr (New York City), have introduced their students to regionally and ethnically specific accordion repertoires. While more accordionists know more styles and repertoires, a major change is apparent in the domain of the commercial music world, in which a wide variety of musical styles have infiltrated radio, MTV, and the Internet. Alongside the older Palmer and Deiro method books for accordion, Mel Bay's and many others introduced in the last two decades showcase ethnic and folk music styles. Bay's *Teach Yourself Accordion*, which I used to teach myself accordion, features Lithuanian, French, Mexican, Finnish, and Scottish tunes; they are part of my repertoire alongside the "standard" accordion fare of polkas, waltzes, and Italian popular songs. Another big change is that many people who are discovering the accordion now, unlike the postwar generation, are conscious of the accordion's role in the music of many cultures and interested in learning about these traditions, becoming engaged in the language and related dance and cultural traditions. Accordion conventions traditionally focused on competitions and classics have broadened their offerings. At a recent Accordion Teachers Guild convention in Minneapolis, a Balkan musical group was invited to demonstrate (and perform) dance rhythms in compound meters. At the 2010 National Accordion Convention in Dallas, attended primarily by classical and jazz players, workshops were offered in klezmer and Celtic musics, German-language song, and learning to play the diatonic button accordion for piano accordionists. The rising level of musicianship in the scene, beyond making new cultural and musical experiences possible, is enabling the evolution of such genres as the polka into a multicultural musical experience. The virtuosity in some of this music is also an important part of its appeal, and the rather high bar set by such players as Guy Klucevsek, Carl Finch, and Linda Seakins is a constant source of awe and inspiration. Recognizing the significance of virtuosity beyond the classics, the American Accordionists Association conducts an annual search for the "Hottest Accordionist" at the Welk Resort Center. In 1999 the winner was Creole button accordionist Dwayne Dopsie, son of the famed Rockin' Dopsie.

Accordion culture has established itself as a recognizable niche. A considerable number of participants have been present since the golden age, performing, composing, and promoting the accordion together for a quarter of a century. The accordion conventions and clubs are no longer the primary meeting place for like-minded people—there are new festivals, workshops, YouTube instructional videos, blogs, MySpace, and Facebook groups. The original vision of elevating the accordion and its role in enhancing musical participation has really come to fruition, as many musicians, experienced and novice, come to celebrate this convergence of people joined by a shared love for the accordion and free-reed instruments. "What a wonderful thing the accordion has been in my life," said Joan from Frederick, Maryland, who learned accordion from her father and travels the convention and festival circuit. "I've made all my dearest lifelong friends in the accordion world." For many, the accordion has become not just a thing they play but a life they live. Like any living thing, accordion culture, with the piano accordion at its center, continues to change, responding to the changing needs of its participants, who are in themselves changed by the experience.

CONCLUSION

WHEN HELMI HARRINGTON, a musicologist and curator of the World of Accordions Museum, responded to my 2003 request for information about the history of the accordion, she said earnestly, "it's about time someone approached this topic in a serious-minded way." Echoing many other accordion devotees I interviewed, Harrington suggested that her interpretation of the scene as a whole, as well as her explanations for her own involvement in it, would depart from my own. When I visited her collections on two separate occasions in 2005 and 2009, she made sure to remind me that this was the case. In this way, each person I've interviewed has amplified a different aspect of the accordion and dismissed others. Some have suggested idealistic and far-fetched interpretations of the accordion. There is no doubt that each could have made interesting contributions to this work, and I hope that Harrington's own research on this topic will soon come to light. But even if it were possible to cover them all in one book, it would be hard to reconcile them all. Individuals' perceptions and understandings of the accordion and their relationship to it are constantly being modified, argued, and realigned. Formulating an answer to one of my interview questions involved making a statement and does not necessarily reflect the subtleties and nuances. The nature of material objects is dialogic; it involves a multitude of contrasting meanings that are in a continuous state of creation and recreation, negotiation and renegotiation. Musical instruments occupy a special place as icons of local and national culture, in Europe and the Americas; one need only consider the Italian accordion factories—instruments serve to accompany their people's heroic stories and come to stand for the people themselves. Within the commercial and capitalist world in which it emerged, the accordion plays a distinctive role that is thinly veiled by the priority given to its internal design technology and visual iconography.[1] Although the accordion industrial complex endowed the instrument with embodied social meanings and successfully disseminated them, they lost control over this discourse.

The accordion was swept into musical eclecticism and the expansion of the world music market in the 1980s and 1990s and became part of the larger process by which local and subcultural musical practices became co-opted and redefined within the parameters of the commercial music scene. Therefore, the biographical study of the accordion seems well suited to illuminate new approaches to the musical instruments and other material objects by emphasizing their shifting and multilayered meanings, and their "entangledness" in discourses of commercialism, exchange, and power. As Nicholas Thomas notes, "objects are not what they are made to be, but what they have become."[2]

The multiplicity of these meanings, visual, verbal, and sonic, has the focus of this cultural biography of the accordion. I have elaborated on what seemed to me the densest areas of overlap, trying to include some of the context in which many conversations occurred. Therefore, this conclusion and the book as a whole are not an ending but a beginning. I have documented some of the continuities and discontinuities involved in accordion communities in various segments of American society, over the course of more than a century's worth of American history. The fact that the accordion was predominantly a matter of choice and affinity for some of its practitioners and part of an ethnic heritage for others resulted in a wide range of explanations and justifications for people's involvement with the accordion. In many cases, polemics and ideology were at the forefront of the discussion, being considered at least as significant for accordion culture as repertoire and musical content.

Those deeply immersed in the scene are often too close to it to be able to see other points of view as relevant to their own. It is commonplace for people to see the history of a thing as beginning with their own involvement in it. There is often a sense among contemporary accordionists, particularly in New York City and San Francisco, that the history of the accordion has nothing to do with them. It is highly unlikely that anyone who plays accordion in a burlesque band in Oakland would have become interested in the instrument because of Guido Deiro. It is be more likely that someone would want to play the accordion after having seen Polkacide at the Cotati festival (as was the case with Maggie Martin of the Mad Maggies) or They Might Be Giants' John Linnell jamming with Doc Severinson's orchestra on the *Tonight Show*. How could one know, when seeing a band with an accordion, the many goals the instrument served fifty years ago? It would be outlandish to try to draw conclusions that would apply as well to the polkas of Slovenian coal miners in Ohio as to the conjunto music of Texas-Mexican migrant farmworkers. How could these two groups of people possibly share a common perspective on the accordion? Still, the long history of ideas, practices, and values attached to the accordion is an aspect of American cultural history that current participants are as much a part of as the early accordion advocates were. Individual understandings of the classical art music aesthetic, preconceptions of the accordion's social value, and particular responses to unfamiliar music are all culturally grounded.

The milieus of experimental accordion artists in New York and the Bay Area exist parallel to the numerous accordion clubs and handful of studios still in operation throughout the country, the schools that include accordion in their programs, and a variety of ethnic music festivals. Although currently synchronic, each movement has succeeded the previous as the most significant and public of its day, and each is no longer what it was. The once mighty AAA, which still harbors ambitions to elevate the accordion as a classical instrument, is only a shadow of its former self. Even if a single accordion, like my Delecia Carmen, is played over the course of fifty years, every time it's picked up it will mean something different. Yet its meaning is not completely up for grabs. It remains tied to a history, to place, to the trajectories of people who use it and to its physical qualities, however many reeds break or how much the bellows leak. But this is the cultural biography of "the" accordion, not one accordion, and the network of peoples and ideas I've looked at in this book is much more dynamic than a single instrument. Throughout this historical period, the accordion and its repertoire, polka or zydeco, classical and avant-garde, has proven very fluid and adaptable to a range of social demands. And throughout all the different time periods and uses, even when certain principles stood in opposition to each other, common threads were apparent.

In tracing the accordion's transmission from Europe to immigrant communities in America, I noted the great ease with which the accordion has circulated. Its mobile global travel patterns have been taken for granted, even by scholars who have focused on free-reed instruments. Cultural hegemony is one piece of the analysis; target marketing is another. Careful consideration of how local and regional musical practices have incorporated the accordion, as in the transition from brass band instrumentation to accordion that occurred in Czech and German polka styles, could do much to illuminate the extraordinary appeal of the accordion across cultures. Portability, rhythmic function, and sonic density are just some general features of the accordion's appeal; the list is potentially long. Of interest is not just the fact that the accordion has circulated but also that this circulation is accompanied by speedy recognition of musical kinship between the old traditions and what the new instrument represents. As I have shown, at accordion festivals accordionists find each other and get together with ease. Piano accordionists can learn from diatonic button box and melodeon players, incorporating their style and repertoire. Rock musicians with no memories of Lawrence Welk have little difficulty with accordions, and a few well-regarded guitarists and keyboardists have succeeded in becoming accordionists. Diverse repertoires and practices can be accommodated—one beginning accordionist I interviewed described herself as an "ethnic music glutton."[3] A naïve eclecticism is at the heart of such projects, sometimes leading to interpretations of the music that are inconsistent with those that tradition bearers might consider to be correct or appropriate. But in the accordion world, diverse and creative approaches can be accommodated and negotiated with ease and facility.

In each case, some form of community has figured prominently. In the Latino, Creole, and Scandinavian communities, the accordion was used to express ethnic identity and cultural heritage for much of the twentieth century. But the folks in American Accordionists Association, the Accordion Teachers Guild, and the local accordion clubs were bound by membership and affinity rather than regional belonging. As American culture has seen a development in the idea of individual self-fulfillment in the late twentieth century, the aims of the accordion community have splintered.

Other important changes can be seen in the steady move toward material calculated to show the accordion in an elevated light—concerts, competitions, and serious method books and arrangements emphasizing the accordion as a symphonic instrument and its classical repertoire. Differences in accordion culture have also developed around geographical regions of the country, with the East Coast studios and teachers at the forefront of the accordion industrial complex. Many participants in these communities found accordion playing to be a good, clean, and moral activity, a bulwark against the what they perceived as the encroaching decadence of rock 'n' roll, and an affirmation of middle-class family values. Others have seen their choice of the accordion as self-empowerment and as their chance to "come out of the closet" and celebrate who they are as individuals. For some, the accordion has been a refutation of mainstream culture; for others, living proof of its triumphs.

What would Tom Torriglia and Lou Seakins have in common with Pietro Deiro and Anthony Galla-Rini? What does David Byrne have in common with Frankie Yankovic? In what way could Lawrence Welk and Dick Contino have the slightest shred of appeal to contemporary music fans, weaned on rap, hip-hop, and punk?

All these individuals, and the movements they represent, have to some degree idealized the past, with a sense that it represents strong communal bonds expressed through music making. The traditions of the accordion are seen as cultural remedies for the shallowness of American popular music. The accordion as a low-tech, antipostmodern antidote to synthesizer saturation was at the heart of its reincarnation in the 1970s and 1980s. It is no accident that the accordion revival converged with the Balkan, Celtic, and klezmer "revivals" of the period. However, the whole nexus of ideas and practices surrounding the accordion has been used not to reject contemporary popular music but to help "humanize" it—to add warmth and depth to its sound textures and to create a space for different repertoires and styles of music. Some of Bruce Springsteen's and John Mellencamp's projects seem like the embodiment of this seeming contradiction. Their working-class sensibilities and a back-to-basics instrumentation has harmonized with their rock aesthetic.

Whether the accordion has been just another weapon in the rock band arsenal, whether it has been seen as cool or uncool, it has been understood as rich, deep, fascinating, exotic, and valuable. Playing the accordion and engaging oneself in its folk, international, and traditional repertoires, was meant to bring one closer to an authentic musical experience and, perhaps, closer to one's own cultural heritage. The San Francisco accordion picnics (Marin Park) were also celebrations of Italian-American food and culture. Some of the tables resembled mini–Italian delicatessens, with their wide assortment of salami, sausage, macaroni, cheese, spaghetti, ravioli, cannoli, scallopini, panettone, rolls, and sourdough bread. Such events were attended by people of many backgrounds, and demonstrate that involvement in the accordion was an extension of Italian family heritage. Memories of these kinds of events clearly have real meaning—meaning that can travel through the generations.

Playing the accordion, though it might almost be considered a spiritual experience, has been thought to bring one closer to the essence of humanity by mirroring the physical dynamics of breathing. Such was the powerful image of the accordion that fascinated me during my visit to Main Squeeze Accordions. This statement is indicative of two notions that persist throughout the historical period described in this book. The first is that there is something more "real" that Americans are looking for and the truth is that it can be found right here, close to home. That truth is to be regained by drawing on the source, the mother lode (i.e., polka music), that is uncontaminated by modernity. A second notion is that Americans, in acknowledging that something is missing from their music (and their lives), can recover it and save it from destruction.

These ideas have traveled from accordion festival to convention and across generations of accordion players. Some pop artists, whether as part of their own cultural heritage or as a strategic maneuver to appeal to their audiences, find in the accordion a symbol of their "folk roots." Some of the personal stories I have related here suggest that some accordion players, particularly those who have switched from keyboard and electronic instruments, are seeking an experience of musical Otherness.[4] Whether or not this is a sign of crisis, as Veit Erlmann has emphasized with regard to post-Marxian pessimism, these are visible conditions of the contemporary world music scene from the outset. Fascination with the perceived "authenticity" of the accordion is often juxtaposed with the "newness" of rock and its expressive forms. The authentic, as I have shown, transcends the boundaries of the culture that created it and becomes universal and organic.

Numerous cultural tropes persistent in the American mainstream continue to shape individual responses to the accordion and its repertoire. I have described ways that people stumble upon the accordion and recognize something familiar about it. Most Americans have clear opinions about Lawrence Welk and his champagne music. Representations of generic, mediocre accordionists are hard to escape in a variety of media, from newspapers to television and films. Such associations are familiar enough to be lampooned in cartoons, comic sketches, and music videos. Even if people did not grow up watching Lawrence Welk or Myron Floren, they have most likely been exposed to the idea of accordionists as banal hacks. If one has not seen a real accordionist, it is likely that one has an image of a middle-aged man in a powder-blue suit and a toupee playing "Lady of Spain." These tropes offer some direct clues to the accordion's "revival" in the 1990s and the attitudes of some contemporary accordion artists and their listeners. For further exploration of this issue, Maria Sonevystki's article is helpful in explaining the ironic idea of "whiteness" that has surfaced in Lawrence Welk's music and image.[5]

For the accordion to be salvaged from Welkian squareness requires an activist approach. It is enough to look at the posters, fliers, and album covers of groups like Mad Maggies, 5 Cent Coffee, Amber Lee and the Anomalies (on the West Coast) and Rachelle Garniez, Phoebe Legere, and Debutante Hour (on the East Coast) to realize that "the accordion" can mean avant-garde, edgy, even sexy.

A study of the accordion's visual iconography would be fascinating in its own right. Deeply rooted in grassroots romanticism, the representation of the accordion community is amply illustrated in promotional materials for festivals

The New York City–based trio Debutante Hour. Left to right: Mia Pixley, cello and vocals; Susan Hwang, percussion and vocals; Maria Sonevytski, accordion and vocals. (Photo and artwork courtesy Maria Sonevytski)

and conventions. Each year the Cotati festival committee commissions a local artist to design a poster (and T-shirt) that is sold at the festival; these provide a substantial revenue base for the festival. The designs for some of these posters, featuring (in different years) accordion-playing bears, chickens, and whimsical representations of Dick Contino and Cotati festival king Jim Boggio in a crown and ermine cape capture the festive and whimsical approach that characterizes these projects.

Another unexpected dimension of accordion culture are displays of empowered female sexuality such as that cultivated by the all-female Main Squeeze Orchestra. Founded by the Main Squeeze's owner (and my first accordion teacher), the orchestra adopts a bold and calculated strategy for subverting the listener's expectations of an accordion band: "When these girls strap it on and squeeze like hell, you stand up and listen. The secret lovechild of Lawrence Welk and Eartha Kitt, The Main Squeeze Orchestra is every wildest accordion dream come true. These twelve gals with accordions, conducted by local accordion master Walter Kuhr, deliver a rare and irresistible repertoire (Bach, Queen, Joy Division, Madonna and more) that has been enchanting New York audiences since 2002."[6]

An even more ambitious exercise in subverting the accordion's nerdy, sexless image is the West Coast Accordion Babes Pinup Calendar. Produced by button box player Renee de la Prade, it features color photo portraits of female

New York City's all-female Main Squeeze Orchestra with founder and conductor
Walter Kuehr. (Photo by Hai Zhang)

indie accordion artists in highly theatricalized and sometimes ironic (campy)
poses, like de La Prade herself on the cover as an accordion-playing angel. De
la Prade also created a compilation of their songs on an accompanying CD.
Fanny Mae Farrell of the Bay Area band Below the Salt and Suzanne "Kitten
on the Keys" Ramsey cultivate a sultry, Mae West–style glamour with their
vintage accordions as props.

Other models make use of whimsy, posing with accordions in a bathtub or
bowling alley, in order to make the accordion appear incongruous with its surroundings. In many of these photos, just as in the artists' live performances, the
accordion is featured as an accessory fitting for a sexually desirable and powerful
woman—in direct opposition to its image of nerdy maleness. The accordions
themselves—Big Lou's blue and gold vintage Colombo, Roxanne Oliva's gold
and white Scandalli are among the most spectacular and well preserved—ac-
cessorize the splendidly costumed and made-up performers like jewelry and
take a central visual role in these artfully composed photographic compositions.
As in San Francisco's erstwhile Ms. Accordion Pageant, the "hook" here is the

West Coast cabaret artist, accordionist, and off-color songwriter Suzanne
"Kitten on the Keys" Ramsey (Photo by Larry Utley)

idea that the accordion has become "hot." According to Tara Linda, one of the project's facilitators, the calendar had the aim of promoting the work of women accordionists as well as a sense of community around the accordion in general.

Accordion memorabilia, clothing, and accordions themselves give direct visual clues for the viewer to understand the values and ethics of the accordion community. Joan Grauman, through her virtual Squeezinart store and her display booths at accordion conventions, collects and trades thousands of accordion-playing angels, clowns, Bavarian peasants in lederhosen, trolls, mice, and bears, as well as wall clocks, magnets, alarm clocks, stationery, and many other household and personal items representing the accordion. (Grauman also serves as historian for the American Accordionists Association.)

At accordion festivals and conventions, T-shirts with humorous accordion slogans are the norm. Wearers often feel that T-shirts are a way to identify themselves as members of a community, which is part of their attraction to the accordion. At the Cotati festival and on the streets of San Francisco, regular appearances by costumed street musician Frank Lima ("the Great Morgani"), contribute to the creation of this imagined world, creating a unique and distinct ambience. Lima, a former stockbroker from Santa Cruz, specializes in designing and making one-of-a-kind costumes that cover his body, face, and accordion. His performances bring standard strolling-accordionist fare (he plays French, Italian, jazz, and popular repertoire) into the realm of fantasy and make-believe, transforming the instrument's bland, pedestrian visual and sonic references and transposing unfamiliar and exotic references onto it, such as a colorful tribute to the Vatican Swiss Guards (with papal miter in the foreground).[7]

Ideological meanings aside, people are looking for a deeper musical experience and for an instrument that is uncommon. They recognize in the accordion the potential for powerful, visceral emotional expression that is different from that of the piano, the guitar, or any other instrument with which they may be familiar. I can personally relate to perceptions of the accordion as direct, strong, haunting, and visceral. The value assigned to the accordion comes in part from the ideological background in which it is framed as old, traditional, and proven valuable over decades, but also from the aesthetic experience of the sound and physical dynamics (as discussed in chapter 1). Playing in an accordion band demands close coordination among the sections. The bond between musicians that results from playing the same instrument is real and meaningful. Through such experiences, participants work to create an artistic outlet and social space for themselves—one that had been denied to them in American public schools, conservatories, and concert halls. Along the road, many encounter and create opportunities to connecting with new people, cultures, and places. For example, over years of playing solo with accordion bands and symphony orchestras, and touring, Texas accordionist Lynlee Alley has enjoyed musical experiences and an exposure to the world that she never imagined when she was a child prodigy. A student of Palmer and Hughes at the University of Houston, she has played professional jobs in hotels, cruise ships, and corporate events and has toured Europe several times with a German polka band. She traveled to Europe and back playing accordion on cruise ships and was invited to be a guest of the Hohner factory in Trossingen, Germany. As a noted classical artist, she made a solo appearance in 1957 with the Houston Symphony, the only accordionist to do so, earning her the admiration of conductor Leopold Stokowski.

Many other musical communities provide for a kind of alternative musical education, enabling people to be actively involved in music making, regardless of their age or skills. Many segments of American society have discovered what Mark Slobin, Martin Stokes, and other scholars have described as an "affinity community."[8] For example, the contra dance, Balkan, klezmer, bluegrass, old-time, Celtic, and even early music scenes bear a great deal of resemblance to the accordion world. There is much crossover in membership and similarity in organization, infrastructure, and adopted values between various folk scenes. An important distinguishing feature of the accordion scene is the vast and growing number of divergent cultural traditions it gathers under one umbrella, a diversity that is reflected in the global reach of the "world music" scene.

Attitudes toward repertoire, aesthetics, and performance practice generate tension, confusion, and change within the accordion world. Participants often feel a need to justify their musical choices as well as a need to compare, evaluate, and exclude others. One example of this is the bitter opposition Tom Torriglia has described between the "old guard" in the San Francisco Accordion Club, many of them club date musicians and strolling accordionists with a core repertoire of "standards," and the younger players, who gravitate toward ethnic music and edgier repertoire. Issues of representation and authenticity are more often about the people themselves than they are about accordion culture. In addition, there are actual "real" accordion cultures, such as zydeco and conjunto, with their own traditions and points of view. These traditions actually exist side by side with mainstream American accordion culture, and there are real opportunities for new players of the accordion to enjoy first-hand experiences of these musical cultures, as Ry Cooder did when he apprenticed with Flaco Jimenez. Even though musicians involved in such activities are not trying create authoritative renditions of conjunto, zydeco, or polka, they are modeling their playing after their personal responses to the music and the way they imagine it.

Many accordionists particularly enjoy buying, selling, repairing, and accumulating information about accordions. People take great pride in their accordion collections, sharing their knowledge with other accordionists and guiding the uninitiated. "You know, a lot of accordionists are engineers, computer geeks, and people who are interested in gadgets; they want all the paraphernalia that goes along with it."[9] To others, accordions convey luxury and "retro" art deco style. "I love accordions, because they're just so beautiful, all dressed up for a party with rhinestones, mother-of-pearl, and semiprecious stones."[10] The desire to accumulate and collect is most evident in the desire for new songs and repertoire. A certain hierarchy of authority is built into the scene, helping to set milestones for future achievements. In this way, one can establish authority, making it possible to quantify and assess one's own knowledge and dedication.

The fact that for some the accordion is "inherited" rather than a result of individual and personal preference makes the process of evaluating people's musical choices more complicated. Even in making a musical choice clearly within heritage options—recall the comment about Spagnoli's Valtaro music being part of his DNA—some accordionists (Yankovic and Spagnoli himself) have been eager to expand their heritage, looking to commercial American musical forms such as blues, country, and jazz in search of deeper links to their inherited music. Issues of ethnicity and musical choice were made even more complex at the inception of the world music phenomenon in the 1980s. In conversations with Carl Finch and other accordionists who ventured into polka, zydeco, and conjunto, I detected a deep belief that culture, at least for today's accordionists, is a matter of choice. Finch, Cooder, and Dan Newman—a Minneapolis-based accordionist I interviewed who specializes in French musette and many other ethnic styles of music—may talk at length about "authentic" repertoire and style, but they have yet to grapple with issues of representation of the Other or pursue a deeper understanding of the culture and people whose music they "borrow." Many in the accordion world do not realize that they are not playing "conjunto," "French musette," or "polka" but their own constructed interpretations of these repertoires.

Despite a minefield of ideological pitfalls and controversies (idealization of the folk, rigid adherence to classical principles, and the like) the accordion community has much to show for itself. Its members' commitment to their instrument and their openness to different repertoires creates a space for something that is unique in American culture—seeing an instrument choice as the basis of a community that includes people of different backgrounds, ages, and playing abilities. A suitable metaphor can be found at the Cotati Accordion Festival, at which several performances take place simultaneously; for example, a fais-do-do in the zydeco tent, a self-consciously campy one-woman accordion vaudeville act on the mainstage, and a Bay Area accordion band playing four-part arrangements of popular standards, completely free from irony, in the Accordion Club tent. The richness of what the accordion world has created and its proven resonance with different segments of American society are likely to ensure its continuing vitality well into the future. In addition, the recent trend toward manufacturing accordions in China has resulted in a proliferation of new accordions in the under-$1,000 range and, possibly, deeper dissemination among new players who might otherwise not be able to afford the instrument. As the quality of these Chinese instruments is not well appreciated by many longtime players and collectors who prefer Italian instruments, this trend is likely, as well, to spark bitter debates about aesthetics. Those who stumble into the accordion world will continue to find a place for the accordion in their own lives and in the social, cultural, and artistic spheres they see as appropriate. Whether or not the twenty-first century will produce an accordion icon on a par with Guido Deiro or Dick Contino, new generations of players will surely find their own reasons and meanings and will have their own motivations for sustaining "accordion culture." And most likely, these ideas and practices, made from materials recycled from the classical tradition and a variety of folk cultures, will inspire a new chapter in the cultural biography of the accordion.

NOTES

Abbreviations

ABAM   Alex & Bell Accordion Museum, New York
CFRt   The Classical Free-Reed (website of Henry Doktorski: www.ksanti.net)
GDA   Guido Deiro Archives, Graduate Center, City University of New York
MDF   Museo della Fisaharmonica, Castelfidardo, Italy
PDA   Pietro Deiro Archives, Graduate Center, City University of New York
WOA   World of Accordions Museum, Superior, Wisconsin

Introduction

1. For helpful summations of some of these methods, see Sue Carole DeVale, "Issues in Organology," *Selected Reports in Ethnomusicology* 8 (Los Angeles: Department of Ethnomusicology, University of California, 1990), and DeVale, "The Classification of Musical Instruments: Changing Trends in Research from the Late Nineteenth Century, with Special Reference to the 1990s," *Ethnomusicology* 45 (winter 2001): 283–314, Margaret Kartomi, *Concepts and Classifications of Musical Instruments* (Chicago: University of Chicago Press, 1990).

2. Alan Merriam, "The Ethnographic Experience: Drum-Making among the Bala (Basongye)," *Ethnomusicology* 13 (1964), 74–100.

3. Paul Berliner, *The Soul of Mbira: Music and Traditions of the Shona People of Zimbabwe* (Berkeley: University of California Press, 1978).

4. These include Kevin Dawe, *Music and Musicians in Crete: Performance and Ethnography in a Mediterranean Island Society* (New York: Scarecrow Press, 2007), Steve Waksman, *Instruments of Desire: The Electric Guitar and the Shaping of Musical Experience* (Cambridge, Mass.: Harvard University Press, 1999), Richard Leppert, *Music and Image: Domesticity, Ideology, and Sociocultural Formation in Eighteenth-Century England* (Cambridge: Cambridge University Press, 1988), Karen Linn, *That Half-Barbaric Twang* (Urbana-Champaign: University of Illinois Press, 1994), and a special issue of *World of Music* devoted to accordion culture, which I edited (2008, vol. 3).

5. Linn, *That Half-Barbaric Twang*, 21.

6. James Clifford, "Traveling Cultures," in *Cultural Studies*, ed. Laurence Grossberg, Cary Nelson, and Paula Treichler (London: Routledge, 1992), 96–116.

7. Karl Neuenfeldt, *The Didjeridu: From Arnhem Land to Internet* (Sydney: John H. Libbey, 1997).

8. Kevin Dawe and Andrew Bennett, *The Cultural Study of Musical Instruments* (New York: Routledge, 2003).

9. Sydney Hutchinson, "Becoming the Tiguera: Female Accordionists in Dominican Merengue Tipico," *Worlds of Music* 3 (50)(2008): 37–57, Cathy Ragland, "'With His Accordion in His Hand': The Impact of the Accordion during the Formative Years of Modern Texas-Mexican Conjunto Music (1930s–1950s)," *Free-Reed Journal* 2 (2001), 25–33.

10. Arjun Appadurai, *The Social Life of Things: Commodities in Cultural Perspective* (New York: Cambridge University Press, 1986), Igor Kopytoff, "The Cultural Biography of Things: Commoditization as Process," in *The Social Life of Things* (Cambridge: Cambridge University Press, 1986), 64–94.

11. Kevin Dawe, *Guitar Cultures* (Oxford: Berg, 2001), 201.

12. Kopytoff, "Cultural Biography of Things," 90.

13. Dawe, *Guitar Cultures*, 222.

14. Jon Frederickson, "Technology and Music Performance in the Age of Mechanical Reproduction," *International Review of the Aesthetics and Sociology of Music* 20 (2) (1989), 193–220.

15. Timothy D. Taylor, *Strange Sounds: Music, Technology and Culture* (New York: Routledge, 2001), Paul Théberge, *Any Sound You Can Imagine: Making Music/Consuming Technology* (Middletown, Conn.: Wesleyan University Press, 1998).

16. Théberge, *Any Sound You Can Imagine*, 18.

17. See Helmi Harrington and Gerhard Kubik's authoritative entry on the accordion in *New Grove Encyclopedia of Music and Musicians*, ed. Stanley Sadie (London: Grove's Dictionary of Music, 2001), 57–65. Harrington, who is curator of the World of Accordions Museum in Superior, Wisconsin, is currently preparing a taxonomy of accordion-family instruments and a catalog of her museum's collection. When these works are published, they are sure to add new and important insights to the field. The only other scholars who have focused in large part on the history of the accordion include Toni Charuhas, *The Accordion* (New York: Accordion Music, 1955), and the following authors. Daniel Binder, *A Formal and Stylistic Analysis of Selected Compositions for Solo Accordion, with Accompanying Ensembles by Twentieth-Century American Composers, with Implications of Their Impact upon the Place of Accordion in the World of Serious Music* (Ph.D. diss., Ball State University, 1981), analyzes contemporary classical repertoire for accordion. James Leary, *Polkabilly: How the Goose Island Ramblers Redefined American Folk Music* (New York: Oxford University Press, 2006), offers snapshots of diverse polka styles in Michigan's Upper Peninsula. Leary explores the significance of the accordion in these styles in "Accordions and Working Class Culture along Lake Superior's South Shore," in *The Accordion on New Shores*, ed. Helena Simonett (Champaign-Urbana: University of Illinois Press, in press). This anthology will explore the different contexts and meaning of the accordion in a range of North and South American traditions from conjunto to Te-

jano to American contemporary avant-garde music. Likewise, a special issue of *World of Music* (2008, vol. 3) devoted to accordion culture explored the instrument's global travels and specific accordion-based music cultures and styles. Scholarly articles on specific accordion traditions and accordion artists appeared in the *Free-Reed Journal* until it ceased publication in 1991 (complete tables of contents and back issues are available from the Center for the Study of Free-Reed Instruments, http://web.gc.cuny.edu/freereed/journal .html. Musicians, journalists, and accordion enthusiasts without scholarly credentials have made valuable contributions. Ronald Flynn and Eddie Chaves, *Golden Age of the Accordion* (Schertz, Tex.: Flynn, 1984; reprint, 1991) compiles profiles and interviews with accordion luminaries, accordion manufacturers, and other helpful information on the accordion's evolution in the United States. For German-language readers, journalist Christoph Wagner documents the accordion's "wild career" in *Das Akkordeon: Eine Wilde Karriere* (Berlin: Transit-Buchverl, 1993).

18. Wade Hall, *Hell Bent for Music: The Life of Pee Wee King* (Lexington: University of Kentucky Press, 1996), is commendable for its excellent scholarship and highly original approach (it is written in the first person from King's perspective). Mainly for fans are a biography of 1950s accordion icon Dick Contino—Bob Bove, *Accordion Man* (Tallahassee: Father and Son, 1994)—and autobiographies of Myron Floren, *Accordion Man* (Brattleboro, Vt.: Stephen Greene Press, 1981), and Lawrence Welk, *Wunnerful, Wunnerful: The Autobiography of Lawrence Welk* (Englewood Cliffs, N.J.: Prentice-Hall, 1971).

19. By this definition (Harrington's), mouth-blown free reeds such as the harmonica and melodica and handheld free reeds such as the concertina and the bandoneon are classified not as accordions but as "accordion-family instruments."

Chapter 1. Advent of the Piano Accordion

1. There is still some uncertainty about the "oldest accordion." The two contenders are Friedrich Buschmann's "Hand-Aeoline" (Berlin 1821) and the Lohner (Sweden c. 1816). See Henry Doktorski, "Birth of the Accordion," CFR, www.ksanti.net/free-reed/history/ birth.html, accessed January 10, 2010; and Doktorski, "Interview with Friedrich Dillner, Owner of What May Be the World's Oldest Accordion," www.ksanti.net/free-reed/index .html, accessed March 2, 2010.

2. Demian's accordion patent, May 23, 1829, available at CFR, www.ksanti.net/free-reed/ history/demian.html.

3. Paralleling the rise of the piano accordion in the United States was the popularity of the English concertina, which found a home in London music halls. See Allan Atlas, "Concertina," in *New Grove Encyclopedia of Music and Musicians,* ed. Stanley Sadie (London: Grove's Dictionary of Music, 2001), 4:236–240; and Atlas, *The Wheatstone English Concertina in Victorian England* (Oxford: Oxford University Press, 1996), 12–15.

4. Sears Roebuck Catalog, 1902, 10, WOA.

5. An expert accordion repair technician notes: owing to the corrosive effects of dust and moisture, as well as dryness (producing cracks and leaks in the bellows), most accordions are only playable for about fifty years (Helmi Harrington, personal communication, June 11, 2005).

6. See Beniamino Bugiolacchi, *A Man and His Dream: An Illustrated History of the Accordion* (Castelfidardo, Italy: Loreto Cassa di Risparmio Foundation, 2005).

7. The one-row Cajun button accordion adopted by bayou musicians necessitates frequent bellows changes, which players exploit and incorporate as elements of their percussive and syncopated musical style. Players of the Irish traditional music favor the two- and three-row B/C melodeons, which can play more notes on a single draw. See Graeme Smith, "The Irish Button Accordion," *World of Music* 3 (1) (2008), 285–311.

8. Harrington, personal communication, June 11, 2005, Superior, Wisconsin. The Anglo concertina and the bandoneon featured in Argentine tango are diatonic members of the accordion family.

9. Ibid., 18.

10. The circumstances of the accordion's dissemination to Italy remain mysterious. Several Italian historians state that young Paolo Soprani received a Demian-like instrument from an Austrian pilgrim, either as a gift or in exchange for lodgings at the family's farmhouse in Castelfidardo, but there is no evidence to support these claims.

11. Report of the Italian Academy of Industrial and Exhibiting Inventors, 1899, MDF.

12. Production data provided by MDF.

13. Beniamino Bugiolacchi, "Castelfidardo: International Centre of Accordion Production in Italy," available at the website of MDF, www.accordions.com/museum, accessed July 2, 2008.

14. Ibid.

15. MDF.

16. According to Bugiolacchi, "Castelfidardo." I have yet to track down the definitive source for this proposal.

17. The button in the major chord row (the third row) diagonally adjacent to the C in the fundamental row is a C major chord. When this button is pressed, a coupling mechanism inside the accordion produces a C major triad (the accordionist plays a whole chord with the touch of one button). Diagonally adjacent to this C major chord, in the minor chord row, a C minor chord button sounds the C minor triad. In the next row is a C seventh chord, and in the last row is a C diminished chord. Above the C fundamental button is the G fundamental with its diagonal row of major, minor, seventh, and diminished chords. This pattern of fundamental with its own row of major, minor, seventh, and diminished chords is found up and down the whole bass section. Although the sight of 120 bass buttons on the accordion's left side appears daunting to the uninitiated, most accordion players only need to learn several finger patterns in order to master it. The so-called alternating bass—with the major, minor, seventh, and diminished chords on C—can be repeated throughout the whole bass keyboard. In addition, the finger pattern needed for playing a C major scale in the bass can be replicated on any fundamental tone, to play all twelve major scales. Among the various sources of information on this topic, Donald Balestrieri's representation of the registers, switches, and buttons of the standard Stradella keyboard is useful: it appeared in *Accordion Quarterly* 1 (2) ([1940s, 1950s?]), reprinted in *Accord* (January-February 1979).

18. Donald Tricarico, *The Italians of Greenwich Village* (New York: Center for Migration Studies, 1984), 78.

19. The Hohner company began making accordions at the turn of the century. Their instruments are also well regarded for tone quality and durability. See Martin Haffner et al., *Legende Hohner Harmonika* [Hohner: The living legend] (Bergkirchen, Germany: Edition Bochinsky, 2006).

20. Marion Jacobson, "Searching for Rockordion: The Changing Image of the Accordion in the United States," *American Music* 25 (2) 2007: 216–243.

21. Although the Guerrini company in San Francisco's catalogs advertised high-end artist's models in the range of $500-$800, a basic "starter" accordion could be had for $75–100 (ibid., 218).

22. Bugiolacchi, "Castelfidardo."

23. For an exploration of the Italian labor migrations to the United States and Argentina, see Patrizio Audenino (1986), and especially John Zucchi's study of the Italian child street musicians in the nineteenth century, *Little Slaves of the Harp* (Liverpool: Liverpool University Press, 1999), whose instrument of choice was the harp.

24. Bugiolacchi, "Castelfidardo."

25. See Alan Trachentenberg and Eric Foner, *The Incorporation of America: Culture and Society in the Gilded Age* (New York: Hill and Wang, 1982).

26. Ronald Flynn, Edwin Davison, and Edward Chavez, *The Golden Age of the Accordion* (Schertz, Tex: Flynn, 1990).

27. The term "vaudeville" (from the French term *voix de ville*), first used in 1883, is generally translated as "voice of the city." See F. Cullen, F. Hackman, and D. McNeilly, "Vaudeville History," in *Vaudeville, Old and New: An Encyclopedia of Variety Performers in America* (London: Routledge, 2007), xi–xxxii.

28. Trachtenberg and Foner, *Incorporation of America*, 12.

29. Joe Laurie, Jr., *Vaudeville: From the Honky Tonks to the Palace* (New York: Holt, 1953), 29.

30. These small free-reed instruments were handy for tucking away inside a bowtie, or for special effects, such as water-squirting concertinas (see Stuart Eydemann, "The Life and Times of the Concertina, with Particular Reference to Scotland" (Ph.D. diss., Open University, Edinburgh, 1995), available at the website of Robert Gaskins, www.concertina .com/eydmann/life-and-times/, accessed June 1, 2010.

31. Information about Ming and Toy is available at the website of the vaudeville scholar "Trav S.D.," http://travsd.wordpress.com/, accessed June 10, 2010.

32. Ove Hahn, *Anthony Galla-Rini:On His Life and the Accordion* (Nils Fläcke Musik, Stockholm, 1986), 38.

33. Ibid., 38.

34. Lawrence Welk with Bernice McGeehan, *Wunnerful, Wunnerful! The Autobiography of Lawrence Welk* (Englewood Cliffs, N.J.: Prentice Hall), 59.

35. Italo-American advertisement, 1930s, available at www.guidodeiro.com, a website devoted to the life and works of Guido Deiro, owned and operated by his son Robert Deiro, accessed January 2, 2010.

36. Guido Deiro, "My Life Story," unpublished manuscript, GDA.

37. Ibid., 5.

38. Robert Deiro (Guido's son), personal communication, January 18, 2011.

39. Undated Des Moines newspaper clipping, ca. 1911, GDA.

40. Deiro, "My Life Story."

41. Guido Deiro, Royal Method for Accordion, 2 vols. (n.p.: Nicomede, 1936).

42. Ibid.

43. Guido Deiro biography, available at www.guidodeiro.com, accessed January 15, 2011, and Robert Deiro, personal communication, January 21, 2011.

44. "Deiro Plays Unique Instrument," *Pittsburgh Post*, May 11, 1911. Both Deiro brothers claimed to have designed their own accordions, contributing to the hype surrounding the accordion in the vaudeville era.

45. *Buffalo Courier*, April 16, 1912; undated review, GDA; *Pittsburgh Post*, May 11, 1911, respectively.

46. Undated review, GDA.

47. Undated, unsigned review, GDA.

48. New York: Biaggio Quattrociocche, n.d. [1930s].

49. Anthony Galla-Rini, letter addressed "To Whom It May Concern," August 10, 2001, GDA.

50. Robert Deiro (Guido's son), quoted in Henry Doktorski, "The Brothers Deiro and Their Accordions," unpublished manuscript provided by Doktorski, 46.

51. Mae West, Goodness Had Nothing To Do With It (New York: Belvedere, 1981).

52. Doktorski, "The Brothers Deiro and Their Accordions."

53. Guido Deiro: The World's Foremost Piano-Accordionist, Vitaphone no. 2968. Filmed at the Warner Brothers studio in Burbank, California, in 1928, the film has been restored and is housed in the UCLA film archives.

54. "Who Was First? The Deiro Brothers Controversy," Accordion News (August 1935), 4–10, available at www.accordions.com/index/art/who_was_first.shtml, accessed November 9, 2008.

55. Peter C. Muir, "Looks Like a Cash Register and Sounds Worse," *Free-Reed Journal*, available at CFR, 86–129.

56. Unsigned review, May 11, 1911, GDA.

57. Guido Deiro, Royal Method, 14.

58. Unsigned review, n.d. [c. 1916], GDA.

59. Minneapolis Journal, December 16, 1912.

60. Accordion News (June 1935), 10.

61. Flynn et al., *Golden Age of the Accordion*, 15.

62. Frederic A. Tedesco, "Organizing an Accordion Band," *Accordion News* (January 1937), 10.

63. "The Accordion Band," Accordion World (February 1937).

64. Harrington, personal communication, August 11, 2008.

65. Flynn et al., *Golden Age*, 8.

66. Middleton, Richard. *Voicing the Popular: On the Subjects of Popular Music* (New York: Routledge, 2006), 89.

67. The "Italian" repertoire and playing style that influenced Italian-American accordionists, and the status of the accordion as "Italian icon," are explored in Jacobson, "Valtaro Musette: Cross-cultural Musical Performance and Repertoire among Northern Italians in

New York," in *Italians in the Americas*, ed. Joseph Sciorra (New York: Fordham University Press, 2010).

68. Muir, "Looks Like a Cash Register," 89.

69. Hahn, *Anthony Galla-Rini*, 38.

70. Ibid., 39.

71. Louis Siquier, "Your Paper," *Accordion News* (October 1934), 5.

72. Russell Brooks, "The New Four-Piece Combination with Accordion," *Accordion World* (1939), 11.

73. Enoch Light, "The Accordion in the Big Band," Accordion News (December 1936), 4.

74. Ibid., 4.

75. See Louis Erenberg, Swingin' the Dream: *Big Band Jazz and the Rebirth of American Culture* (Chicago: University of Chicago Press, 1998).

76. One of the unintended effects of the attempt to promote accordion culture was that it encouraged the appropriation and distillation of black and ethnic music that could be reinterpreted, arranged, and performed by white accordion artists. Accordionists, who were white without exception, worked within a racially segregated music business.

77. Hilding Bergquist, "The Hot Accordionist," Accordion News, n.d., n.p., personal collection.

78. Erenberg, *Swingin' the Dream*, 121.

79. Bergquist, "Hot Accordionist."

80. Vincent Pirro, "The Orchestra Job," Accordion World (March 15, 1936), available at www.ksanti.net/free-reed/essays/pirro.html.

81. A complete discography of early accordion recordings is beyond the scope of this book. However, detailed information on many of these recordings can be found in Peter C. Muir, "The Deiro Recordings: Italian-American and Other Ethnic Issues, 1911–1934, With a Complete Discography of the Recordings of Guido and Pietro Deiro," *Free-Reed Journal* 4 (2002). The Wikipedia article on Charles Magnante offers a comprehensive discography of his records in a wide range of styles: "Charles Magnante," http://en.wikipedia.org/wiki/Charles_Magnante, accessed June 17, 2010. Several publications have addressed, more broadly, the significance of ethnic recordings: Judith McCullough, *Ethnic Recordings in America: A Neglected Heritage* (Washington, D.C.: American Folklife Center, 1982), and Richard K. Spottswood, *Ethnic Music on Records: A Discography of Ethnic Recordings Produced in the United States, 1893–1942* (Champaign-Urbana: University of Illinois Press), 7 vols.

82. Muir, "Deiro Recordings," 190.

83. Ibid., 190.

84. Ibid., 8.

85. See "Charles Magnante," Wikipedia.

86. Gage Averill addressed a similar problem in early recordings of men's quartets. See Averill, *Four Parts, No Waiting: A Social History of American Barbershop Harmony* (New York: Oxford, 2003), 61.

87. Pietro Deiro, "The Accordionist on the Airwaves," *Etude* (January 1938), n.p.

88. All three volumes were published by Pietro Deiro Publications, New York.

89. Myron and Randee Floren, *Accordion Man* (Brattleboro, Vt.: S. Greene, 1981), 112.

90. Charles Magnante," Background for Success: Making Good in Front of the Mike Requires Skill as a Soloist and Orchestra Accordionist," *Accordion World* (August 1938), 10.

91. Flynn et al., Golden Age, 215.

92. Ibid., 2. Cirelli moved to San Rafael in the 1980s.

93. Flynn et al. also mention John Anconi, Alfred Alemstad, John Pezzolo, Reno Pucci, and Michael Parti (ibid., 3).

94. Ibid., 116.

95. Helmi Harrington, personal communication, June 11, 2005.

96. Flynn et al., *Golden Age*, 3.

97. Guerrini Catalog, c. 1920, 53, WOA.

98. Vincent Cirelli, interview by the author, August 25, 2008, Cotati, California. Cirelli, age eighty-eight at the time of our interview, repairs and collects some of the earliest Guerrini accordions. His shop, Cirelli Accordion Repair Service, was located in the Mission District until the 1980s.

99. Palmer patent, 1925, Patents file, WOA.

100. Flynn et al., *Golden* Age, 8.

101. Ibid., 26.

102. Colombo Catalog, 1920s, WOA; also cited in Flynn et al., *Golden Age*, 74.

103. I am indebted to Helmi Harrington for this explanation of the evolution of these early accordions.

104. Colombo Catalog, 1920s, WOA.

105. Ibid., 74.

106. Harrington, personal communication, June 11, 2005.

107. Standard's catalog advertised the fact that all its models were custom made by a single craftsman (Flynn et al., *Golden* Age, 97). Vincent Cirelli confirms, in addition, that Guerrini only made custom instruments; Cirelli himself made many instruments from start to finish (Cirelli, personal communication, August 25, 2008).

108. Bugiolacchi, "Castelfidardo."

109. Virtual Museum of the City of San Francisco, "The Panama Pacific Exposition of 1915," www.sfmuseum.org/hist9/ppietxt1.html, accessed November 7, 2008.

110. List of Guerrini Accordions at the 1915 Panama Pacific Exposition, San Francisco, available at the website of H. A. Layer, http://online.sfsu.edu/~hl/a.html, accessed November 9, 2008.

111. Siquier, "Your Paper."

112. Louis Siquier, "Looking over 1936," Accordion News (December 1936), 2.

113. Ibid., 3.

114. "Meet Stanley Darrow: Director, Westmont Philharmonic Accordion Orchestra," *Accordion World* (September 1958).

Chapter 2. Squeezebox Bach

1. Joe Biviano, "History Is Made at Carnegie," *Accordion World* (April 1939), available at the website of CFR, www.ksanti.net/free-reed/essays/historyatcarnegie.html, accessed June 10, 2010.

2. Unsigned review of Magnante concert (n.d.), *Cue*, April 1939, Available at www.ksanti
.net/free-reed/essays/historyatcarnegie.html, accessed May 27, 2009.

3. Minutes of the first meeting of the AAA, March 9, 1938, reprinted in American Accordionists Association, *Fiftieth Anniversary Souvenir Journal and Program*, 1988, 10–11,
personal collection of the author.

4. The Classical Free-Reed, Inc., available at http://free-reed.net/, accessed June 10, 2010.

5. Lawrence W. Levine, *Highbrow/Lowbrow: The Emergence of Cultural Hierarchy in
America* (Cambridge, Mass.: Harvard University Press, 1988)

6. John H. Reuther, "Report of the 1936 Music Trades Convention at Chicago," *Accordion World* (August 1936), 16.

7. Ronald Flynn, Edwin Davison, and Edward Chavez, *The Golden Age of the Accordion*
(Schertz, Tex.: Flynn, 1990), 119.

8. Reuther, "Report of the 1936 Music Trades Convention at Chicago," 16.

9. Ibid., 16.

10. Helmi Harrington, personal communication, June 17, 2008.

11. Flynn et al., *Golden Age*, 118.

12. "An Accordion Built on Truly Artistic Lines," *Accordion News* (January 1935), 12.

13. Ibid.

14. Ibid.

15. Henry Doktorski, "Accordion Registrations," *New Music Box* (February 1, 2005),
available at www.newmusicbox.org/article.nmbx?id=4178, accessed July 9, 2010, explains
the various reed combinations and their tone colors.

16. John Reuther, "Report of the 1936 Music Trades Convention at Chicago," *Accordion
World* (August 1936), 16.

17. Willard Palmer, "Should Accordionists Play Bach?," *Accordion World* (April 1949),
n.p.

18. "John Serry, Sr.," www.wikipedia.org/wiki/john_serry_sr., accessed July 14, 2007.

19. In northern Europe in the 1950s and 1960s, accordionist-composer Mogens Ellengard had popularized the free-bass accordion, and many composers in his native Denmark
had begun to write works for him. In 1968, Ellengard introduced the manufacture of free-
bass accordions with nothing but free-bass layouts to accommodate beginning players.

20. Joan Sommers, personal communication, July 15, 2009.

21. Since 1965, only one American accordionist, Peter Soave, has claimed the first prize
in the Coupe Mondiale. Soave, like most winners of that competition, plays chromatic
button accordion.

22. Information provided by the Deiro family at www.guidodeiro.com, a website devoted
to the life and works of Guido Deiro, owned and operated by his son Robert Deiro, accessed July 1, 2009. John Barsuglia opened and operated some of Guido Deiro's California
studios. To establish the Jackson, California, studio in 1938, Guido himself performed a
concert at the Amador Theater, according to a poster announcing the concert (available at
www.guidodeiro.com/accordionteacher1.html).

23. Among the dozens of leading accordion teachers and performers I have interviewed
who were influenced by these door-to-door pitches is Robert Young McMahan, who was
"dazzled" by the impromptu accordion demo given by a representative of the Guild Accordion School at his home in Washington, D.C.

24. "US Musical Instrument Sales 1909–1965," National Association of Music Merchants, Library and Resource Center, Carlsbad, California.

25. "O. Pagani," *Accordion World*, 1936.

26. Ibid.

27. Ibid.

28. Anthony Galla-Rini, "The Accordion in the Serious Field of Music," *Musical Merchandise* (October 1948).

29. Frederic A. Tedesco, "Organizing an Accordion Band," *Accordion News* (January 1937), 10.

30. For example, the Santo Santucci method, the Murray Golden Piano Accordion Method, and many others.

31. Willard Palmer and Bill Hughes, *Palmer-Hughes Accordion Course,* vol. 7 (New York: Alfred Music, 1952).

32. Flynn et al., *Golden Age of the Accordion,* 96.

33. Charles Nunzio, personal communication, June 4, 2004.

34. These and other method books, originally published by AMPCO, Pagani, and Deiro Publications, are available from Ernest Deffner Publications.

35. Accordion teachers credit Anthony Galla-Rini with establishing these conventions. There is very little published information on accordion notation. The oddity about AAA notation is that it does not represent exactly what is being played. Most accordions play the seventh and the diminished seventh as triads, omitting the fifth. This allows for the creation of different chords or tonal combinations by adding additional notes or chords. For this reason, the Accordion Teachers Guild objected to AAA notation on the grounds that it encouraged musical illiteracy among accordionists. The Guild advocated notating each of the actual tones produced by the chord buttons. For more on this controversy, see Henry Doktorski, *The Brothers Deiro and Their Accordions* (Oakdale, Pa.: Classical Free-Reed, 2005), 21.

36. Concert programs, GDA.

37. Galla-Rini, "Accordion in the Serious Field of Music."

38. Pietro Deiro, *Ukrainian Folksongs and Dances,* ed. Michael Storr, PD no. 870 (New York: AMPCO, n.d.), 1.

39. A lone exception to this was Deiro's *Hebrew and Jewish Songs and Dances,* ed. Elsie Bennett (n.p., n.d.), PD no. 847, PDA, which was designed to be used in "Centers, Camps, Synagogues, Hebrew Schools, and all types of youth and adult sings." It could also be used in congregational singing, campfire song fests, and dance groups (publisher's introduction).

40. Doktorski, *Brothers Deiro and Their Accordions,* 16.

41. Ibid.

42. Hilding Bergquist, "A Symphonic Seat for the Accordion," *Accordion World* (July 1948).

43. Galla-Rini, "Accordion in the Field of Serious Music."

44. Helmi Harrington recalled that when she was a graduate student in her twenties, she approached accordion virtuoso Carmelo Pino to compliment him on a presentation, with carefully worded observations that would mark her as a knowledgeable colleague in the accordion field. He dismissed her remarks as "sweet." Harrington also reported that Pino

later apologized, acknowledging the implied sexism in his remarks, and vowed to change his attitudes toward women. Helmi Harrington, personal communication, June 16, 2008.

45. Faithe Deffner, "The Contest Learning Experience," *Accord* 1 (1979–80), 5.

46. Mickey Bisilia, "Building Accordion Champs," *Accordion World* (October 1957).

47. William Schimmel, personal communication, June 1, 2004.

48. Henry Kingsbury, *Music, Talent, and Performance: A Conservatory Cultural System* (Philadelphia: Temple University Press, 2001).

49. See, for example, William Grant Still, "Lilt" (New York: Pietro Deiro Publications, 1968, and William Schimmel, "The Spring Street Ritual" (Mineola, N.Y.: Ernest Deffner, 1979), both reprinted from *Accord* (January-February 1979), 16–17.

50. Joan Sommers, personal communication, July 15, 2009.

51. Bisilia, "Building Accordion Champs."

52. In the late 1920s, Hohner came up with a new idea for promoting the accordion through "accordion orchestras," no doubt providing the model for American accordion symphonies and bands in the 1940s and 1950s. The Hohner Symphony, an ensemble of thirty skilled lay accordionists, toured extensively throughout Germany and neighboring countries until the Nazis rose to power and repurposed the Hohner factory for the manufacture of weapons. See Christoph Wagner, *Das Akkordeon: Eine Wilde Karriere* (Berlin: Transit-Buchverl, 1993). Both accordion bands and orchestras performed with other instruments. Accordion bands tended to include guitar, bass, and drums. Accordion orchestras were accompanied by symphonic instruments (strings, winds, and percussion).

53. Jacob C. Neupauer, interview with the author, June 18, 2009.

54. Ibid.

55. According to AAA historian Joan Graumann, Galla-Rini rejoined the AAA in 1960. The "new" notation was no longer objectionable to him.

56. Neupauer also conveyed this impression to the author of a biographical article on him, "Slovak American Personality: Dr. Jacob C. Neupauer," in Holy Trinity Society newsletter, Branch 796 KJ, Egypt, Pennsylvania, n.d. [1986?].

57. At many institutions, such as Columbia University, accordionists have been hired as adjunct professors to instruct composition and theory students who play accordion, but no college or university other than UMKC offers an accordion major.

58. Joan Sommers, personal communication, July 15, 2009.

59. Robert Young McMahan, personal communication, May 29, 2009.

60. Bennett, "Commissioning Music for the Accordion," *Accordion Horizons* 1 (1) (1964), 22.

61. These included Hindemith's *Kammermusik No. 1*, Virgil Thomson's *Four Saints in Three Acts*, and a brief accordion appearance in the tavern scene of Berg's *Wozzeck*.

62. For these observations, I am indebted to Robert McMahan, who interviewed Elsie Bennett in 1995 and documented some of these observations in a fine article, "The Accordion Works of William Grant Still," *Free-Reed Journal*, **n.d.**, available at www.ksanti .net/free-reed/essays/mcmahan.html, accessed May 29, 2009.

63. Personal communication, Robert Young McMahan, June 1, 2009.

64. Bennett, "Commissioning Music for the Accordion," 22.

65. Elsie Bennett, *Paul Creston's Concerto for Accordion and Orchestra*, report from the

AAA Commissioning Committee (1957), 10, in Bennett files, personal collection of Robert Young McMahan.

66. McMahan, "The First Commissioned Work of the AAA," American Accordionists Association Sixtieth Anniversary Jubilee Program (July 8–12, 1998), New Orleans, 5, personal collection of the author. McMahan assumed Bennett's responsibilities for the Commissioning Committee on her death in 2005.

67. Ibid.

68. McMahan, "The Twentieth Commissioned Work of the AAA," American Accordionists Association Seventieth Anniversary Festival, August 13–17, Arlington, Va. (2008), 4, personal collection of the author.

69. McMahan, "Accordion Works of William Grant Still."

70. Unfortunately there is no published recording available of the work. McMahan was kind enough to share his own performance on CD, part of a recording project in progress.

71. McMahan, personal communication, May 29, 2009.

72. At www.ameraccord.com.

73. Helmi Harrington, personal communication, July 15, 2009.

74. Stravinsky was reputed to dislike the organ, so it comes as no surprise that he would have felt the same way about the accordion. McMahan, personal communication, May 29, 2009.

75. McMahan, "The Ninth, Tenth, and Eleventh Commissioned Works of the AAA," American Accordionists Association, 2002 Festival Program, July 10–14, Minneapolis, personal collection of the author.

76. McMahan, The Fifth, Sixth, and Seventh Commissioned Works of the AAA," American Accordionists Association, 2000 Festival Program, July 12–16, Washington, D.C., personal collection of the author.

77. McMahan, "The Twelfth, Thirteenth, and Fourteenth Commissioned Works of the AAA," American Accordionists Association, Sixty-Fifth Anniversary Celebration Program, Philadelphia, July 9–13 (2003), 8, personal collection of the author.

78. Ibid.

79. The Commissioned Works of the AAA, pt. 3, 3.

80. McMahan, personal communication, June 15, 2009.

81. Ibid.

82. The compositional practice of one such composer is the subject of Jacobson, "The Accordion in New Scores: Paradigms of Authorship and Identity in William Schimmel's Musical 'Realities,'" in *The Accordion on New Shores*, ed. Helena Simonett (Urbana: University of Illinois Press, forthcoming).

Chapter 3. Squeezebox Rock

1. Nicholas DeVores, "Uncle, May We Swap You a Ship for Some Accordions?" *Accordion World* 8 (June 1944), 2.

2. "Accordion Goes All the Way to War," *Accordion World* 8 (June 1944), 11.

3. Ibid., 11.

4. Ibid., 12.

5. Nicholas DeVores, "Rumblings of Unrest," *Accordion World* 3 (1) (n.d.).

6. "Historical Sketch," unpublished manuscript, Inventory of the Graham W. Jackson, Sr., Papers, Auburn Avenue Research Library on African-American Culture and History, Atlanta-Fulton Public Library System, available at www.dlg.galileo.usg.edu/aafa, accessed March 29, 2010. In 1945, a photograph in *Life* of Jackson playing the accordion and weeping at Franklin D. Roosevelt's White House funeral became a national symbol of grief and mourning. The photo by Ed Clark can be viewed at www.gettyimages.com/detail/50596355/.

7. Charles Nunzio, personal communication, June 4, 2003.

8. Sigmund Spaeth, "The Accordion: A Natural for School Music," *Accordion World* (1940), 2.

9. Frank Gaviani was among the accordion teachers who received their certification under the GI bill. Ronald Flynn, Edwin Davison, and Edward Chavez, *The Golden Age of the Accordion* (Schertz, Tex.: Flynn, 1990), 136.

10. At www.dickcontino.com.

11. Bob Bove, *Accordion Man: Dick Contino* (Tallahassee: Father and Son Press, 1994), 7.

12. At www.dickcontino.com.

13. Bove, *Accordion Man*, 26.

14. Ibid., 28.

15. Ibid., 29–30.

16. Ibid., 51.

17. Ian Whitcombe, "My Uncle Wrote Lady of Spain," available at the website of Ian Whitcomb, www.picklehead.com/ian/uncle.html, accessed October 15, 2009.

18. Contino appeared in the Hollywood films *Daddy-O* (1958) and *Big Night* (1959).

19. James Bacon, "Dick Contino Challenges Liberace to Musical Duel." *Pittsburgh Post-Gazette*, August 27, 1955, 20.

20. Bove, *Accordion Man*, 86.

21. Ibid., 87.

22. Ibid., 198.

23. Samuel Honigsberg, "Lawrence Welk" (review of Edgewater Beach Hotel engagement), *Billboard*, August 12, 1939, 13; and George T. Simon, *The Big Bands*, 4th ed. (New York: Schirmer Books, 1981), 449–51.

24. Simon, *Big Bands*, 87.

25. Myron Floren, *On the Accordion: Waltzes, Polkas and Schottisches* (Brunswick, Me., n.d. [c. 1960]).

26. As accordion performance artist Frank Lima proclaims on his website promoting his services for events: "I play anything . . . except 'Lady of Spain' and Metallica"; available at www.greatmorgani.com, accessed June 10, 2010.

27. Paul Friedlander, *Rock 'n' Roll: A Social History* (Boulder, Colo.: Westwood Press, 1997), 29.

28. Reebee Garafalo, *Rockin' Out: Popular Music in the USA* (Upper Saddle River, N.J.: Pearson-Prentice-Hall, 2005).

29. US Musical Instrument Sales, 1909–1965, unpublished document, Library and Resource Center, National Association of Music Merchants, Carlsbad, California.

30. George Nelson describes this phenomenon convincingly in *Where Did Our Love Go? The Rise and Fall of the Motown Sound* (New York: St. Martin's Press, 1985).

31. Jerry Trecroce, email correspondence with author, September 2, 2003.

32. "The Angry: Canton, Ohio, 1962–1966," available at the website of Keith Buckley and Dan Angott, www.myfirstband.com/FirstBandAngry.html, accessed February 16, 2007.

33. Michael Hicks, personal communication, February 16, 2007.

34. William Schimmel, personal communication, June 15, 2003.

35. Bill Bullock, "Keep Rock 'n' Roll under Control," *Accordion World* (January 1957), 5.

36. "So You Lost a Student?" *Accordion World* (June 1956), 8.

37. Ralph Dougal, "How I Changed to Rock 'n' Roll," *Accordion and Guitar World* (October 1962), 10.

38. Elsie Bennett, "Commissioning Music for the Accordion," *Accordion Horizons* (1962), 43.

39. Rebecca R. Furco, "Accordions Do Rock 'n' Roll as Well as Lawrence Welk," *Menomonee Falls (WI) News* (February 1996), available at the website of Baldoni Accordions, www.baldoni.com/Family_History.html, accessed July 14, 2007.

40. Faithe Deffner, personal communication, September 17, 2003.

41. "Tiger Combo 'Cordion Introduced," press release, n.d., provided by Ernest Deffner Affiliates, Long Island City, New York.

42. Ibid.

43. Some of my informants have claimed that this high-gloss paint actually came from the Fiat factory in Italy.

44. "Introducing the Tiger Combo 'Cordion," press release, n.d. [1965?], from Deffner Associates.

45. Alan Polivka, personal communication, September 11, 2003.

46. Bove, *Accordion Man*, 41.

47. Faithe Deffner, "In Memory of Dr. Willard ('Bill') Palmer," *Free-Reed Journal* (July 1996), reprinted in *Free-Reed Journal*, available at the website of CFR, www.ksanti.net/free-reed/essays/palmerbio.html, accessed July 14, 2007.

48. "Celebrity Interview with Faithe Deffner," www.accordions.com/mterviews/deffner/index.shtml, accessed July 14, 2007.

49. Ralph Stricker, personal communication, January 15, 2007.

50. Delfin Vigil, "Squeeze Play," *San Francisco Examiner*, June 4, 2006, arts sec., 1.

51. Many accordion jokes are available online at www.accordions.com/index/fun/jok/fun_jok.shtml. Also see Richard March's forthcoming analysis of this phenomenon in "Accordion Jokes," in *The Accordion on New Shores*, ed. Helena Simonett (Urbana-Champaign: University of Illinois Press, forthcoming).

52. William Schimmel, personal communication, June 16, 2004.

53. According to his biography, Barbutti, an accomplished accordionist, once operated two studios in his hometown of Scranton, Pennsylvania.

54. Schimmel, personal communication, June 16, 2004.

Chapter 4. Crossover Accordionists

1. Turpeinen is referred to in this manner in various postings on a Finnish-American genealogy website, http://finlander.genealogia.fi/archive/index.php/.

2. Victor Greene, *A Passion for Polka: Old-Time Ethnic Music in America* (Berkeley: University of California Press, 1992), 238.

3. Columbia Records released "Just Because" on Frank Yankovic and His Yanks, *All-Time Hits* (FL 9503 and CL-6303); "Blue Skirt Waltz" was released on their *Waltz Parade* (Columbia Records FL-9529).

4. Greene, *Passion for Polka*, 239.

5. James Leary, "Accordions and Working Class Culture along Lake Superior's South Shore," in *The Accordion on New Shores*, ed. Helena Simonett (Champaign-Urbana: University of Illinois Press, forthcoming).

6. For a discussion of mainstream American polka and a comprehensive survey of regional styles, see—and hear—James Leary and Richard March's *Down Home Dairyland*, packaged with forty half-hour radio programs produced for Wisconsin Public Radio (Madison: University of Wisconsin-Extension, 1996), reissued with twenty compact discs (Madison: Center for the Study of Upper Midwestern Cultures, 2004), distributed by University of Wisconsin Press.

7. Jerry Schneider, "Etwas schoen von Chilton," cited in program book for Leary and March, *Down Home Dairyland*, 45.

8. Leary, "Accordions and Working Class Culture," 1.

9. Ibid., 3.

10. Leary and March, "The Accordions," *Down Home Dairyland*, CD 17, program 33.

11. Ibid.

12. James Leary, *Yodeling in Dairyland: A History of Swiss Music in Wisconsin* (Mount Horeb, Wisc.: Wisconsin Folk Museum, 1991).

13. See James Leary, *Polkabilly: How the Goose Island Ramblers Redefined American Folk Music* (New York: Oxford University Press, 2006).

14. Greene, *Passion for Polka*, 241.

15. *Accordion World* 12 (April 1948), 8.

16. James Leary, *In Tune with Tradition: Folk Instruments in Wisconsin* (Mount Horeb, Wisc.: Wisconsin Folk Museum, 1990), 30.

17. According to the 1920 census, Michigan and Minnesota were the states with the largest Finnish-American populations. The total Finnish-speaking population in America at the time numbered about twelve thousand.

18. Leary, "Legacy of Viola Turpeinen," 6.

19. Ibid., 6.

20. Greene, *Passion for Polka*, 187.

21. Taru Spiegel, "Finns in America," online reference information, European Reading Room, Library of Congress, Washington, D.C., available at the website of the Library of Congress, www.loc.gov/rr/european/FinnsAmer/finchro.html, last accessed March 2, 2010.

22. Jacket notes to "Major Bowes Radio Check," *Viola Turpeinen: American Hanuriprincessa*, vol. 1. Released on the Finnish label Fifty Records, these records are distributed in

the United States by Accordions Worldwide on their website, www.musicforaccordions. com/recordings.

23. Ibid.

24. Spiegel, "Finns in America."

25. Leary, "Accordions and Working Class Culture."

26. Leary, "Legacy of Viola Turpeinen," 8.

27. Greene, *Passion for Polka*, 190.

28. Ibid., 190.

29. Jacket notes to "Major Bowes Radio Check," *Viola Turpeinen*, vol. 1.

30. Ibid.

31. Ibid.

32. "Major Bowes Radio Check," *Viola Turpeinen*, vol. 1.

33. Leary, "Legacy of Viola Turpeinen," 27.

34. Ibid., 188.

35. Brugnoli's region of origin, Emilia, is now known as Emilia-Romagna, as it merged with Romagna to become a single administrative region of Italy in 1947. Until Italy unified in 1861, Emilia had been part of the Duchy of Parma. For more specifics, see "Emilia Romagna," available at the website of the Italy World Club, www.italyworldclub.com/emilia/, accessed December 31, 2008.

36. Carol Schiavi, "Peter Spagnoli: New York Valtaro Accordionist."

37. See Marion Jacobson, "Valtaro Musette: Cross-cultural Musical Performance and Repertoire in Manhattan's Northern Italian Community," in *Italian American Folk Culture*, ed. Joseph Sciorra (Bronx, N.Y.: Fordham University Press, 2010), 134–50.

38. A pair of ethnic dance music folios for accordion published by Ernest Deffner in 1953.

39. Peter Spagnoli, interview with author, c. February 11, 2006.

40. See Louis Erenberg, *Swingin' the Dream* (Chicago: University of Chicago Press, 1999), for an exploration of the jazz scene in the 1920s and 1930s.

41. This event was held at the City University of New York Graduate Center on March 23, 2001, sponsored by the John Calandra Italian American Institute at Queens College and the Center for the Study of Free-Reed Instruments.

42. James Periconi, "Vergogna e Risorgimento: The Secret Life of an Italian-American Accordionist," *Free-Reed Journal* 4 (2002), 49.

43. Mary Boatti, personal communication, New York City, December 3, 2008. The spatial divisions sought after by some of the residents of these neighborhoods reflected a long-standing system of social stratification ranking northerners as *alt'Italiani* (high Italians) and southerners as *bass'Italiani* (low Italians). See Donald Tricarico, *The Italians of Greenwich Village: the Social Structure and Transformation of an Ethnic Community* (Staten Island, N.Y.: Center for Migration Studies of New York, 1984). According to some scholars—and my informants—perceived differences in status and economic standing set up serious barriers between these two groups.

44. Dominic Karcic, "John (Gianod Scud'lein) Brugnoli's Val-Taro Musette Orchestra," *Washington Metropolitan Accordion Club News,* available at www.washingtonaccordions .org/ValTaro.htm#brugnoli, accessed February 11, 2009. This article also appeared in Italian translation in *Gazzetta di Parma* (September 10, 2002).

45. For further exploration of the ballo liscio tradition and its repertoire, see Goffredo Plastino, jacket notes to *Italian Journey: Emilia-Romagna*, Alan Lomax's historic 1950s recordings from central Italy (Rounder CD, 2002).

46. Carol Schiavi, "Peter Spagnoli."

47. Ibid.

48. Ibid.

49. Dominic Karcic, "John Brugnoli and the Val-Taro Musette Orchestra," *Washington Metropolitan Accordion Club News* (2002), available at www.washingtonaccordions.org/ValTaro.htm, accessed June 21, 2007.

50. Schiavi, "Pete Spagnoli."

51. Pete Spagnoli, personal communication, February 11, 2006.

52. Ibid.

53. In her 2002 address to the Society for Ethnomusicology meeting in Toronto (published in *Ethnomusicology* in 2005), Barbara Kirshenblatt Gimblett highlighted folklorization as a process by which artists strategize ways to add value to their work by highlighting its authenticity.

54. Rounder's Italian Treasury series of recordings by Alan Lomax and Diego Carpitella contain some representative performances of Italian polkas.

55. See James Leary and Richard March. "Dutchmen Bands: Genre, Ethnicity, and Pluralism in the Upper Midwest," in *Creative Ethnicity: Symbols and Strategies of Contemporary Ethnic Life*, ed. Stephen Stern and John Allan Cicala (Logan, Utah: Utah State University Press, 1991), 21–44.

56. Without explaining why, my accordion teacher—who had played with a Polish polka band in Dearborn, Michigan—always instructed me to select a single-reed switch (Clarinet) or the two-reed switch (Bandoneon).

57. Alan Polivka's article on wet versus dry tuning provides some useful insights into the cultural construction of texture in accordion playing; available at the website of Hans Palm, www.accordionpage.com/wetdry.html, accessed June 23, 2008.

58. See ibid.

59. See Luisa Del Giudice, "From Autobiography to Advocacy: Italian Traditional Song in Toronto," *Journal of Canadian Studies* 29 (spring 1994), 1–17.

60. Accordionist Ray Oreggia has claimed that he was "listening to Valtaro before he was born" (Schiavi, "Peter Spagnoli.")

61. Dominic Karcic, personal communication.

62. The same might be said of Valtaro singers Mario Nicolich and Eugene Gercovich, who performed Valtaro repertoire on the Colonial Italian Sing-Along albums. Nicolich, a native Italian speaker, was born in a part of Croatia that was formerly under Italian rule. Although Croatian, he considers himself to be an admirer of and advocate for Italian culture and Valtaro music specifically and continues to perform the Valtaro repertoire today.

63. For a discussion of the "twilight" phenomenon, which has been disputed by other scholars, see Richard Alba, *Italian Americans: Into the Twilight of Ethnicity* (New Jersey: Prentice Hall, 1985).

64. Luisa Del Giudice discusses the shift in Italian musical tastes in "Italian Traditional Song in Toronto: From Autobiography to Advocacy," *Journal of Canadian Studies* 29 (1) (1994), 1–17.

65. Although the resorts of the Catskills region are known most famously as the borscht belt, this area was home to a number of resorts catering to Italian Americans, such as Villa Roma, Villa Bocilli, and Beverly Farms. Accordion music (solo and ensemble performance) was, according to Dominic Karcic, the featured musical entertainment at the Italian establishments, drawing clientele from other resort communities on weekends.

66. Sing Along in Italian albums, such as Colonial LP 231 and Colonial LP 212, are out of print and only available in private collections.

67. Peter Spagnoli recorded two long-playing records on that label with John Brugnoli, featuring folk songs of Valtaro, *Balliamo e Cantiamo Con Valtaro* and *Cantano I Due Menestrelli* (Fiesta Records FLPS 1542), and an instrumental album, *Valtaro Musette: Popular Italian Favorites* (Fiesta Records FLPS 1515).

68. Available at the website of Milwaukee Festa Italiana, www.festaitaliana.com/, accessed April 23, 2008.

69. Ibid.

70. See Robert Dolgan, *America's Polka King: The Real Story of Frank Yankovic* (New York: Gray, 2006).

71. Greene, *Passion for Polka*, 232.

72. Frank Smodic, Jr., "Frank Yankovic through the Years," unpublished manuscript, available at www.polkas.com/yankovic/yankbio.htm, a website maintained by Nancy Hlad, issued in celebration of Yankovic's seventy-fifth birthday, August 12, 1990, 2.

73. Quite valuable for understanding the evolution of the genre is the website www .polkas.nl, maintained by a knowledgeable Dutch collector of Slovenian-style polka music. The site has biographical information and complete audio clips and is regularly updated to include contemporary practitioners such as accordionists Lynne Marie and Alex Meixner.

74. Dolgan, *America's Polka King*, 276.

75. Smodic, "Frank Yankovic's Life Story," 2.

76. Ibid., 2.

77. Greene, *Passion for Polka,* 232. Comprehensive discographical information on all of Yankovic's recordings can be found on a Dutch website devoted to Slovenian-style polka, available at www.polkas.nl (accessed June 10, 2010).

78. Ibid., 2

79. Smodic, "Frank Yankovic's Life Story," 2.

80. Bill Kennedy, "Hollywood Goes Polka Slap Happy: Dotted Ties and Dresses Worn in Dance Revival," *Redbook* (May 1950).

81. Don Dornbrook, "Roll Out the Polka, Bugs' Jitters Cease," *Milwaukee Journal* (June 10, 1948), 11.

82. Dolgan, *America's Polka King*, 3.

83. Televised performance of "Hoop De Do Polka," c. 1960, available at www.youtube .com/watch?v=e2BJtv9TnqQ, accessed June 14, 2010.

Chapter 5. New Main Squeeze

1. Bob Doerschuk, "Rock's New Main Squeeze," *Keyboard*, December 1987, 66.

2. Cover photo, *Keyboard*, December 1987.

3. Laura Accinelli, "How the Accordion Went from Wunnerful to Cool," *New Times Los Angeles*, [1996–2002], undated clipping in author's files.

4. Faithe Deffner, "Groups Start Using Accordion," *Music Trades*, October 1967.

5. Deffner, "The Accordion in Advertising," available at the website Accordions World Wide: The Largest Accordion Resource on the Web, www.accordions.com/index/squ/squ_96_11_29.shtml#1196product, accessed June 10, 2010. See also "Seeing Accordions," unpublished manuscript by anonymous author and compiler of hundreds of "accordion sightings" in advertisements, movies, and other popular culture outlets, WOA.

6. Frank Busso, an officer in the AAA, told a National Public Radio interviewer that he was delighted by the Volkswagen advertisement, which was televised in 2003.

7. Undated letter from Art West to Helmi Harrington, WOA.

8. *MTV Unplugged*, taped at Brooklyn Academy of Music, February 14, 1995.

9. Aaron Howard, "Flaco Jimenez Talks about Fame and Music on the Texas Border," *RootsWorld*, www.rootsworld.com/interview/flaco.html, last accessed January 22, 2010.

10. Ibid.

11. We need to be cautious about Buckwheat's assessment. Zydeco has been seen as an urban music, reflecting the influence of rock and R & B, and Buckwheat himself has been part of that process of transformation and change. Most of zydeco's leading practitioners live and work in the culturally diverse urban metropolitan area of Houston. The music has a wide harmonic range; hence, many of its practitioners favor the piano accordion. For an excellent discussion of zydeco's roots see Roger Wood, *Texas Zydeco* (Austin: University of Texas Press, 2006).

12. *Polkasonic* was released on Cleveland International Records, CIR-1023-2; *Let's Kiss!* on Dentone Records. A complete discography of Brave Combo's work is available at their official website, www.brave.com.

13. According to *Billboard*, their eponymous album, *Gipsy Kings,* sold one million copies in 1995. "World Music: Year to Date Charts," *Billboard* 107 (December 23, 1995), 68.

14. See, for example, Timothy D. Taylor, *Global Pop, Global Markets* (New York: Routledge, 1997); Simon Frith, "The Discourse of World Music," in *Western Music and Its Others: Difference, Representation and Appropriation*, ed. Georgina Born and David Hesmondhalgh (Berkeley: University of California Press, 2000); Jan Ling, "Is World Music the Classic Music of Our Time?," *Popular Music* 22 (2) (May 2003), 235–40; Louise Meintjes, "Paul Simon's *Graceland*, South Africa, and the Mediation of Musical Meaning," *Ethnomusicology* 24 (winter 1990): 37–73.

15. Carl Finch, personal communication, January 26, 2010.

16. Brave Combo's first (vinyl) records are no longer in print, but many of their early song compositions and arrangements can be found on the CD *Musical Varieties*, 1987, Rounder CD 11546.

17. Brave Combo, *Mood Swing Music.* 1996, Rounder CD 11756.

18. Carl Finch, personal communication, January 26, 2010.

19. Timothy D. Taylor's discussions of some of these artists in *Global Pop, Global Market*, are helpful in framing their cultural, political and educational agendas.

20. Ibid.

21. Guy Klucevsek, "Accordion Misdemeanors: A Musical Reminiscence," *Free-Reed*

Journal, available at CFR, www.ksanti.net/free-reed/essays/misdemeanors.html, accessed May 29, 2009.

22. Klucevsek, personal communication, January 25, 2010.

23. Ibid.

24. Ibid.

25. Klucevsek, "Accordion Misdemeanors," 3.

26. Klucevsek, personal communication, January 25, 2010.

27. Ibid.

28. Annie Proulx and various musicians, *Accordion Crimes,* audio CD (Prince Frederick, Md.: Recorded Books, 1996).

29. Klucevsek, "Accordion Misdemeanors," 5.

30. Ibid.

31. Ibid.

32. William Schimmel, personal communication, June 11, 2004.

33. David Byrne, "Machines of Joy: I Have Seen the Future and It Is Squiggly," *Leonardo Music Journal* 12 (2002), 7–9.

34. Byrne, "Machines of Joy," 9.

35. Doerschuk, "Rock's New Main Squeeze," 70.

36. Charlie Giordano's recording credits are listed at the website of The All Music Guide, www.allmusic.com/cg/amg.dll?p=amg&sql=11:3nftxq95ldhe~1~T40B, accessed June 1, 2010.

37. Michael Gallant, "Accordion Americana: Interview with Charlie Giordano," *Keyboard* (June 2007), 17, www.keyboardmag.com/PrintableArticle.aspx?id=29074, accessed January 1, 2010.

38. Ibid.

39. Doerschuk, "Rock's New Main Squeeze," 71.

40. Stephen Holden, review of *Gigantic: A Tale of Two Johns* (documentary feature film about *They Might Be Giants*), *New York Times*, May 23, 2003.

41. Doerschuk, "Rock's New Main Squeeze," 80.

42. Ibid., 80.

43. Ibid., 81.

44. Ibid., 81.

45. Ibid., 81.

46. Ibid., 81.

47. Jack Thurston, "Squeezing Out a Living," *WCAX News,* July 1, 2007, available at www.wcaxnewswww.wcax.com/Global/story.asp?S=6734691&nav=4QcS, accessed January 10, 2010.

48. *Baltimore Sun,* July 9, 1998.

49. Richard Guilliatt, "The Main Squeeze," *Sydney Morning Herald*, February 28, 1998, available at the website Accordions Worldwide, www.accordions.com/index/art/mam_squeeze.shtml, accessed April 2, 2007.

50. Joel Rose, "Is the Accordion Making a Hipster Comeback?," radio program created for WHYY, Philadelphia, and broadcast on National Public Radio member stations, July 13, 2003, available at www.npr.org/templates/story/story.php?storyId=1335255.

51. Quoted in Denis Herbstein, "The Hazards of Cultural Deprivation," *Africa Report* 32 (July-August 1987), 35.

52. Lida Dutkova-Cope, "Texas-Czech Ethnic Identity: So How Czech Are You, Really?" *Slavic and East European Journal* 2 (4) (winter 1992), 659.

Chapter 6. Out of the Closet

1. Michelle Keleman, "Is the Accordion Making a Hipster Comeback?," *NPR Weekend Edition,* July 13, 2003, available at www.npr.org/templates/story/story.php?storyId= 1335255.

2. Bob Doerschuk, "Rock's New Main Squeeze," *Keyboard*, December 1987, 66.

3. Pauline Oliveros, "Calling All Accordions!," *Squid's Ear*, www.squidsear.com/cgi-bin/ news/newsView.cgi?newsID=429, accessed January 1, 2005.

4. Torriglia self-identifies as an Italian American.

5. A somewhat exaggerated claim, since the piano accordion as we know it was invented in France. Torriglia would be more accurate if he said that San Francisco was the first place where piano accordions (and chromatics) were manufactured in the United States, around 1908.

6. Tom Torriglia, personal communication, August 27, 2008.

7. "Ready, Set, Accordion!," National Public Radio, http://www.npr.org/templates/story/ story.php?storyId=5473086.

8. Greg Cahill, "Musical Mauraders: Mad Maggies Snatch Bits and Pieces from a World of Sound," *Petaluma Argus-Courier*, October 12, 2005, B7.

9. Lou Seakins's website, www.accordionprincess.com, accessed June 15, 2010.

10. Website of Tara Linda, www.taralinda.com.

11. Website of Those Darn Accordions, www.thosedarnaccordions.com, accessed February 10, 2010.

12. Comments, University of Illinois Press/University of Wisconsin Press/University Press of Mississippi mentoring session, American Folklore Society annual meeting, Boise, October 24, 2009.

13. Richard von Busack, "Squeezebox Fever Grips Cotati," n.d., available at the website of the Cotati Accordion Festival, www.cotataccordionfestival.com.

14. Ibid.

15. Steve Rubenstein, "Obituary for Jim Boggio," *San Francisco Chronicle,* November 20, 1996.

16. Website of the Cotati Accordion Festival, www.cotataccordionfestival.com.

17. Ibid.

18. Virginia Sager Johnson, "A History of the Cotati Festival," August 24, 1991, available at the website of the Cotati Accordion Festival, www.cotataccordionfestival.com.

19. "Dick Contino," available at Space Age Pop, a website devoted to exotica and lounge music, www.spaceagepop.com/contino.htm, accessed January 7, 2011.

20. Marion Jacobson, "Val-Taro Musette and the Negotiation of Northern Italian American Identity in Manhattan," in *Italians in the Americas*, ed. Joseph Sciorra (New York: Fordham University Press, forthcoming), 133–52.

21. Website of City of Santa Rosa, http://santarosa.about.com/od/attractions/ig/Cotati-Accordion-Festival/, accessed November 3, 2009.

22. Website of Sonoma County, www.sonomacountyconnections.org, accessed November 3, 2009.

23. Patti Davi, personal communication, December 29, 2010, Cotati, California.

24. Jack Kugelmass, "Wishes Come True: Designing the Greenwich Village Halloween Parade," *Journal of American Folklore* 104 (1991), 445.

25. Charles Roger Wood, *Texas Zydeco* (Austin: University of Texas Press, 2006).

26. "Czech Texans," *Texas Almanac 2010–2011*, available at www.texasalmanac.com/culture/groups/czech.html, accessed June 15, 2010.

27. "Czech Texans," *Texas Almanac,* available at the website of the Texas State Historical Association, www.texasalmanac.com/topics/culture/Czech/Czech-texans.

28. The name Gabbanelli Accordions may cause some confusion because two companies currently operate under that name. Another branch of the Gabbanelli family, based in Italy, makes accordions in Castelfidardo; however, owing to the outcome of an intellectual property suit, that company is not permitted to operate in the United States.

29. See Cathy Ragland, "'With His Accordion in His Hand': The Impact of the Accordion during the Formative Years of Modern Texas-Mexican Conjunto Music (1930s–1950s)," *Free-Reed Journal* 2 (2001), 25–33.

30. In his remarks at the Accordion Kings Festival, on June 2, 2007, emcee Joe Nick Patoski invoked this idea.

31. Bernadette Conlon, "Tour of he American Accordion Scene," available at the website Accordions Worldwide, www.accordions.com/index/art/bernadette_conlon.shtml, accessed August 25, 2009.

Conclusion

1. Pierre Bourdieu, *Distinction: The Judgment of Taste* (Cambridge, Mass.: Harvard University Press, 1984).

2. Nicholas Thomas, *Entangled Objects: Exchange, Material Culture, and Colonialism in the Pacific* (Cambridge, Mass.: Harvard University Press, 1991), 4.

3. Jane [last name withheld], interview with the author, Houston, March 2, 2007.

4. Veit Erlmann, *Music, Modernity, and the Global Imagination* (Oxford: Oxford University Press, 1999).

5. Maria Sonevytski, "Learning from Lawrence Welk: The Accordion and Ethnic Whiteness," *World of Music* (50) (2) (2008), 88–101.

6. Main Squeeze Orchestra artist website, http://lepoissonrouge.com/events/artist/849, accessed January 7, 2011.

7. Frank Lima, *The Great Morgani: The Creative Madness of a Middle-Aged Stockbroker Turned Street Musician* (Santa Cruz: Great Morgani, 2007).

8. See Mark Slobin, *Subcultural Sounds: Micromusics of the West* (Middletown, Conn.: Wesleyan University Press, 1993), and Martin Stokes, "Music and the Global Order," *Annual Review of Anthropology* 33 (2004), 47–72, for discussion and comparison of the various

types of affinity communities. Among the various ethnographers who have approached their ethnographic "field" as an affinity community are Mirjana Lausevics, *Balkan Fascination* (New York: Oxford University Press, 2007), and Ruth Finnegan, *The Hidden Musicians* (Cambridge: Cambridge University Press, 1989).

9. Matt [last name withheld], interview with the author, Cotati Festival, Cotati, California, August 26, 2008.

10. Gina [last name withheld], interview with the author, New York, January 10, 2004.

INDEX

MARION JACOBSON holds a Ph.D. in music and ethnomusicology from New York University. An accordionist herself, she has performed with klezmer bands and accordion bands, and in old-timey jam sessions, but her favorite spot for gigs is the New York City subway.

The University of Illinois Press
is a founding member of the
Association of American University Presses.

───────────────────────────

Designed by Jim Proefrock
Composed in 11.25/14 Bulmer
with Chippewa Falls display
at the University of Illinois Press
Manufactured by Thomson-Shore, Inc.

University of Illinois Press
1325 South Oak Street
Champaign, IL 61820-6903
www.press.uillinois.edu